MICROSOFT® POWERPOINT

Pamela R. Toliver
Yvonne Johnson

ADDISON-WESLEY

An imprint of Addison Wesley Longman, Inc.

Reading, Massachusetts • Menlo Park, California • New York • Harlow, England
Don Mills, Ontario • Sydney • Mexico City • Madrid • Amsterdam

Senior Editor: Carol Crowell
Production Supervision: Patty Mahtani/Diane Freed
Copyeditor: Robin Drake/Barb Terry
Proofreader: Joyce Grandy
Technical Editors: Martha Johnson, Debbie Minyard, Robin Edwards
Indexer: Irv Hershman
Composition: Compset, Inc.
Cover Illustration: © Frederic Joos/SIS
Cover Designer: Anthony Saizon
Cover Design Supervisor: Gina Hagen
Marketing Manager: Michelle Hudson
Manufacturing Manager: Hugh Crawford

ISBN 0-201-31528-9

Ordering from the SELECT System
For more information on ordering and pricing policies for the SELECT Lab Series and supplements, please contact your Addison Wesley Longman sales representative or call 1-800-552-2499.

Addison-Wesley Publishing Company
One Jacob Way
Reading, MA 01867
http://www.awl.com/he/is/
is@awl.com

2 3 4 5 6 7 8 9 10-DOW-009998

Preface to the Instructor

Welcome to the *Select Lab Series*. This applications series is designed specifically to make learning easy and enjoyable, a natural outcome of thoughtful, meaningful activity. The goal for the series is to create a learning environment in which students can explore the essentials of software applications, use critical thinking, and gain confidence and proficiency.

Greater access to ideas and information is changing the way people work. With Office 97 applications, you have greater integration capabilities and easier access to Internet resources than ever before. The *Select Lab Series* helps you take advantage of these valuable resources, with special assignments devoted to the Internet and with additional connectivity resources that can be accessed through our Web site, **http://www.awl.com/he/is/.**

The *Select Lab Series* offers dozens of proven and class-tested materials, from the latest operating systems and browsers, to the most popular applications software for word processing, spreadsheets, databases, presentation graphics, desktop publishing, and integrated packages, to HTML, to programming. For your lab course, you can choose what you want to combine; your choice of lab manuals will be sent to the bookstore, combined in a TechSuite, allowing students to purchase all books in one convenient package at a discount.

In addition to the individually bound books for each application for Office 97, you also may choose the complete *Select*: *Office 97 Professional,* which covers in one combined text Windows 95, Outlook, Internet Explorer 3.0, Word 97, Excel 97, Access 97, and PowerPoint 97.

Your Addison Wesley Longman representative will be happy to work with you and your bookstore manager to provide the most current menu of *Select Lab Series* offerings, outline the ordering process, and provide pricing, ISBNs, and delivery information. Or call 1-800-447-2226 or visit our Web site at http://www.awl.com/he/is/.

Organization

The "Overview of Windows 95" familiarizes students with Windows 95 before launching into the application. Students learn the basics of starting Windows 95, using a mouse, using the essential features of Windows 95, getting help, and exiting Windows 95.

Each Office 97 application is then covered in depth in five or six projects that teach beginning to intermediate skills. An overview introduces the basic concepts of the application and provides hands-on instructions to put students to work using the application immediately. Students learn problem-solving techniques while working through projects that provide practical, real-life scenarios that they can relate to.

Web assignments appear throughout the text at the end of each project, giving students practice using the Internet.

Approach

The *Select Lab Series* uses a document-centered approach to learning. Each project begins with a list of measurable objectives, a realistic scenario called the Challenge, a well-defined plan called the Solution, and an illustration of the final product. The Setup enables students to verify that the settings on the computer match those needed for the project. The project is arranged in carefully divided, highly visual objective-based tasks that foster confidence and self-reliance. Each project closes with a wrap-up of the project called the Conclusion, followed by summary questions, exercises, and assignments geared to reinforcing the information taught through the project.

Other Features

In addition to the document-centered, visual approach of each project, this book contains the following features:

- An overview of Windows 95 and PowerPoint 97 so that students feel comfortable and confident as they function in the working environment.
- Keycaps and toolbar button icons within each step so that the student can quickly perform the required action.
- A comprehensive and well-organized end-of-the-project Summary and Exercises section for reviewing, integrating, and applying new skills.
- An illustration or description of the results of each step so that students know they're on the right track all the time.

PROJECT 2

Editing a Document

Creating a document is just the beginning of your work in word processing. After you create a document, you usually revise it several times. In this project, you will explore some of the most commonly used revision techniques.

The **Introduction** sets up the real-world scenario that serves as the environment for learning.

Objectives

After completing this project, you will be able to:

- Open a document
- Move around in a document
- Select text to change the attributes
- Work with text
- Check spelling and grammar
- Create an envelope
- Change the view

Clearly defined and measurable **objectives** give students the direction and focus they need to learn new material.

The Challenge

After typing a letter for Mr. Williams to the Sports Marketing Professionals, Mr. Williams wants the letter retyped with the changes shown in Figure 2.1. Instead of sending additional information with the letter as previously planned, Mr. Williams has decided to send the information separately, so you will have to create an envelope for the letter.

WORD-41

The **Challenge** introduces the goal of the project, the document, spreadsheet, database, or presentation to be created.

The **Solution** describes the plan for completing the projects, the tasks leading to the final product.

WORD-72

The Solution

You will format a document and set up the document to print across the long side of the paper in three columns. You will insert a graphic, modify and apply styles, create the bulleted and numbered lists, and format the brochure shown in Figure 3.1.

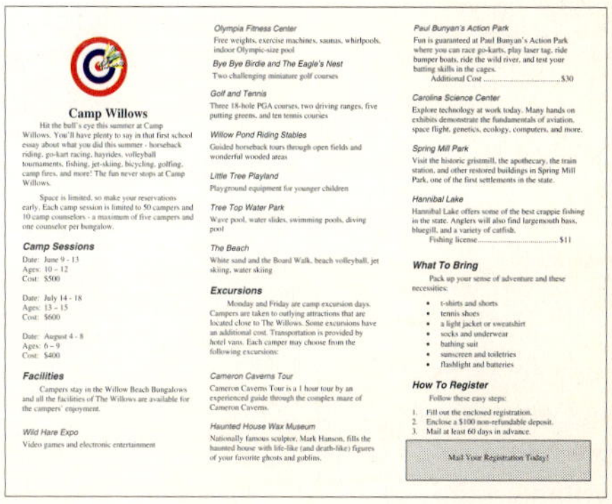

Figure 3.1

An **illustration** shows the outcome of the project.

The Setup

So that your screen will match the illustrations and the tasks in this project will function as described, make sure that the Word 97 settings listed in Table 3.1 are selected on your computer.

The **Setup** tells the students exactly which settings should be chosen to match those in the illustrations.

Clearly defined **tasks** guide students step by step through each process, providing reassurance and increasing confidence for independent or group work.

TASK 3: TO CHANGE TEXT ATTRIBUTES:

1 Select the word "so" in the first paragraph of the letter.

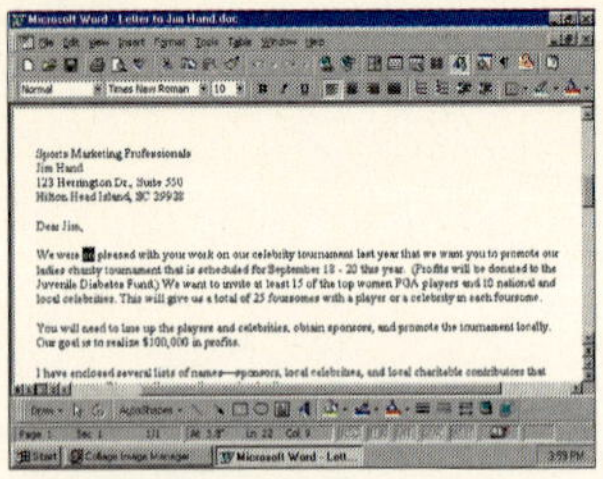

2 Click the Bold button and then press → to deselect the text.

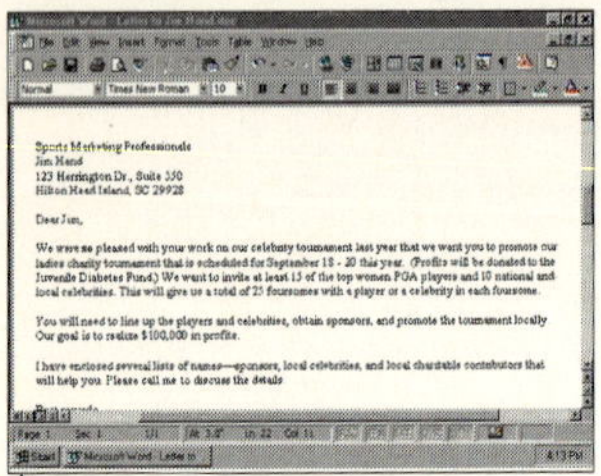

3 Select "so" again and then click the Underline button.
The word is now ***bold*** and ***underlined,*** although it's a little difficult to tell because it's still selected.

4 Click again.
The underline is removed.

Appropriate, full-color illustrations shift the emphasis from text and toward the visual-based Office 97 applications.

Each topic begins with a brief introductory paragraph that explains the concepts and operations students will learn.

2 Point to Programs and choose the Microsoft Word program.
The program opens in a window and creates a document called Document1.

Troubleshooting If Word is already started and you don't see a document on the screen, click the New button. Word creates a new document just for you.

Entering Text

Instead of typing the complete letter you see in Figure 1.1, you will type the letter in sections so that you can focus on some features and commands. As you type, you will be using the ***Enter*** key to end short lines and paragraphs and create blank lines. Don't press the Enter key at the end of each line in a paragraph, because the lines in the paragraph ***wrap*** around automatically.

Caution When you want to move down through the text, use the down arrow, not the Enter key. Remember that you use the Enter key only when you want to start a new paragraph or create a blank line.

TASK 2: TO SPACE DOWN ENOUGH TO ALLOW FOR THE LETTERHEAD:

1 Press CTRL+HOME to ensure that the insertion point is in the upper left corner of the document.
Notice that the status bar displays 1" for the vertical position of the insertion point; you need to allow space for the letterhead.

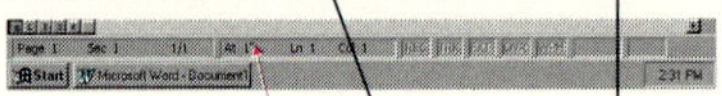

2 Press ENTER repeatedly until the vertical position 2.1" is displayed in the status bar.

Inserting a Date

The date should appear on the first line of the letter. Instead of typing the date, you can have Word 97 insert it for you.

18 Select Align Top.

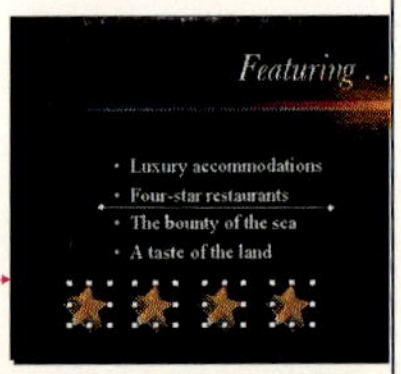

Tip If you want to position an image b... image and choose Draw, Order, and the... tion from the cascading menu.

19 Click the Draw button on the Drawing toolbar, select Align or Distribute, and then select Distribute Vertically.
The stars are evenly spaced from each other.

20 Save the changes to the presentation.

Each project ends with **The Conclusion**, a concise paragraph that wraps up the loose ends and enables the student to present a final, completed project for evaluation.

The Conclusion

Before closing the presentation *The Willows*, print a copy of the presentation as black-and-white handouts with six framed slides per page. Then, if you've completed your work, close the presentation and exit PowerPoint. If you plan to continue with the Exercises and Assignments, close the presentation and leave PowerPoint running.

Tips, Reminders, Cautions, and Troubleshooting sections appear at appropriate spots throughout each project to highlight important, helpful, or pertinent information.

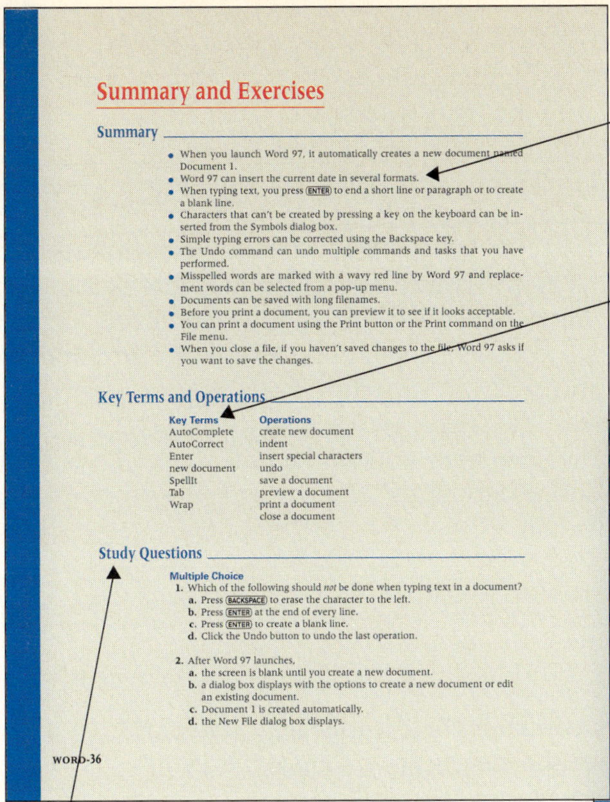

Summary and Exercises

Summary

- When you launch Word 97, it automatically creates a new document named Document 1.
- Word 97 can insert the current date in several formats.
- When typing text, you press (ENTER) to end a short line or paragraph or to create a blank line.
- Characters that can't be created by pressing a key on the keyboard can be inserted from the Symbols dialog box.
- Simple typing errors can be corrected using the Backspace key.
- The Undo command can undo multiple commands and tasks that you have performed.
- Misspelled words are marked with a wavy red line by Word 97 and replacement words can be selected from a pop-up menu.
- Documents can be saved with long filenames.
- Before you print a document, you can preview it to see if it looks acceptable.
- You can print a document using the Print button or the Print command on the File menu.
- When you close a file, if you haven't saved changes to the file, Word 97 asks if you want to save the changes.

Key Terms and Operations

Key Terms	Operations
AutoComplete	create new document
AutoCorrect	indent
Enter	insert special characters
new document	undo
SpellIt	save a document
Tab	preview a document
Wrap	print a document
	close a document

Study Questions

Multiple Choice

1. Which of the following should *not* be done when typing text in a document?
   a. Press (BACKSPACE) to erase the character to the left.
   b. Press (ENTER) at the end of every line.
   c. Press (ENTER) to create a blank line.
   d. Click the Undo button to undo the last operation.

2. After Word 97 launches,
   a. the screen is blank until you create a new document.
   b. a dialog box displays with the options to create a new document or edit an existing document.
   c. Document 1 is created automatically.
   d. the New File dialog box displays.

WORD-36

A bulleted **summary list** further reinforces the objectives and the material presented in the project.

Key Terms are boldface and italicized throughout each project and then listed for handy review in the summary section at the end of the project.

Twenty-four **study questions** (Multiple Choice, Short Answer, and For Discussion) bring the content of the project into focus again and allow for independent or group review of the material learned.

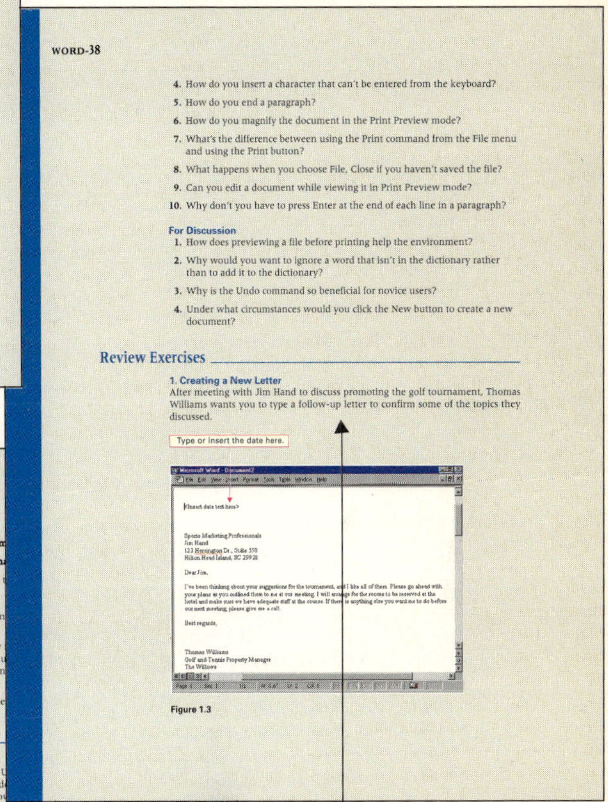

WORD-38

4. How do you insert a character that can't be entered from the keyboard?
5. How do you end a paragraph?
6. How do you magnify the document in the Print Preview mode?
7. What's the difference between using the Print command from the File menu and using the Print button?
8. What happens when you choose File, Close if you haven't saved the file?
9. Can you edit a document while viewing it in Print Preview mode?
10. Why don't you have to press Enter at the end of each line in a paragraph?

For Discussion

1. How does previewing a file before printing help the environment?
2. Why would you want to ignore a word that isn't in the dictionary rather than to add it to the dictionary?
3. Why is the Undo command so beneficial for novice users?
4. Under what circumstances would you click the New button to create a new document?

Review Exercises

1. Creating a New Letter

After meeting with Jim Hand to discuss promoting the golf tournament, Thomas Williams wants you to type a follow-up letter to confirm some of the topics they discussed.

Type or insert the date here.

Figure 1.3

Review Exercises present hands-on tasks for building on the skills acquired in the project.

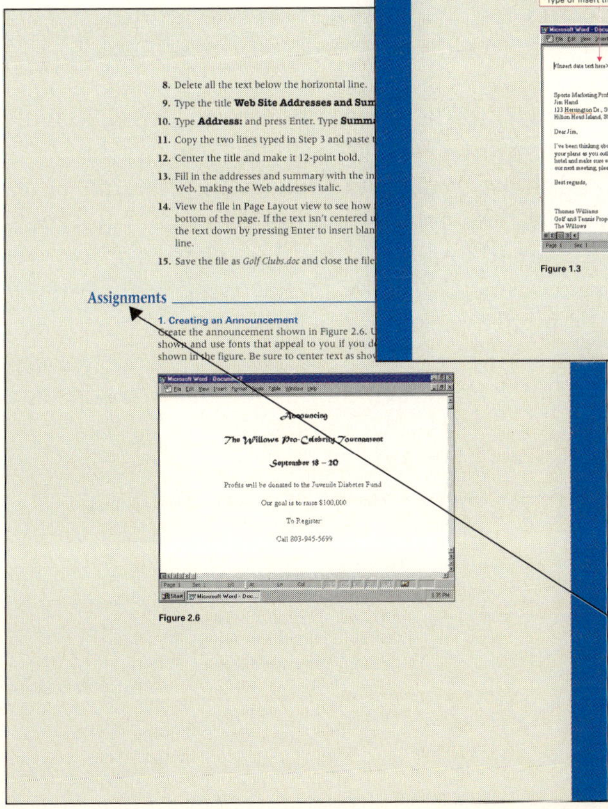

8. Delete all the text below the horizontal line.
9. Type the title **Web Site Addresses and Sum**
10. Type **Address:** and press Enter. Type **Summ**
11. Copy the two lines typed in Step 3 and paste
12. Center the title and make it 12-point bold.
13. Fill in the addresses and summary with the in Web, making the Web addresses italic.
14. View the file in Page Layout view to see how bottom of the page. If the text isn't centered the text down by pressing Enter to insert blan line.
15. Save the file as *Golf Clubs.doc* and close the file

Assignments

1. Creating an Announcement

Create the announcement shown in Figure 2.6. shown and use fonts that appeal to you if you d shown in the figure. Be sure to center text as sho

Figure 2.6

Assignments invoke critical thinking and encourage integration of project skills.

Supplements

You get extra support for this text from supplemental materials, including the *Instructor's Manual* and the Instructor's Data Disk.

The *Instructor's Manual* includes a Test Bank and Transparency Masters for each project in the student text, as well as Expanded Student Objectives, Answers to Study Questions, and Additional Assessment Techniques. The Test Bank contains two separate tests with answers and consists of multiple-choice, true/false, and fill-in questions referenced to pages in the student text. Transparency Masters illustrate over one hundred key concepts and screen captures from the text.

The Instructor's Data Disk contains student data files, completed data files for Review Exercises and assignments, and the test files from the *Instructor's Manual* in ASCII format.

Thanks to . . .

When team members combine their knowledge and skills to produce a work designed to meet the needs of students and professors across the country, they take on an unenviable challenge.

To **Carol Crowell** and **Barb Terry,** thanks for the steady focus and refocus needed to get this project off the ground.

Thanks to **Martha Johnson, Robin Edwards,** and **Deborah Minyard,** who were more than just technical editors, but who also made sure things worked the way we said they would. Thanks to **Robin Drake**—without your great help and comments during development, nothing in this book would match; and to **Chuck Hutchinson,** for excellent editing. To those in production, especially to **Pat Mahtani,** your design efforts have paid off in a highly user friendly book!

To **Michelle Hudson,** thanks for your strong marketing insights for this book.

And, finally, thanks to everyone at Addison Wesley Longman who has followed this project from start to finish.

P. T.
Y. J.

Acknowledgments

Addison-Wesley Publishing Company would like to thank the following reviewers for their valuable contributions to the *SELECT Lab Series*.

James Agnew
Northern Virginia Community College

Joseph Aieta
Babson College

Dr. Muzaffar Ali
Bellarmine College

Tom Ashby
Oklahoma CC

Bob Barber
Lane CC

Robert Caruso
Santa Rosa Junior College

Robert Chi
California State Long Beach

Jill Davis
State University of New York at Stony Brook

Fredia Dillard
Samford University

Peter Drexel
Plymouth State College

David Egle
University of Texas, Pan American

Linda Ericksen
Lane Community College

Jonathan Frank
Suffolk University

Patrick Gilbert
University of Hawaii

Maureen Greenbaum
Union County College

Sally Ann Hanson
Mercer County CC

Sunil Hazari
East Carolina University

Gloria Henderson
Victor Valley College

Bruce Herniter
University of Hartford

Rick Homkes
Purdue University

Lisa Jackson
Henderson CC

Martha Johnson
(technical reviewer)
Delta State University

Cynthia Kachik
Santa Fe CC

Bennett Kramer
Massasoit CC

Charles Lake
Faulkner State Junior College

Ron Leake
Johnson County CC

Randy Marak
Hill College

Charles Mattox, Jr.
St. Mary's University

Jim McCullough
Porter and Chester Institute

Gail Miles
Lenoir-Rhyne College

Steve Moore
University of South Florida

Anthony Nowakowski
Buffalo State College

Gloria Oman
Portland State University

John Passafiume
Clemson University

Leonard Presby
William Paterson College

Louis Pryor
Garland County CC

Michael Reilly
University of Denver

Dick Ricketts
Lane CC

Dennis Santomauro
Kean College of New Jersey

Pamela Schmidt
Oakton CC

Gary Schubert
Alderson-Broaddus College

T. Michael Smith
Austin CC

Cynthia Thompson
Carl Sandburg College

Marion Tucker
Northern Oklahoma College

JoAnn Weatherwax
Saddleback College

David Whitney
San Francisco State University

James Wood
Tri-County Technical College

Minnie Yen
University of Alaska, Anchorage

Allen Zilbert
Long Island University

Contents

Project 3 Adding Art to a Presentation 82

Project 4 Viewing and Editing a Presentation 116

Project 5 Enhancing a Presentation 136

Overview of Windows 95

Overview of Windows 95

Microsoft Windows 95 is an ***operating system,*** a special kind of computer program that performs three major functions. First, an operating system controls the actual ***hardware*** of the computer (the screen, the keyboard, the disk drives, and so on). Second, an operating system enables other software programs such as word processing or spreadsheet ***applications*** to run. Finally, an operating system determines how the user operates the computer and its programs or applications.

As an operating system, Windows 95 and all other programs written to run under it provide ***graphics*** (or pictures) called ***icons*** to carry out commands and run programs. For this reason, Windows 95 is referred to as a ***Graphical User Interface*** or GUI (pronounced *gooey*). You can use the keyboard or a device called a ***mouse*** to activate the icons.

This overview explains the basics of Windows 95 so that you can begin using your computer quickly and easily.

Objectives

After completing this project, you will be able to:

- **Launch Windows 95**
- **Identify the desktop elements**
- **Use a mouse**
- **Use the basic features of Windows 95**
- **Organize your computer**
- **Work with multiple programs**
- **Get help**
- **Exit Windows 95**

Launching Windows 95

Because Windows 95 is an operating system, it launches immediately when you turn on the computer. Depending on the way your computer is set up, you may have to type your user name and password to log on — to get permission to begin using the program. After Windows 95 launches, the working environment, called the ***desktop,*** displays on the screen.

Identifying the Desktop Elements

Figure W.1 shows the Windows 95 desktop with several icons that represent the hardware and the software installed on the computer. ***My Computer*** enables you to organize your work. The ***Recycle Bin*** is a temporary storage area for files deleted from the hard disk. At the bottom of the desktop is the ***Taskbar*** for starting programs, accessing various areas of Windows 95, and switching among programs.

Figure W.1

Note The desktop can be customized, so the desktop on the computer you're using will not look exactly like the one shown in the illustrations in this overview.

Using a Mouse

A pointing device is almost an indispensable tool for using Windows 95. Although you can use the keyboard to navigate and make selections, using a mouse is often more convenient and efficient.

When you move the mouse on your desk, a pointer moves on the screen. When the pointer is on the object you want to use, you can take one of the actions described in Table W.1 to give Windows 95 an instruction.

Table W.1 Mouse Actions

Action	Description
Point	Slide the mouse across a smooth surface (preferably a mouse pad) until the pointer on the screen is on the object.
Click	Press and release the left mouse button once.
Drag	Press and hold down the left mouse button while you move the mouse, and then release the mouse button to complete the action.
Right-click	Press and release the right mouse button once. Right-clicking usually displays a shortcut menu.
Double-click	Press and release the left mouse button twice in rapid succession.

TASK 1: TO PRACTICE USING THE MOUSE:

1. Point to the My Computer icon, press and hold down the left mouse button, and then drag the mouse across the desk.
   The icon moves.
2. Drag the My Computer icon back to its original location.
3. Right-click the icon.

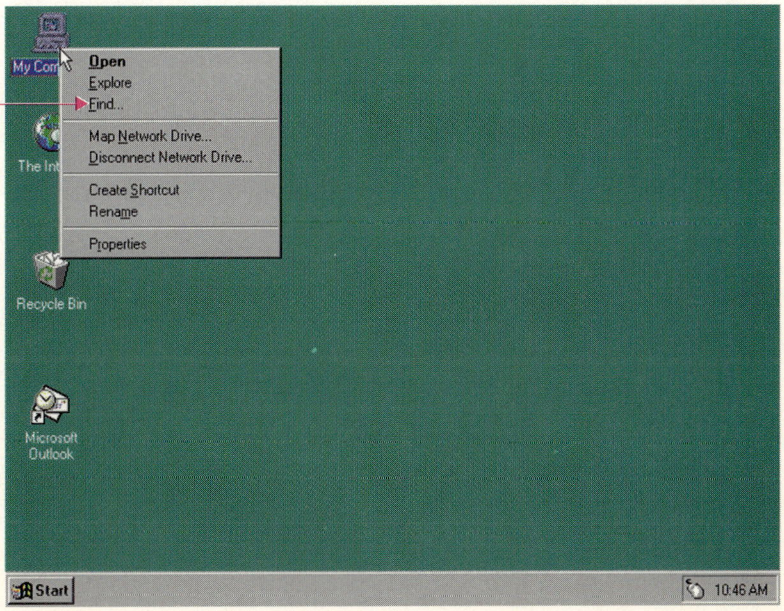

4 Click a blank space on the screen. The shortcut menu closes.

5 Double-click the My Computer icon.

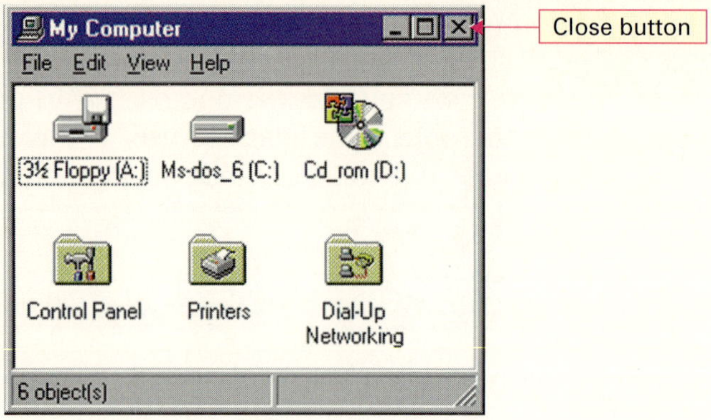

6 Click the Close button to close the My Computer window.

Using the Basic Features of Windows 95

The basic features of Windows 95 are menus, windows, menu bars, dialog boxes, and toolbars. These features are used in all programs that are written to run under Windows 95.

Using the Start Menu

Menus contain the commands you use to perform tasks. In Windows 95, you can use the Start menu shown in Figure W.2 to start programs and to access other Windows options.

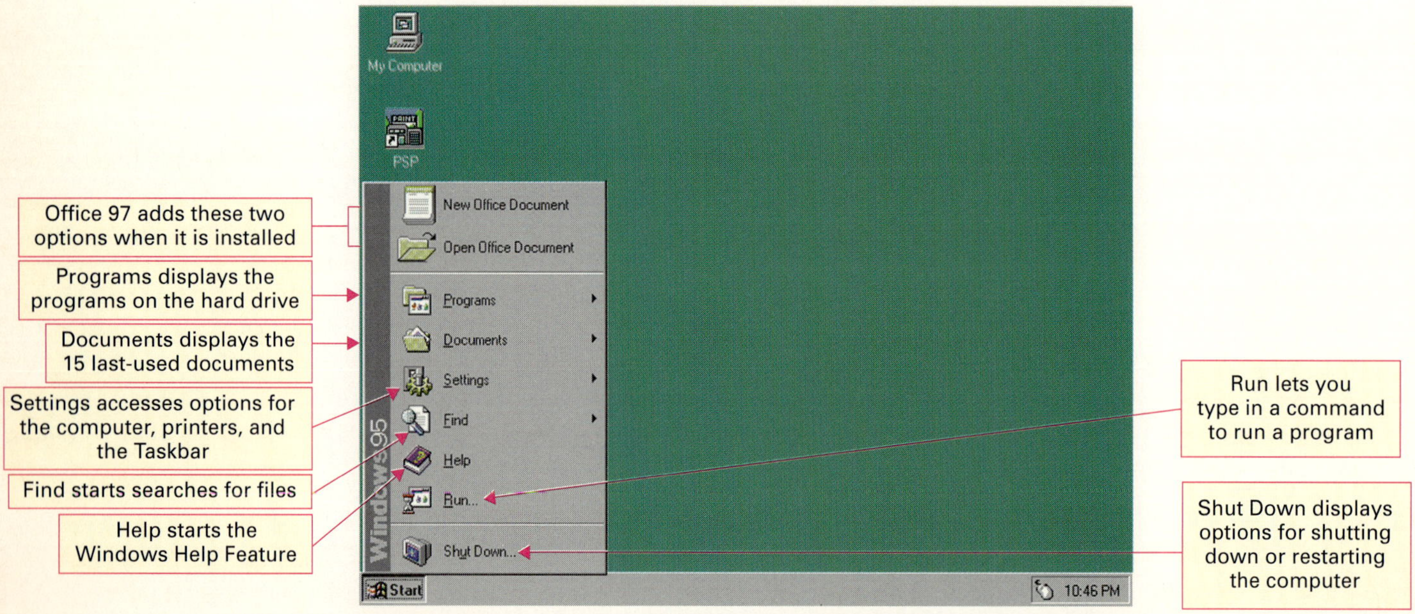

Figure W.2

TASK 2: TO USE THE START MENU TO LAUNCH A PROGRAM:

1 Click the Start button.
The triangles beside several of the menu options indicate that the options will display another menu.

2 Point to Programs and click the Windows Explorer icon.
The Exploring window opens (see Figure W.3). You can use this feature of Windows 95 to manage files.

Using Windows

Clicking on the Windows Explorer icon opened a ***window,*** a Windows 95 feature that you saw earlier when you opened the My Computer window. Figure W.3 shows the common elements that most windows contain.

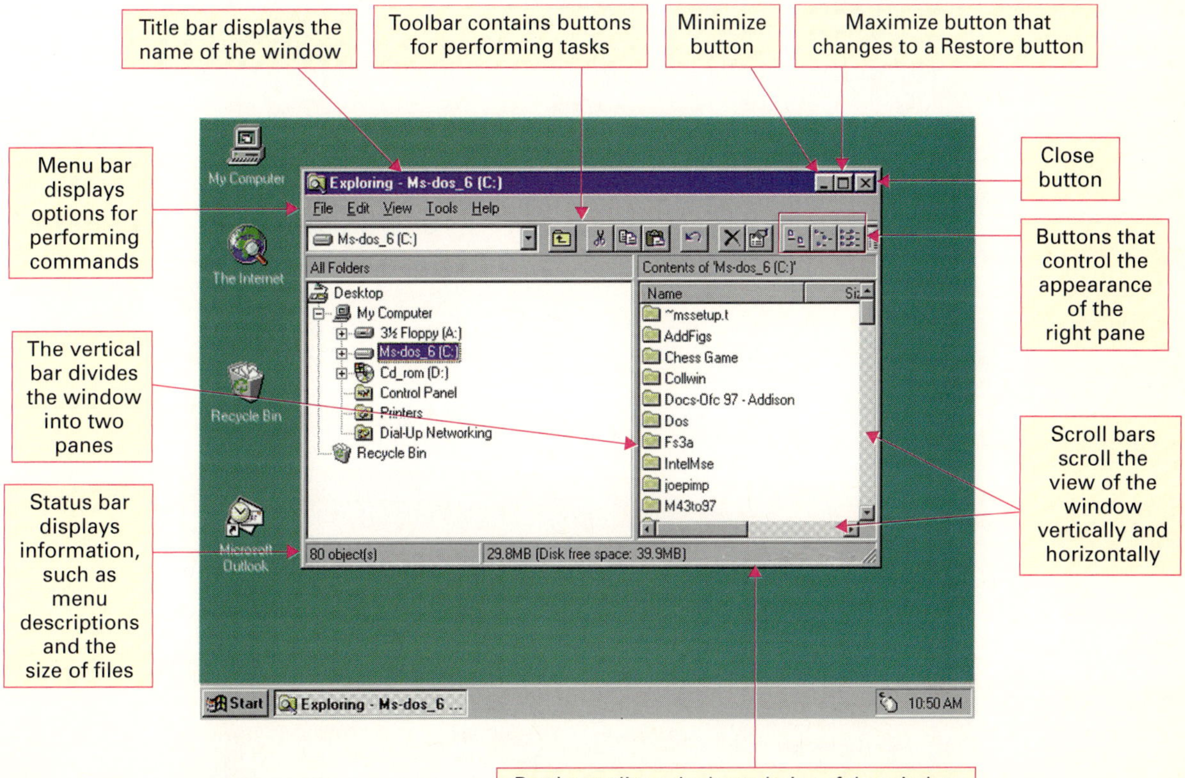

Figure W.3

TASK 3: TO WORK WITH A WINDOW:

1 Click the Maximize button if it is displayed. If it is not displayed, click the Restore button, and then click the Maximize button.
The Maximize button changes to a Restore button.

2 Click the Minimize button.

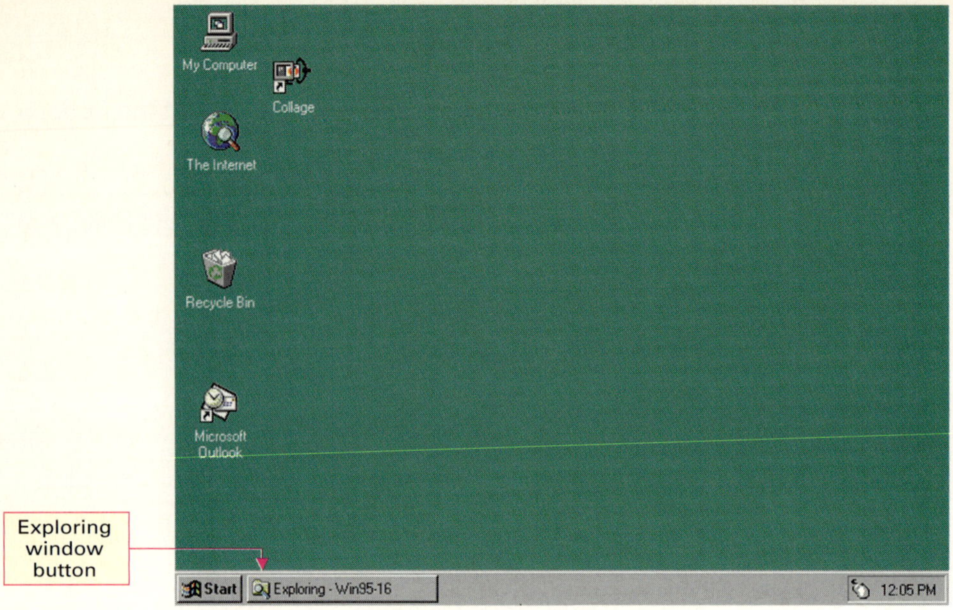

Warning When you minimize a window, the program in the window is still running and therefore using computer memory. To exit a program that is running in a window, you must click the Close button, not the Minimize button.

3 Click the Exploring button on the Taskbar and then click [restore button].

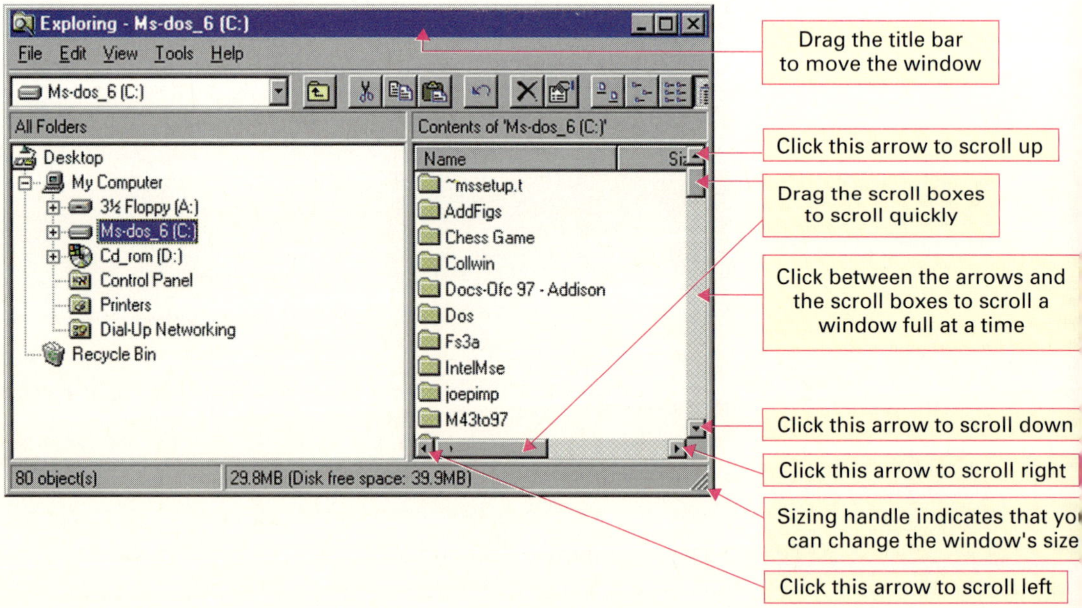

4 Point to the border of the Exploring window until the pointer changes to a double-headed black arrow, and then drag the border to make the window wider. (Be sure that all the buttons in the toolbar are visible.)

5 Practice scrolling.

6 When you are comfortable with your scrolling expertise, click [maximize button].

Using Menu Bars and Toolbars

Menu bars and toolbars are generally located at the top of a window. You can select a menu option in a menu bar by clicking the option or by pressing (ALT) and then typing the underlined letter for the option. When you select an option, a drop-down menu appears. Figure W.4 shows a menu with many of the elements common to menus.

> **Note** Because you can select menu commands in two ways, the steps with instructions to select a menu command will use the word choose instead of dictating the method of selection.

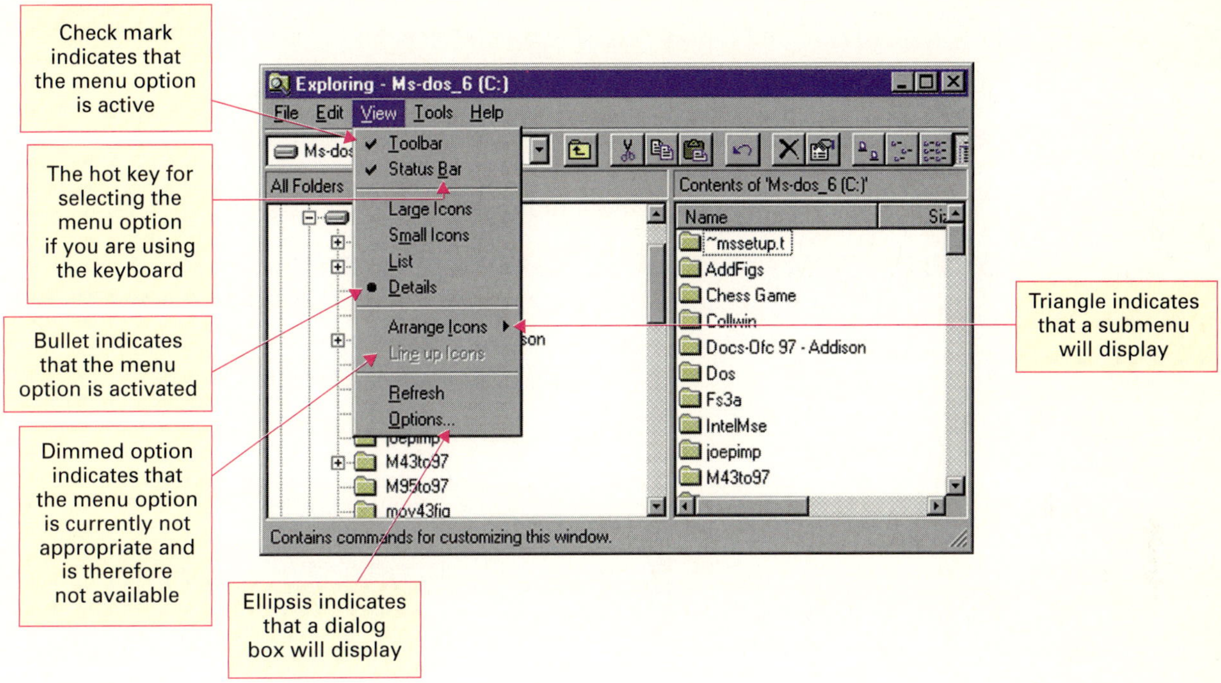

Figure W.4

Toolbars contain buttons that perform many of the same commands found on menus. To use a toolbar button, click the button; Windows 95 takes an immediate action, depending on the button's function.

> **Tip** If you don't know what a button on the toolbar does, point to the button; a ToolTip, a brief description of the button, appears near the button.

TASK 4: TO USE MENUS AND TOOLBARS:

1 Choose View in the Exploring window.
The View menu shown in Figure W.4 displays.

2 Choose Large Icons.

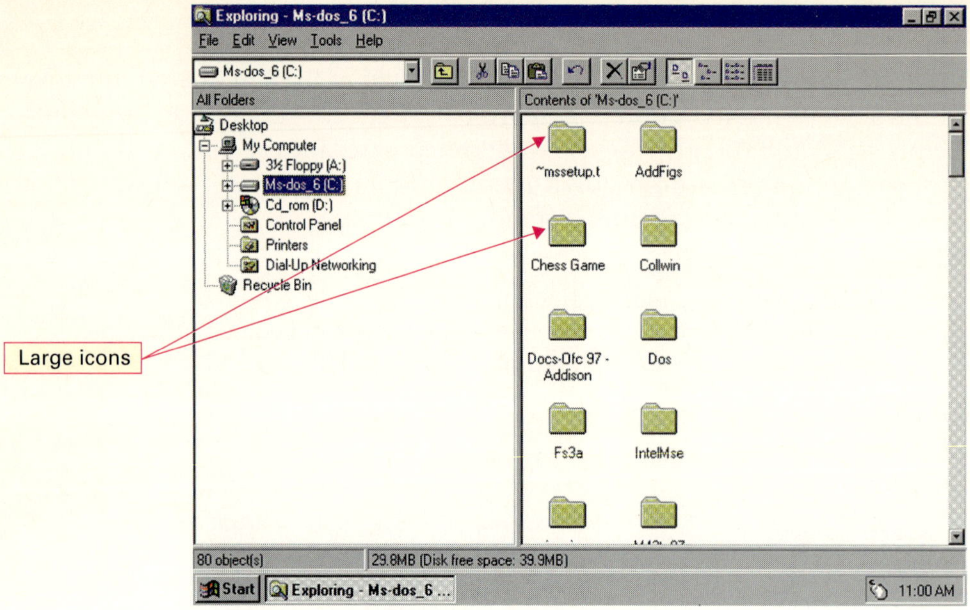

3 Click the Details button on the toolbar.

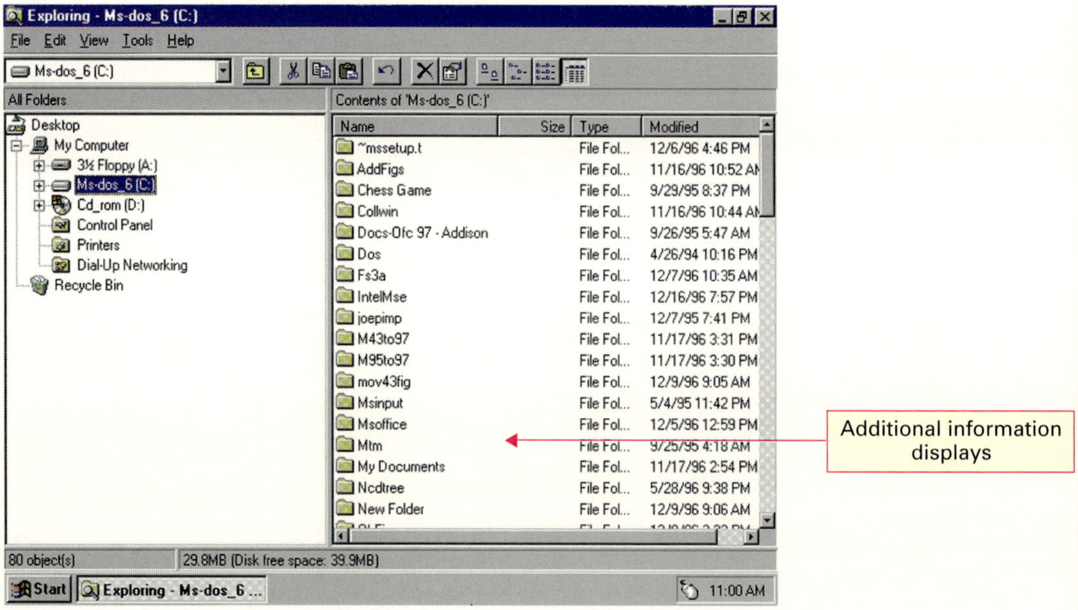

Using Dialog Boxes

When many options are available for a single task, Windows 95 conveniently groups the options in one place, called a ***dialog box.*** Some functions have so many options that Windows 95 divides them further into groups and places them on separate pages in the dialog box. Figures W.5 and W.6 show dialog boxes with different types of options. Throughout the remainder of this project, you practice using dialog boxes.

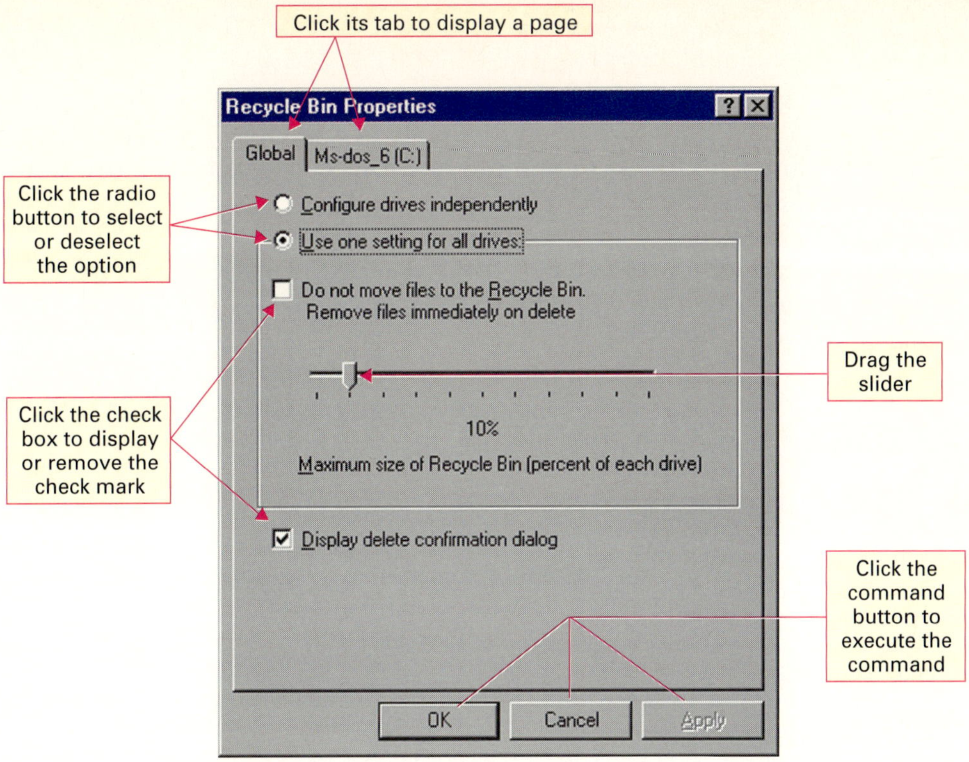

Figure W.5

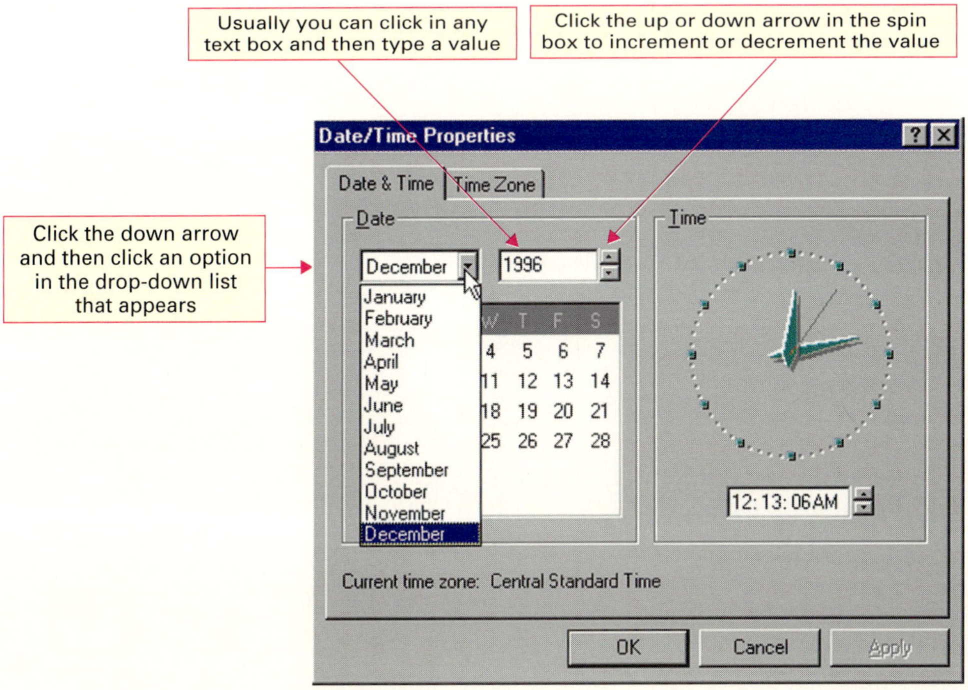

Figure W.6

Getting Help

Windows 95 provides you with three methods of accessing help information: You can look up information in a table of contents; you can search for information in an index; or you can find a specific word or phrase in a database maintained by the Find feature.

Additionally, Windows 95 provides ***context-sensitive help,*** called ***What's This?*** for the topic you are working on. This type of help is generally found in dialog boxes.

After you learn to use Help in Windows 95, you can use help in any Windows program because all programs use the same help format.

TASK 12: TO USE HELP CONTENTS, INDEX, AND FIND:

1 Click the Start button on the Taskbar and click Help.

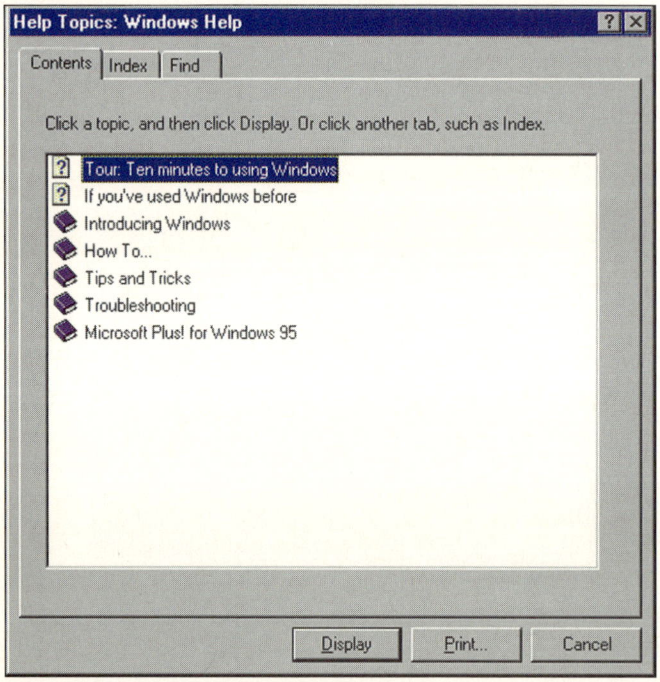

2 Click the Contents tab if a different page is displayed. The Contents page displays.

3 Double-click Tips and Tricks.

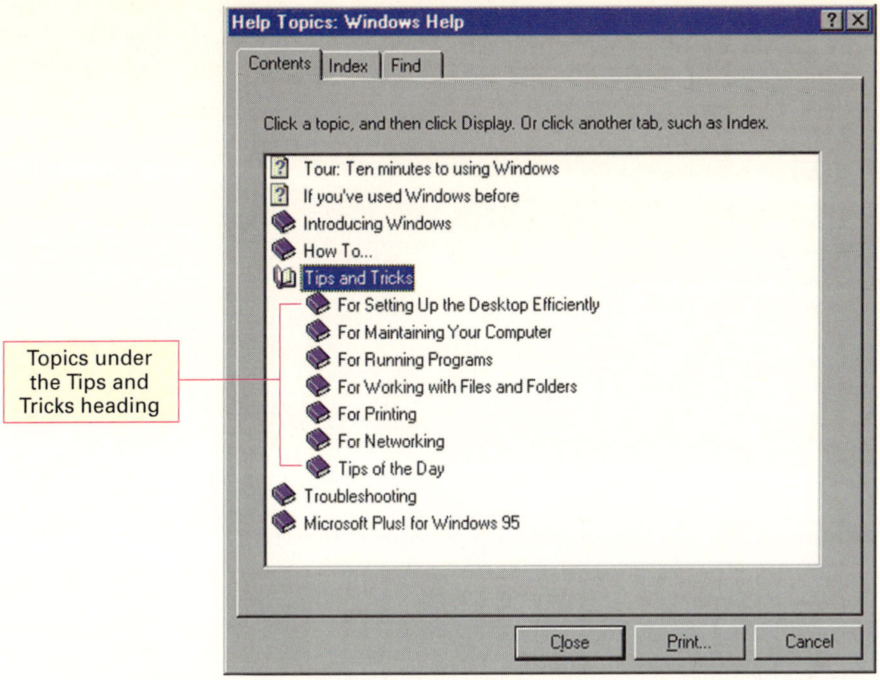

4 Double-click Tips of the Day.

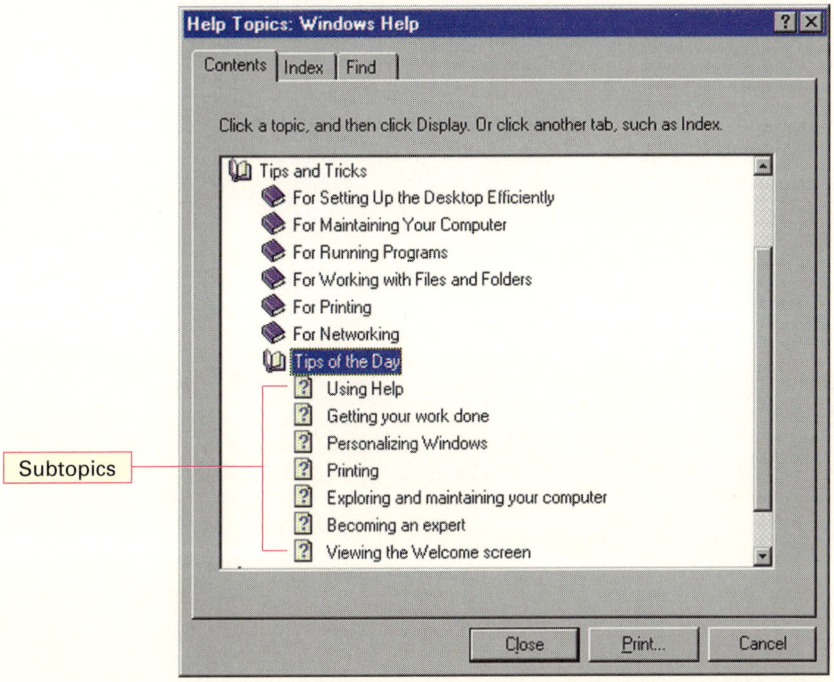

5 Double-click Using Help.

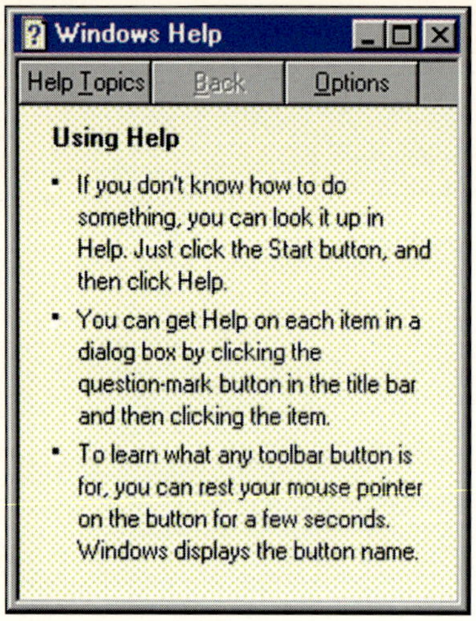

6 Read the information, click the Help Topics button, and then click the Index tab.

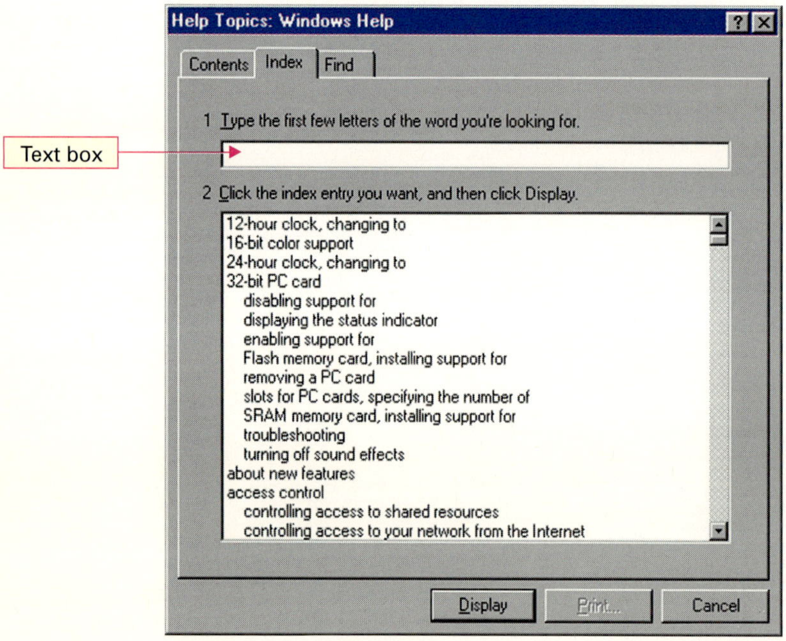

7 Type **shortcut** in the textbox.

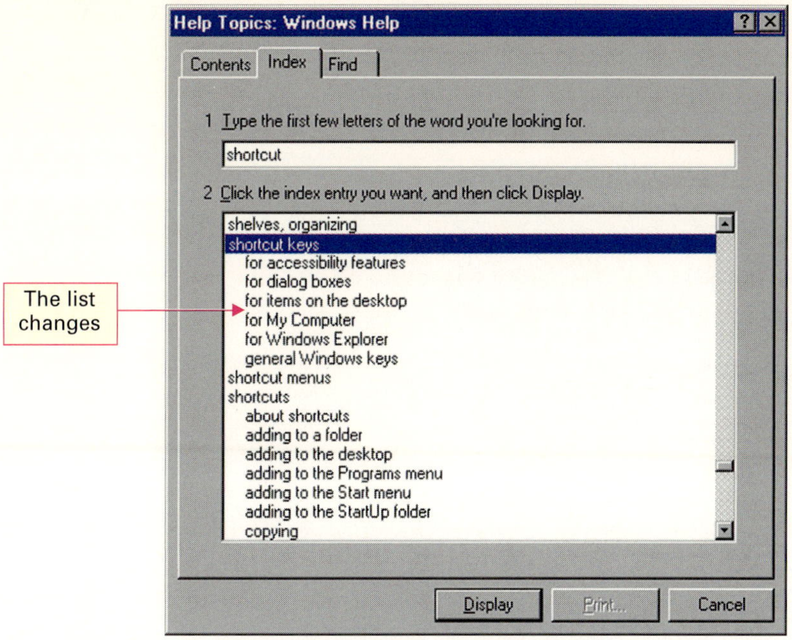

8 Double-click "shortcut menus" in the list.

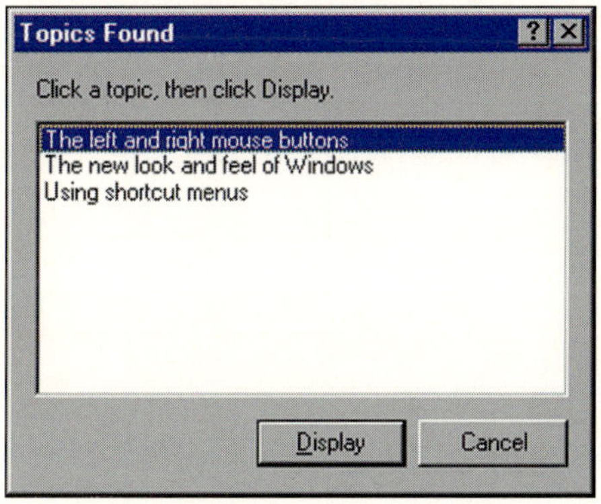

9 Double-click "Using shortcut menus."

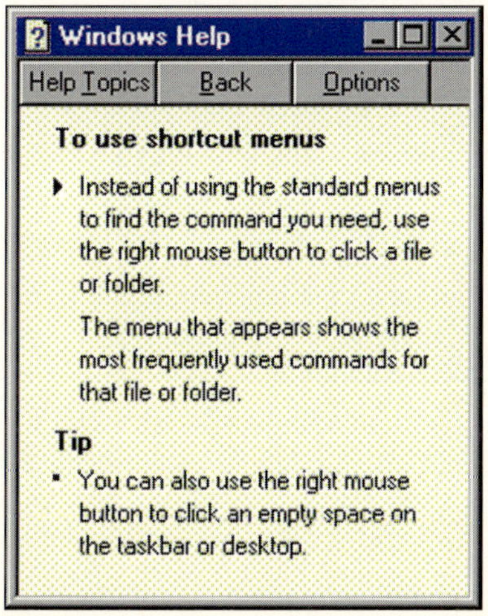

10 **Read the information, click the Help Topics button, and then click the Find tab.**

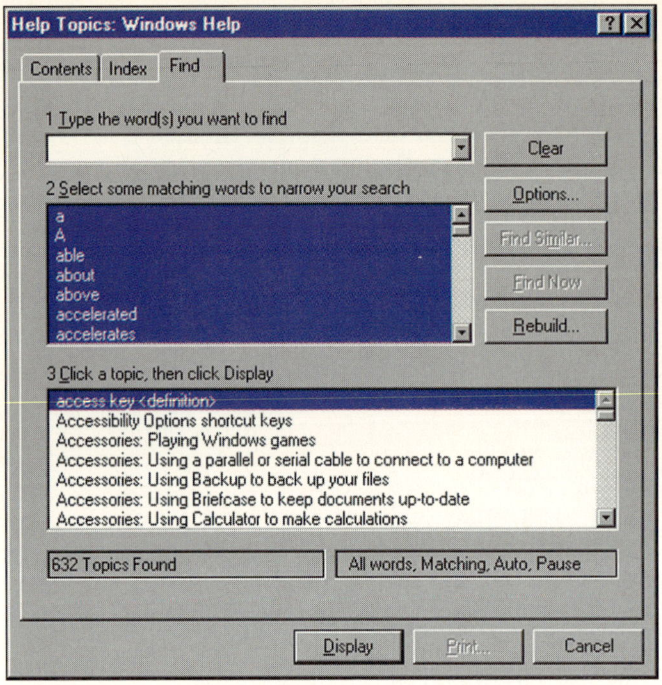

11 **Click the What's This [?] button in the Help Topics title bar. A question mark is attached to the mouse pointer.**

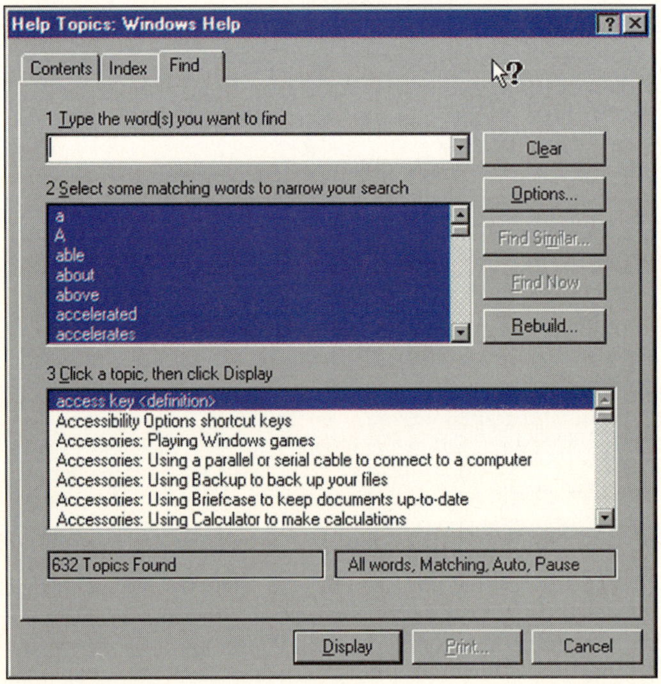

12 Click the Options button.

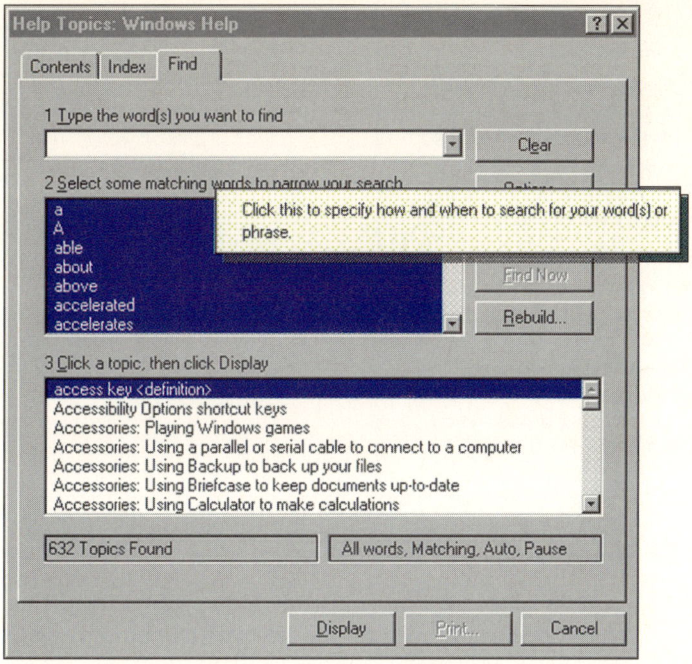

13 Read the pop-up message and then click it.
The message closes.

14 Type **printing help.** (If the list at the bottom of the screen doesn't change, click the Find Now button.)

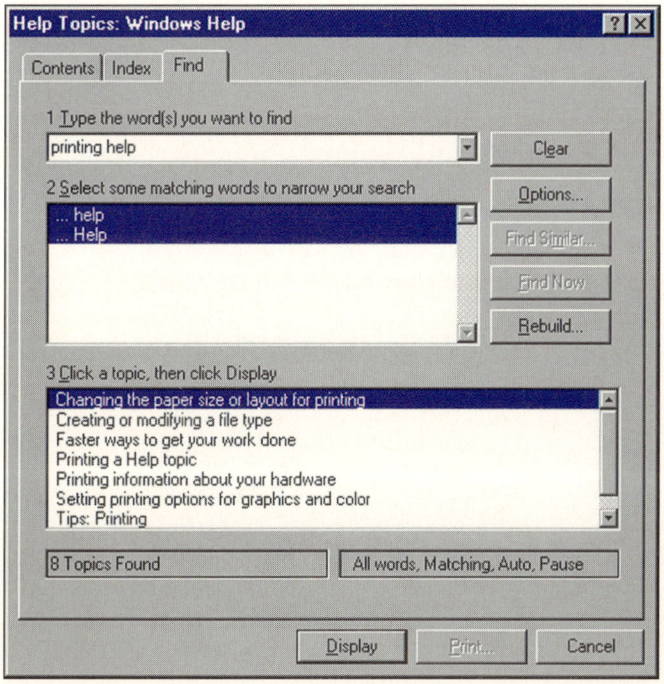

15 If necessary, scroll to "Printing a Help topic" in the list that displays and then double-click it.

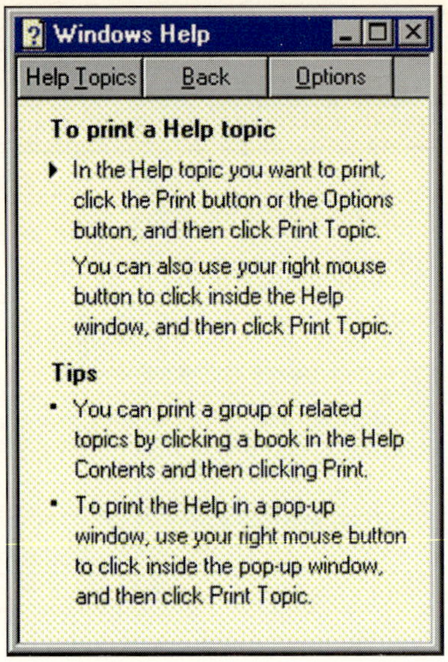

16 Click the close button. The Help dialog box closes.

Tip You can print any help article by right-clicking anywhere in the article and choosing Print Topic.

Exiting Windows 95

When you are ready to turn off the computer, you must exit Windows 95 first. You should never turn off the computer without following the proper exit procedure because Windows 95 has to do some utility tasks before it shuts down. Unlike most of us, Windows 95 likes to put everything away when it's finished. When you shut down improperly, you can cause serious problems in Windows 95.

TASK 13: TO EXIT WINDOWS 95:

1 Click the Start button and then click Shut Down.

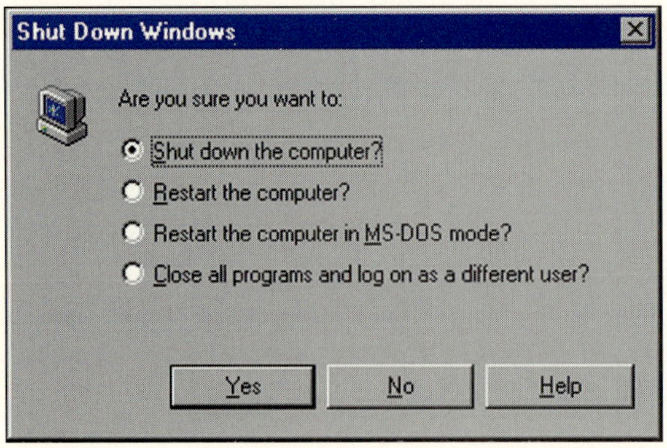

2 Click Shut down the computer? and then click Yes.

3 When the message "It's now safe to turn off your computer" appears, turn off the computer.

Presentation Software
Using Microsoft PowerPoint 97

Overview

Microsoft PowerPoint 97 is a presentation graphics program that enables you to prepare slide shows and present them with style and impact. You can use PowerPoint to print handouts for the audience, speaker notes to aid presentation delivery, and overhead transparencies to use when you have no computer available. In this overview, you identify features unique to PowerPoint and see some old friends from other programs. After you get better acquainted with these basics, you'll be able to put them to use in the other projects in this module and unveil some of the power of PowerPoint.

Objectives

After completing this project, you will be able to:

- **Design a presentation**
- **Launch Microsoft PowerPoint**
- **Identify PowerPoint screen elements**
- **Create a presentation**
- **Display presentations in different views**
- **Work with menus, dialog boxes, and toolbars**
- **Get Microsoft PowerPoint Help**
- **Exit PowerPoint**

Defining PowerPoint Terminology

P*resentations* are collections of related slides that summarize key points of a report or act as a visual aid during an oral presentation. Whether you display slides on a computer screen, project slides onto a flat surface, or use transparencies to present slide images, PowerPoint can help you develop your presentation.

To use PowerPoint effectively, you need to become familiar with the PowerPoint terminology (see Figure O.1):

Term	Description
Slide	Basic unit of a presentation, which may contain numerous slides. Each slide in a presentation is equivalent to a page of a document, workbook, or database record.
Placeholder	Predefined area outlined on a slide, containing slide text, bulleted lists, and objects such as graphs, tables, and charts.
AutoLayout	Preformatted layouts that contain object placeholders.
Masters	Layouts that contain formats for text, bullets, placeholder alignment, headers/footers, and backgrounds.
Templates	Professionally developed slide designs that you can apply to presentations to give a consistent look to all slides in a presentation.

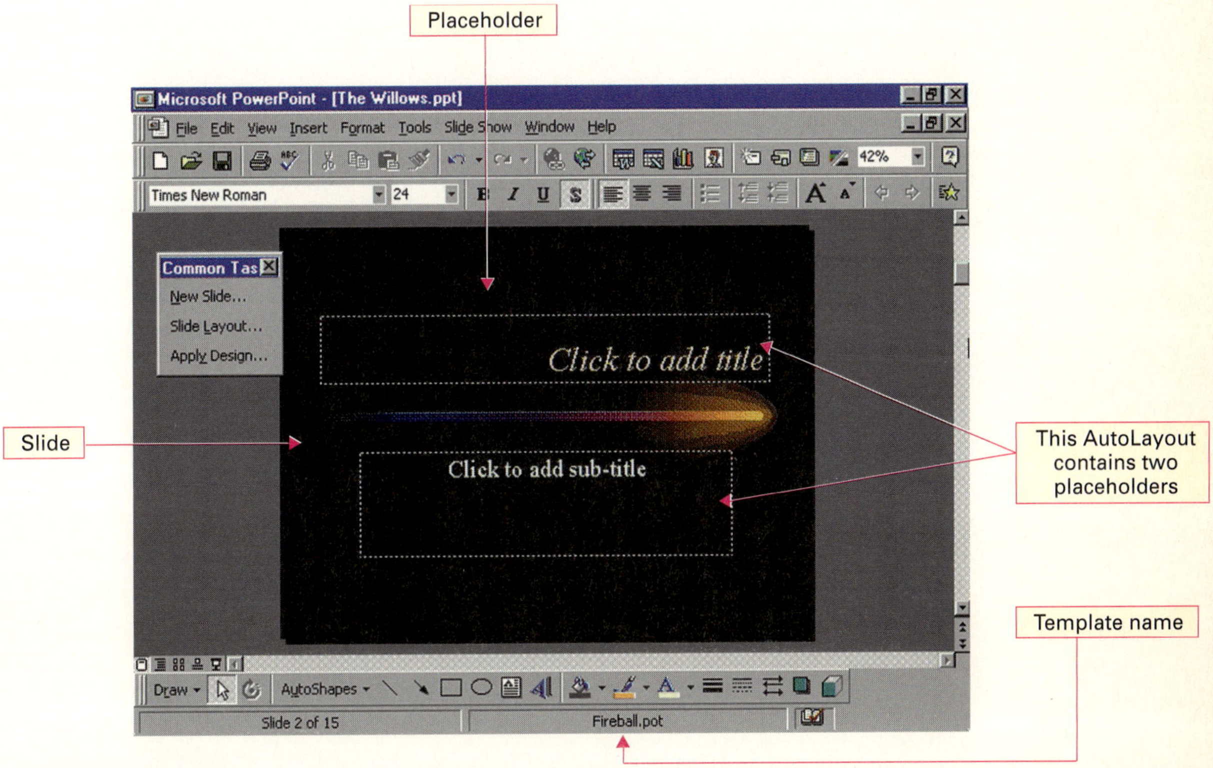

Figure O.1

Designing a Presentation

Because Microsoft PowerPoint comes with a variety of designs you can use to dress up your presentation, you can focus on the content of your presentation as you design it. Some things to consider as you plan your presentation:

- ***Who*** will be in your audience and how many people will attend: managers, corporate executives, salespeople, peers, and so forth.
- ***What*** materials do you want to use with the presentation: slides, handouts, notes, and overhead transparencies.
- ***Where*** is the presentation to be given: consider the size of the room, acoustics of the room, location of the speaker platform, and other factors. Remember that small printed characters are difficult to see from the back of the room, so limit lists to short statements rather than complete sentences and make the characters larger.
- ***When*** will the presentation occur: identify the time of day, placement of the presentation in relation to other presentations, and so on.
- ***Why*** are you giving the presentation: determine the message you want to communicate and the action you want the audience to take.
- ***How*** does the method you will use to deliver the presentation affect the presentation design: color can be used more effectively in on-screen shows than in transparencies; if no color printer is available, handouts and color transparencies might be too dark.

After you consider each of these points, you can develop a presentation targeted to your audience, design a look for the presentation that best conveys the purpose of the presentation, and jot down a brief outline of the topics you want to include in the presentation. Then you're ready to launch PowerPoint.

Launching Microsoft PowerPoint

After you have powered up your computer, logged onto required networks, and responded to messages built into your system, Windows 95 starts automatically.

TASK 1: TO LAUNCH POWERPOINT:

1. Click the Start button.
2. Point to Programs.

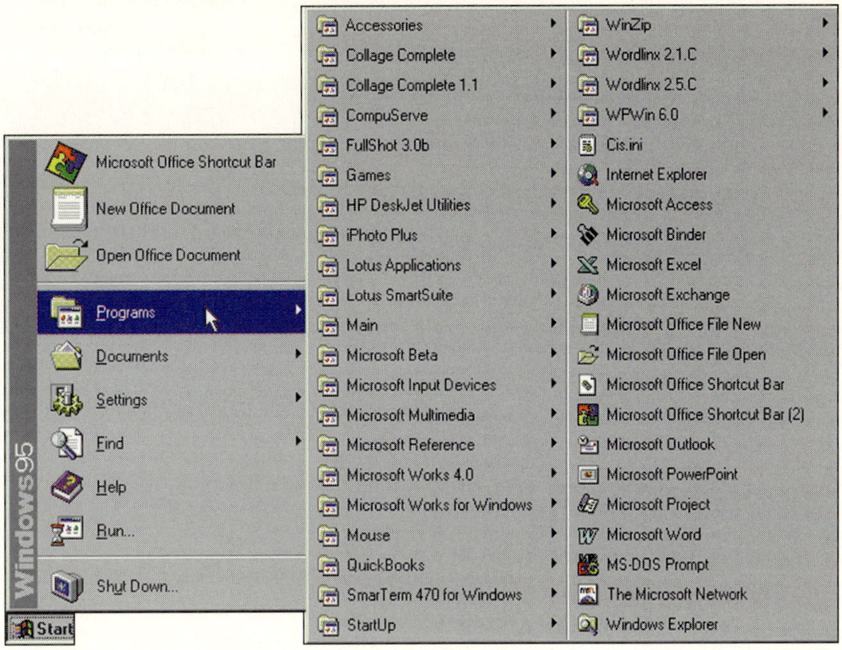

3. Point to Microsoft PowerPoint and click.

Identifying PowerPoint Screen Elements

The PowerPoint screen features a number of elements found in other application windows as well as several elements unique to PowerPoint (see Figure O.2). The first time you launch PowerPoint after it's installed on a computer, the Office Assistant pops up, introduces itself, and offers assistance. After the first time, the Office Assistant sits quietly by or hops up on the toolbar until you need it.

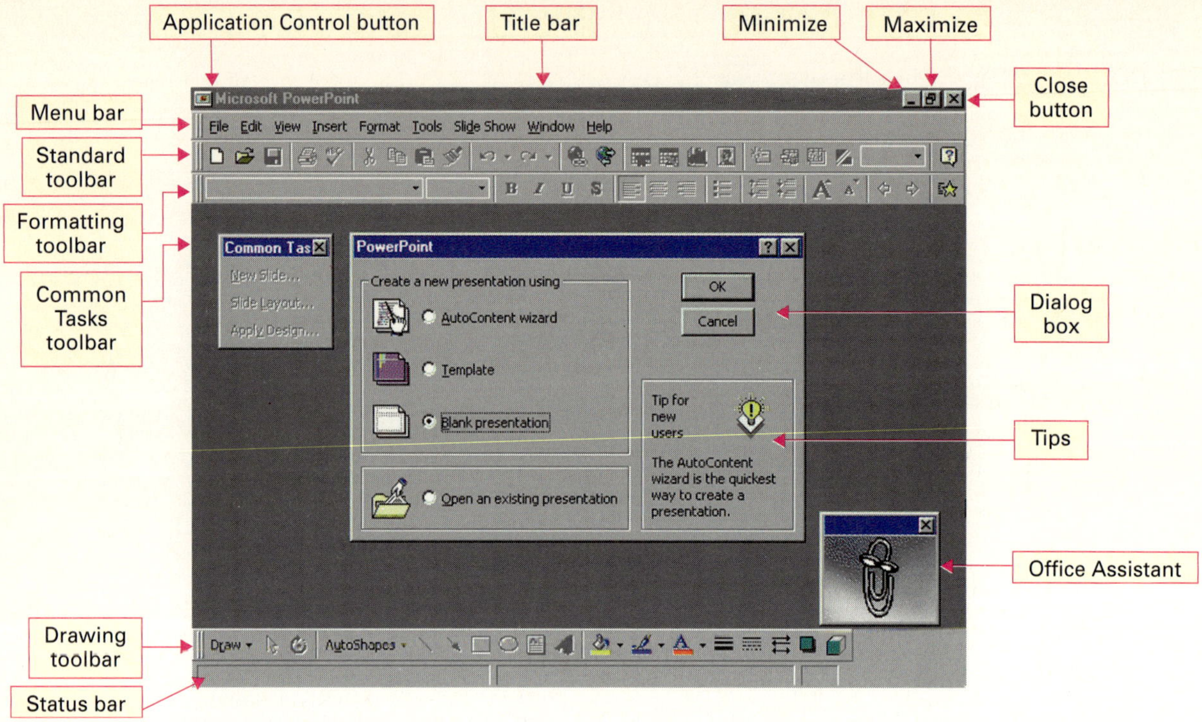

Figure 0.2

Table 0.1 contains a brief description of each PowerPoint screen feature.

Table 0.1 PowerPoint Screen Features

Screen Feature	Description
Menu bar	Provides access to commands used to perform tasks.
Title bar	Identifies the application name and contains the application icon, Maximize/Restore, Minimize, and Close buttons. Until you save a presentation, PowerPoint names the presentations consecutively, using the generic names Presentation1, Presentation2, and so forth. After you save a presentation, the filename you assign appears in the title bar.
Standard toolbar	Contains buttons that serve as shortcuts for performing common menu commands, displaying special toolbars, or changing screen features.
Formatting toolbar	Displays buttons and list boxes to access the most frequently used formatting commands.
Common Tasks toolbar	Displays commands to accomplish the three most frequently performed tasks.
Drawing toolbar	Displays tools for creating and formatting drawn objects.
View buttons	Provides an easy way to display your presentation in a different format. You'll see these after you create your first slide or open a presentation.
Office Assistant	Provides tips as you work and can answer some of your questions about the program.
Status bar	Displays information about the program status, instructions for performing selected tasks, active key information, functions of the toolbar buttons when you point to them, and trouble messages.

Creating a Presentation

Each time you launch PowerPoint, the PowerPoint dialog box shown in Figure O.3 presents options that enable you to create a new presentation or open an existing one.

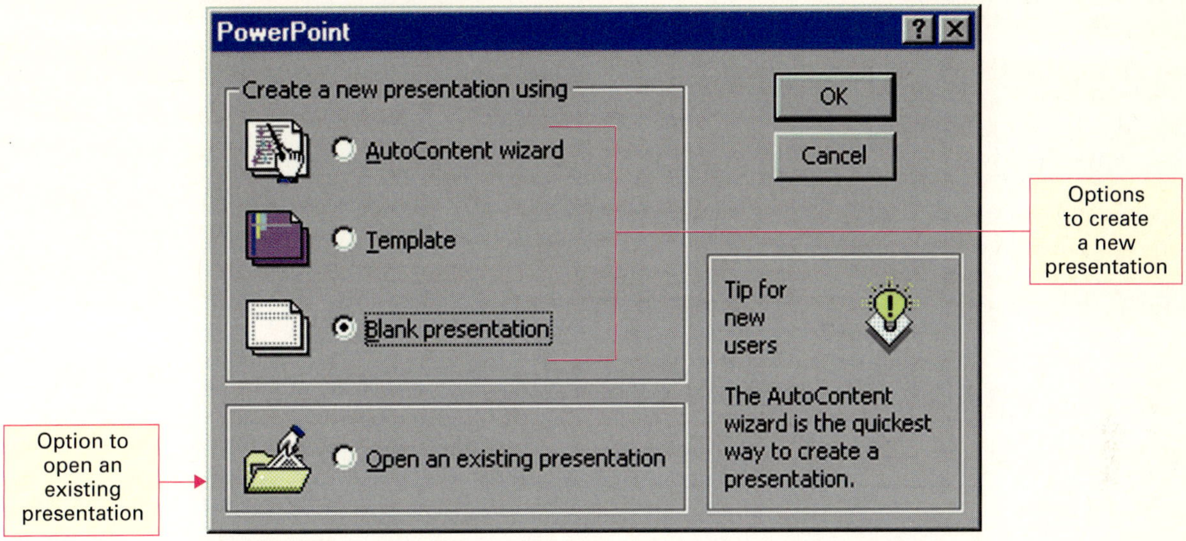

Figure O.3

Options for creating a new presentation include:

- AutoContent wizard: The wizard creates a presentation, based on the purpose of the presentation and choices you select from options the wizard presents. The wizard formats slides in the presentation to contain instructions and information about the presentation content. You then replace that instructional and informative text with the text you want to include on each slide.
- Template: Lets you choose a design for your presentation and then build the presentation from scratch by adding your own text and objects to slides you create.
- Blank presentation: Creates a plain presentation that formats slides with placeholders to contain text and objects.

When you choose to create a new presentation, PowerPoint presents a series of formats for the first slide with the title slide selected. Each placeholder on the title slide contains instructions to help you add text to the slide.

TASK 2: TO CREATE A NEW, BLANK PRESENTATION:

1. Click Blank presentation and then click OK.

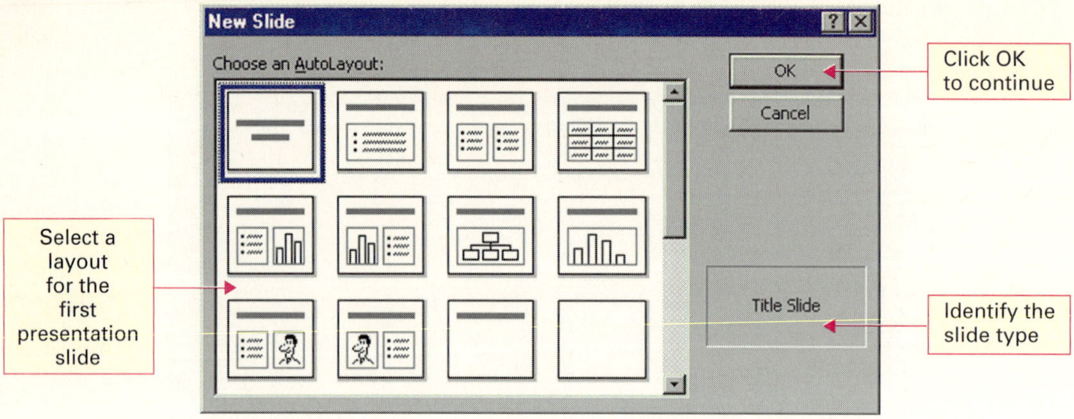

2. Click OK to accept the Title Slide AutoLayout format for the first slide in the presentation.

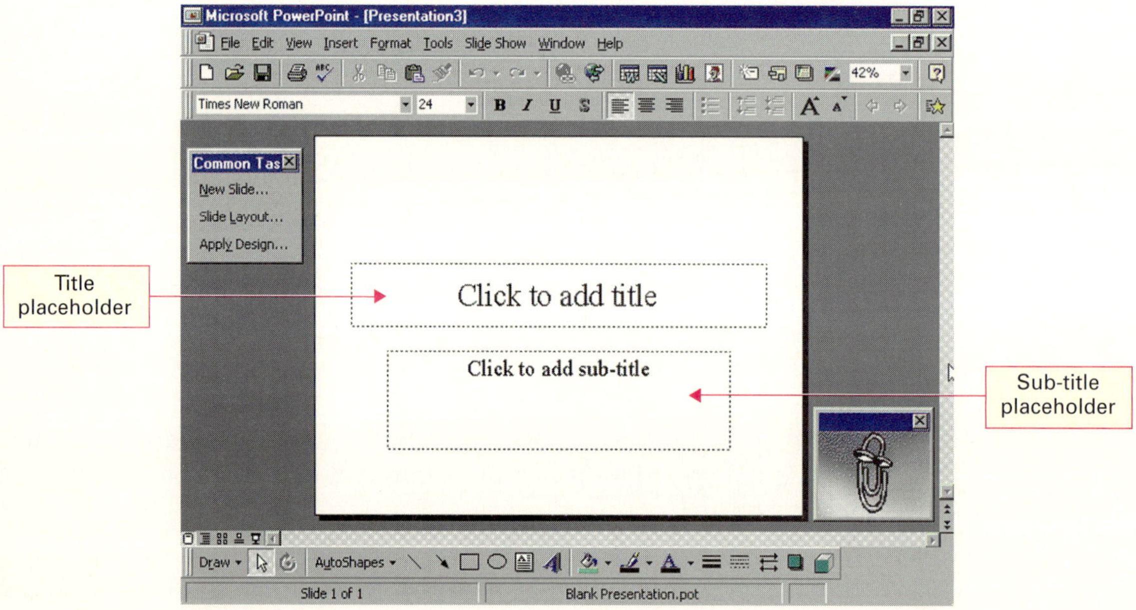

Displaying Presentations in Different Views

PowerPoint provides several views that allow you to display your presentation in different ways. Each view is designed to make working with specific features of a presentation easier:

- Slide view: Displays all slide text, formatting, graphics, charts, and other objects individually on-screen. Slide view lets you add and edit text, create new slides, create drawings, access slide objects, and change the slide format.

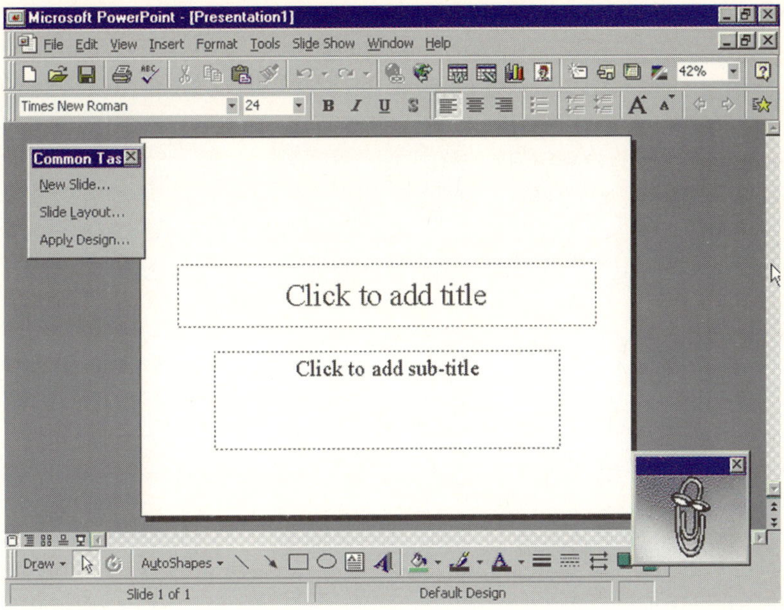

- Outline view: Displays the slide text you type into placeholders in an outline structure. Typing text in Outline view makes creating text for multiple slides more efficient. You can add and edit text, create new slides, and rearrange slides in Outline view, but you can't add other objects to slides.

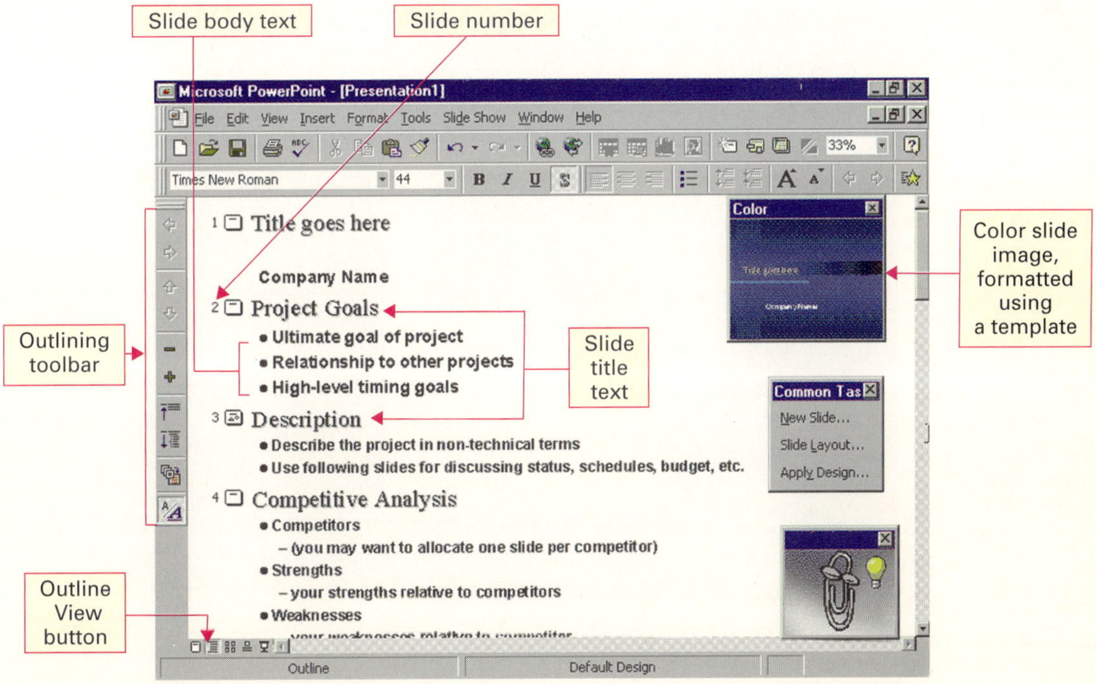

- Slide Sorter view: Displays thumbnail images of multiple slides on-screen at the same time. Slide Sorter view makes rearranging slides more efficient, but slides can't be edited in Slide Sorter view.

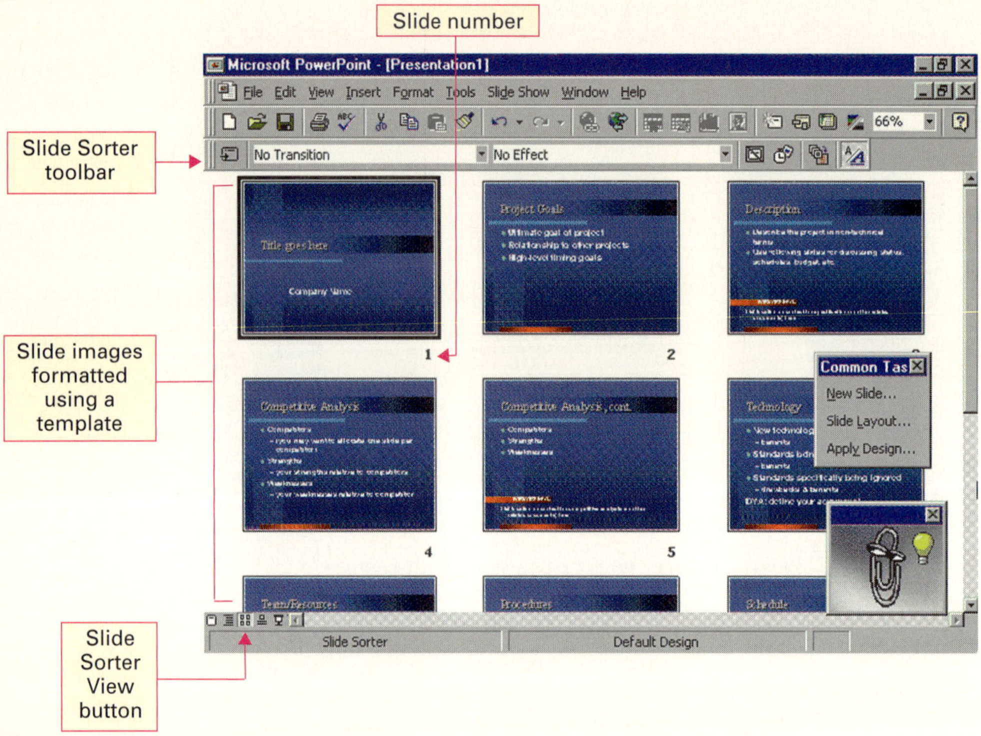

- Notes Pages view: Displays a small slide image at the top of the page and provides space below the image to type notes and supportive information about the slide contents.

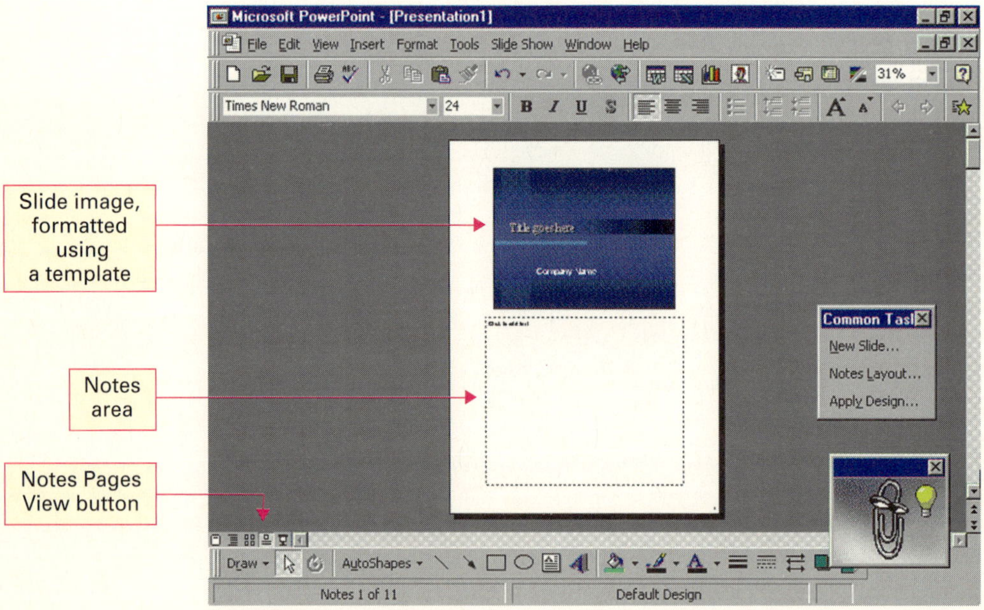

Working with Menus, Dialog Boxes, and Toolbars

Just as menus in restaurants display food items by type, menus and toolbars in PowerPoint group features and commands you use as you perform tasks in PowerPoint. Dialog boxes present options for you to choose as you create presentation files and objects, format slides and handouts, and build your presentations.

Identifying Menu Features

Menus group commands for performing tasks according to type. In PowerPoint, the menu bar remains constant as you work with different presentation objects, but available menu commands change as you switch views and work with objects. To display a list of menu commands, point to the menu item and click. Figure O.4 identifies the standard features of PowerPoint menus you will see:

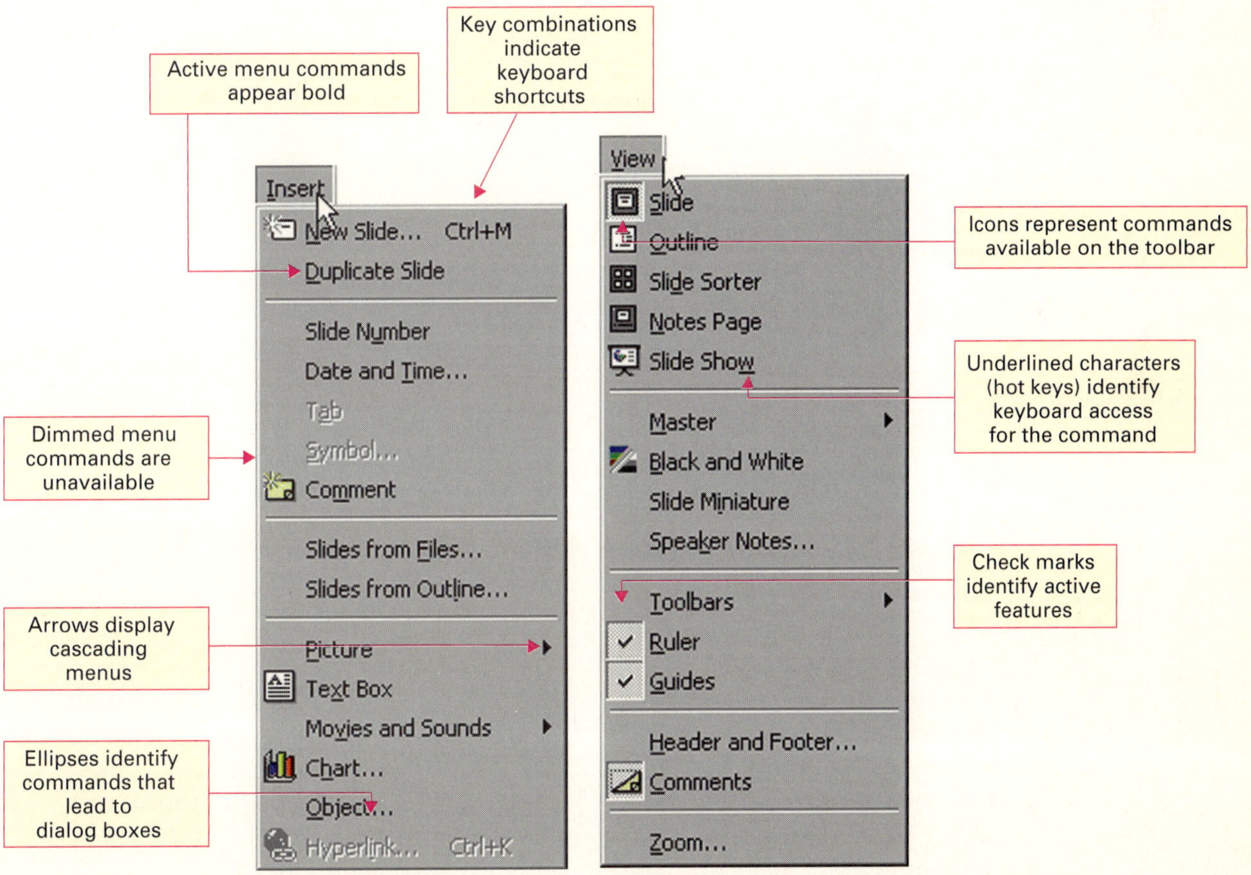

Figure O.4

Working with Toolbars

Tools on the toolbars provide easy access to many of the most frequently used menu commands and dialog boxes. To use the toolbar buttons, point to the button that represents the command you want to perform or feature you want to display, and click. ***ScreenTips*** identify the name of each button on the toolbar, and pop up when you point to the toolbar button.

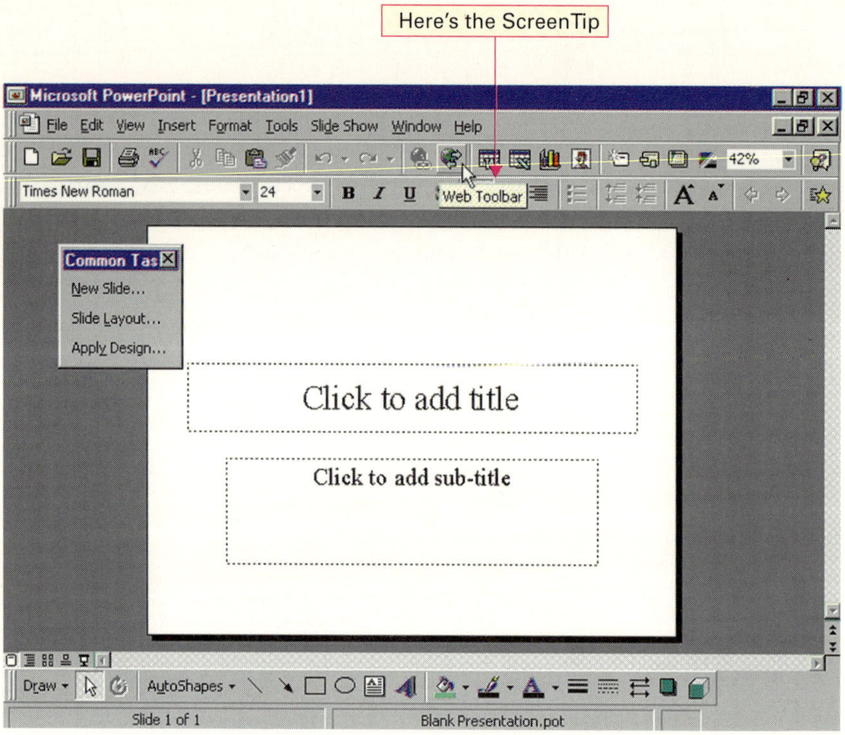

The view buttons at the bottom of the presentation window operate in much the same way as toolbar buttons. When you point to a view button, a ScreenTip identifies the view; when you click a view button, PowerPoint

Note The toolbars displayed in the PowerPoint window change automatically as you work with objects and perform different tasks.

Toolbars (such as the Common Tasks toolbar) that display on-screen with title bars are called ***floating toolbars***; toolbars that appear on-screen with no title bar are called ***docked toolbars***. You can dock a floating toolbar by dragging its title bar until the toolbar forms a narrow horizontal or vertical rectangle on any side of the PowerPoint window. You can also float toolbars by grabbing the toolbar's grip and dragging the toolbar to a new position.

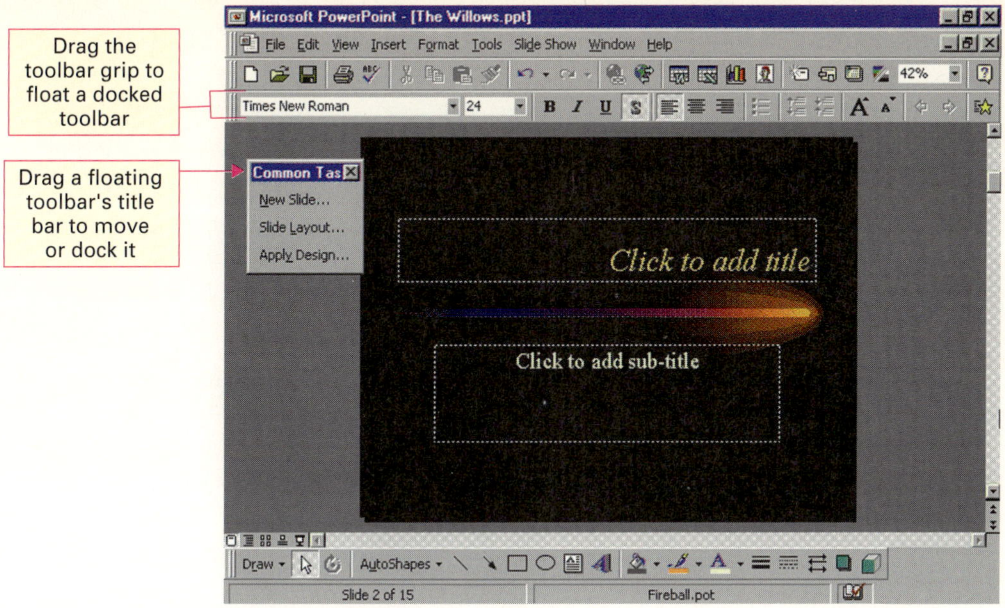

Working with Dialog Boxes

Dialog boxes appear when you select a menu command that's followed by an ellipsis and when you click certain toolbar buttons. Figure O.5 identifies features you'll see as you work with dialog boxes. Not all features will appear in every dialog box.

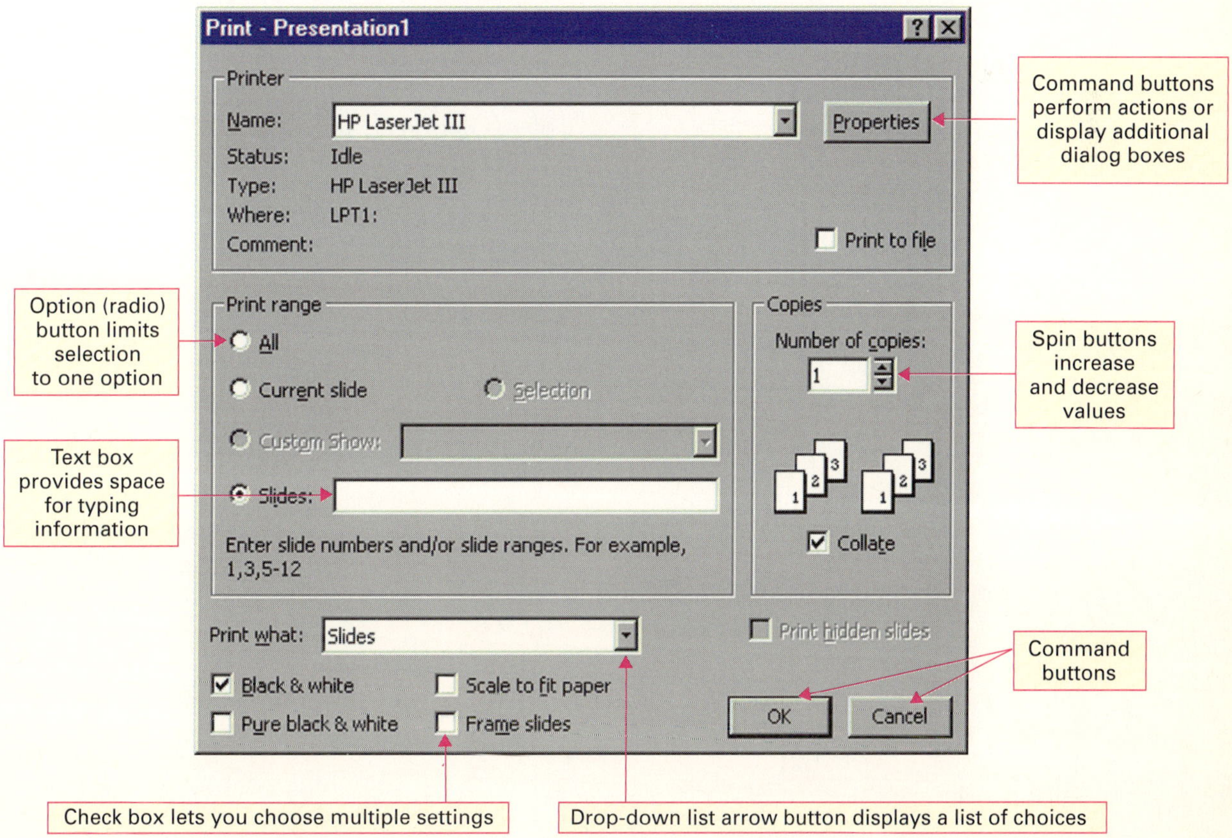

Figure O.5

TASK 3: TO DISPLAY MENUS OR DIALOG BOXES AND USE THE TOOLBAR:

1 Point to the File menu and click.

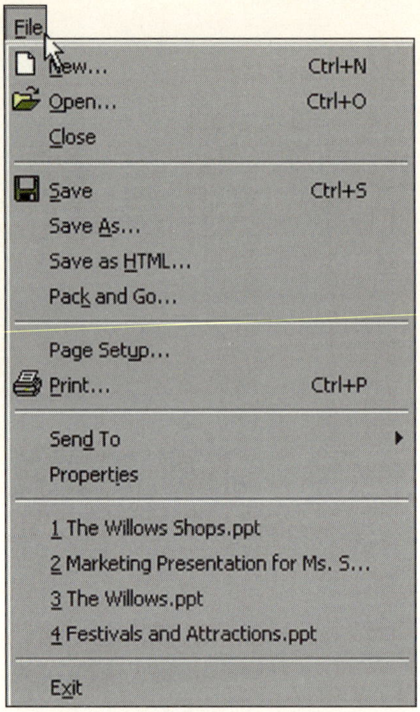

2 Choose Open.

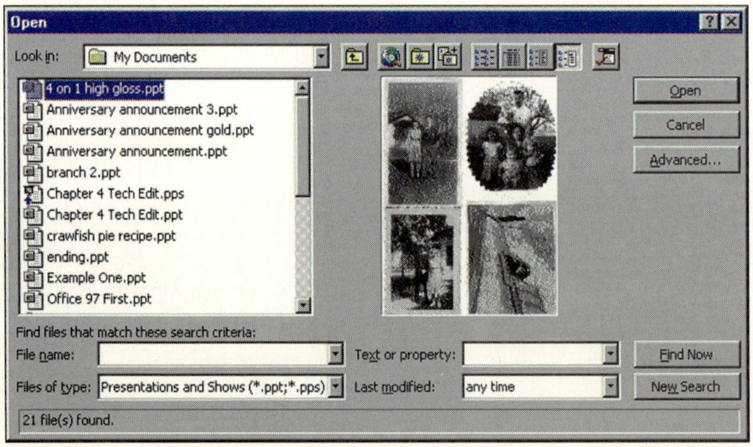

3 Click the Cancel button.
The dialog box closes and the PowerPoint presentation reappears.

4 Point to the Spelling button on the Standard toolbar and pause.

5 Click the title bar of the Common Tasks toolbar and drag it to the lower-right corner of the window.
The toolbar appears where you drop it.

6 Drag the Common Tasks title bar toward the top of the window until it becomes a flat, horizontal toolbar.

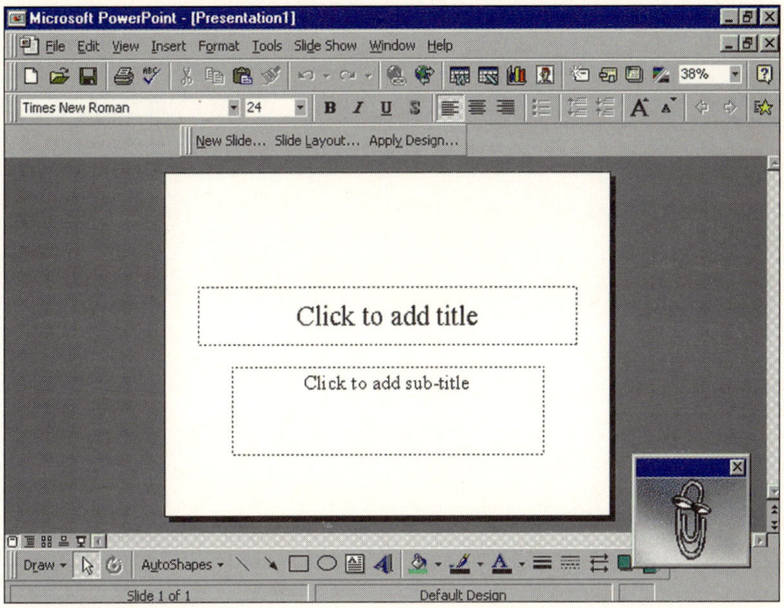

7 Grab the grip on the Common Tasks toolbar and drag it down until the toolbar is shaped as a square.

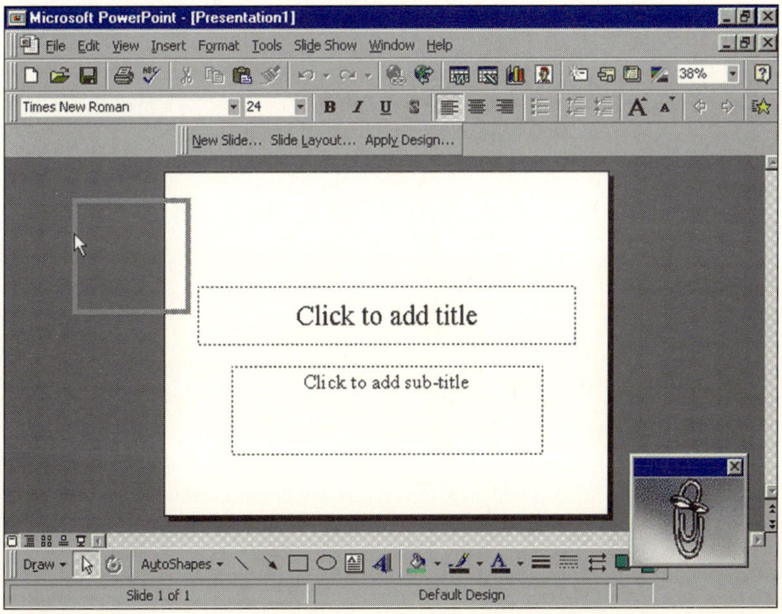

8 Release the mouse button.

9 Choose the Tools menu.

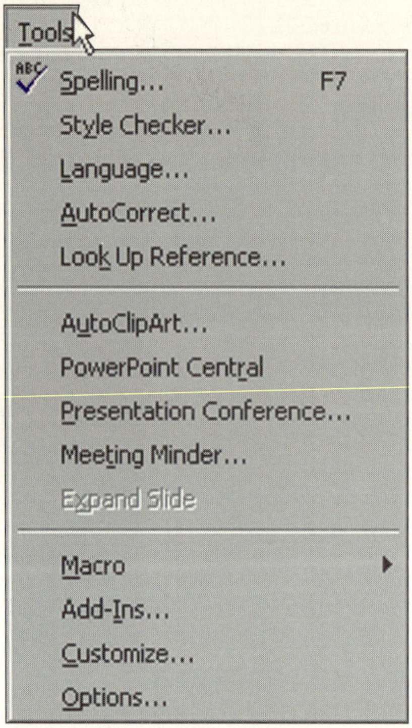

10 Press (ESC) twice to close the Tools menu.

Getting Help

PowerPoint provides numerous ways for you to get online help as you work. From the PowerPoint Help menu, you can access standard features available on the Help menus of other Microsoft Office 97 applications:

- The Office Assistant, which enables you to ask questions about the task you want to perform.
- The standard three-page Windows 95 Help dialog box, which displays Contents, Index, and Find to search for information on the topic or procedure you need.
- What's This?, to obtain a brief description of a button, feature, or command.
- Microsoft on the Web to explore information about new products, obtain answers to frequently asked questions, recommend improvements to the program, and so forth.

In addition, PowerPoint provides context-sensitive help and tips as you work. You will primarily use the Office Assistant to access Help in PowerPoint.

Note Online help has proven to be a more efficient method for obtaining help than searching through voluminous manuals for tips and information about specific programs and tasks. However, "online help" doesn't refer to connecting to the Internet or a communications provider; it simply refers to the help provided by the software that's accessible from your computer.

Using the Office Assistant

The Office Assistant is a feature new to Microsoft Office 97 applications, and already the Office Assistant is growing in popularity. The Office Assistant is easy to use, is personably animated, and provides a focused list of help topics. It opens the first time you launch PowerPoint. After that, it makes eyes at you or waits on the Standard toolbar and appears as a Johnny-on-the-spot each time you call for help.

TASK 4: TO DISPLAY, USE, AND CLOSE THE OFFICE ASSISTANT:

1 Click the Office Assistant button on the toolbar.

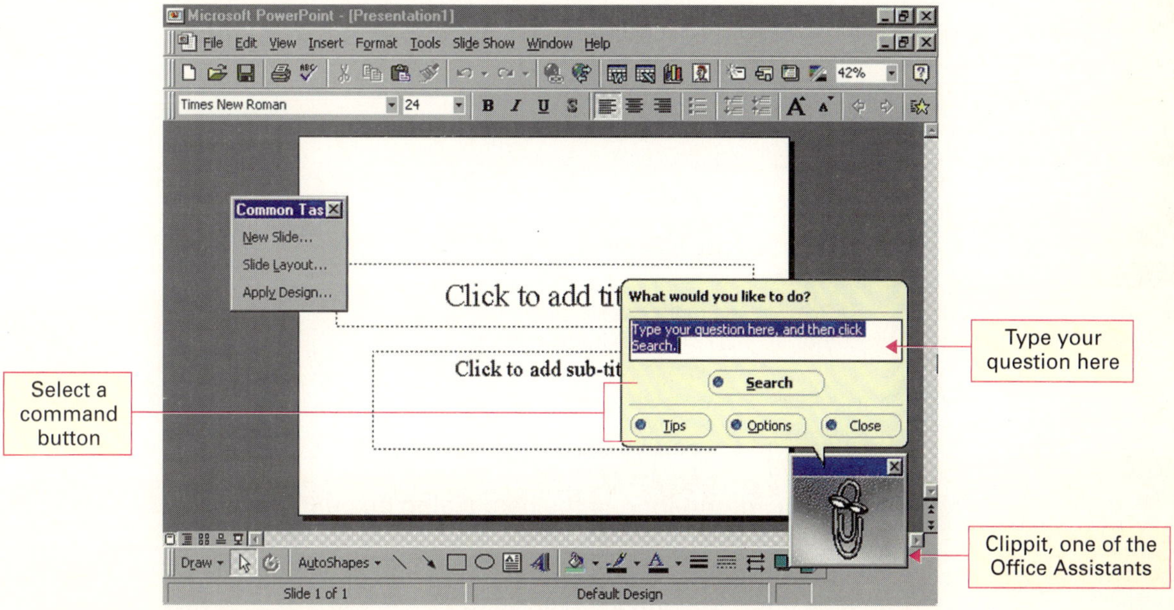

2 Type **Add a slide** in the question textbox; then press ENTER.

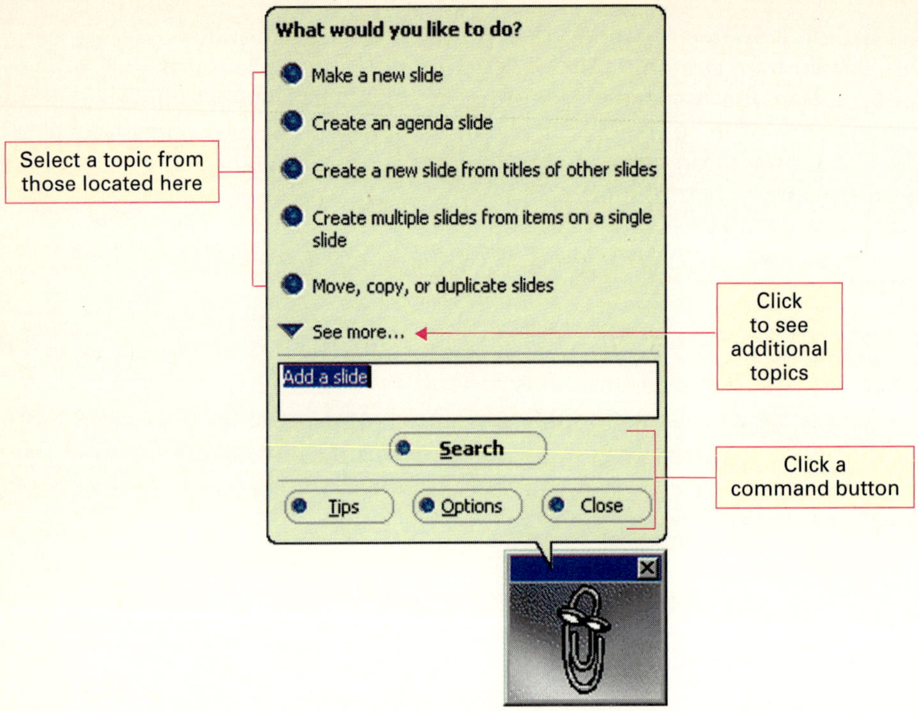

3 Click the button beside Make a new slide, at the top of the related topics list.

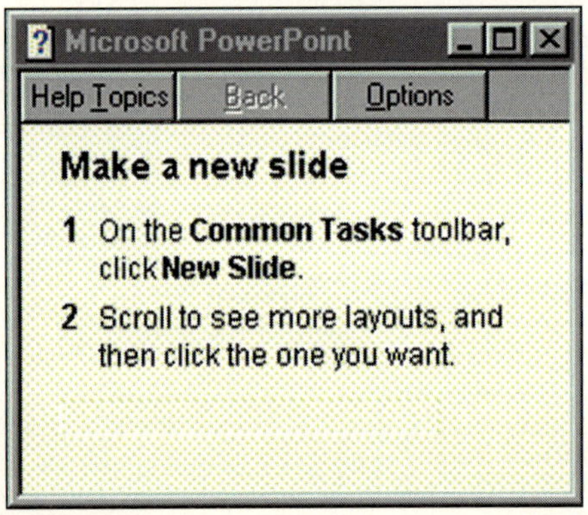

4 Review the information in the help dialog box and then click the Close button.
The list of related topics no longer appears on-screen; the Office Assistant remains on-screen until you close it.

5 Click on the Office Assistant window.

Getting Help from the Microsoft Web Site

If you're connected to the Internet, you can access the Microsoft Web site to obtain additional help information. The Web provides information directly from Microsoft support team members as well as information from other users.

TASK 5: TO ACCESS ONLINE SUPPORT FROM THE WEB:

1 Choose Help, Microsoft on the Web.

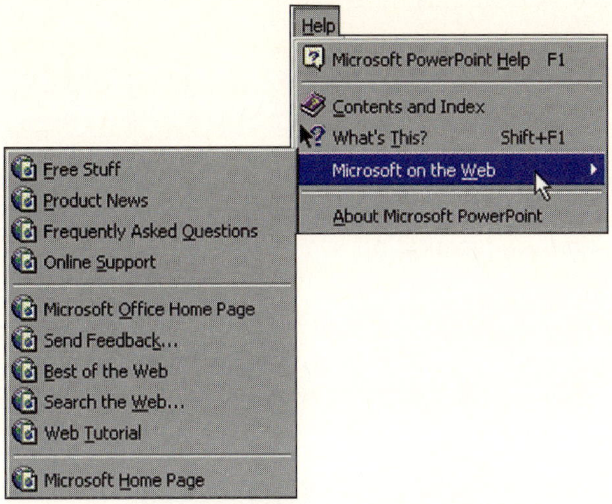

2 Choose Online Support.
Your Internet access window appears.

3 Complete the standard procedure for logging onto the Internet using your service provider.

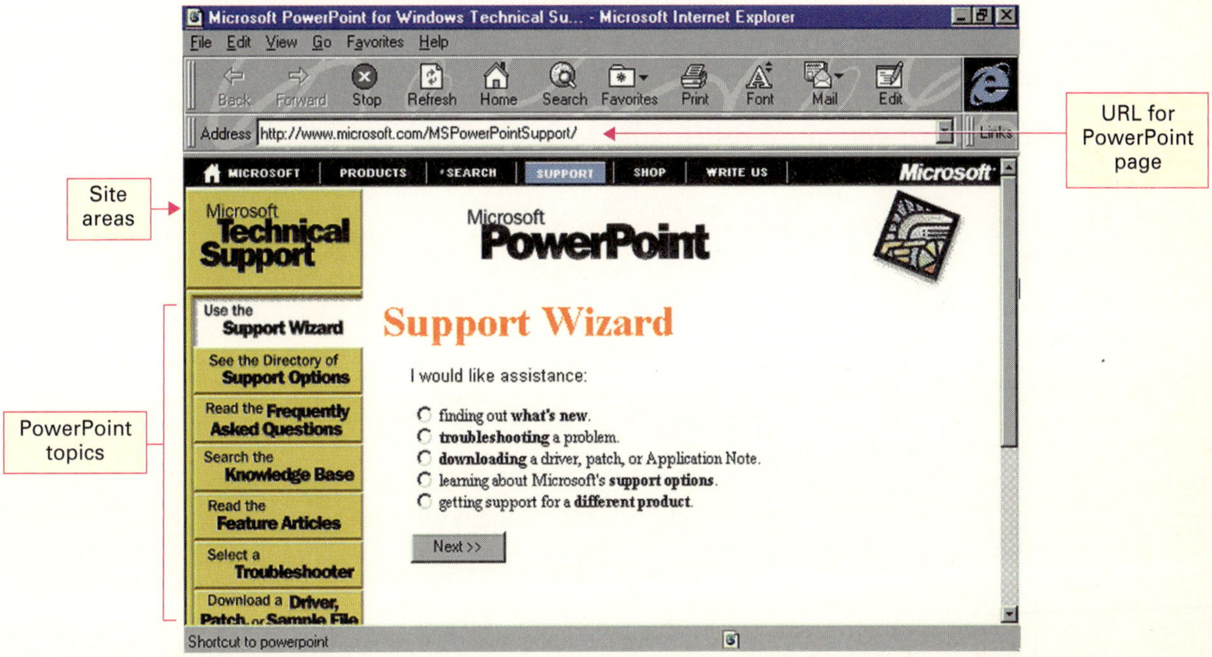

4 Select an option for which you would like assistance and click Next.
Explore several help topics when you log on and get a feel for how to navigate online support and find the information you need. Then log off the Internet.

Closing a Presentation and Exiting Microsoft PowerPoint

When you have completed your work on a presentation, you should close it. When you're finished using PowerPoint, you need to exit PowerPoint.

TASK 6: TO CLOSE A PRESENTATION AND EXIT POWERPOINT:

1. Click ☒ on the presentation window.
   As you close a presentation, PowerPoint examines the presentation and reminds you to save changes by displaying a message window. Click Yes to save changes to the presentation, No to discard changes, or Cancel to return to the presentation.

2. Click ☒ on the application window.
   If you don't save and close your presentation before exiting, PowerPoint reminds you to save changes you have made since you last saved the presentation.

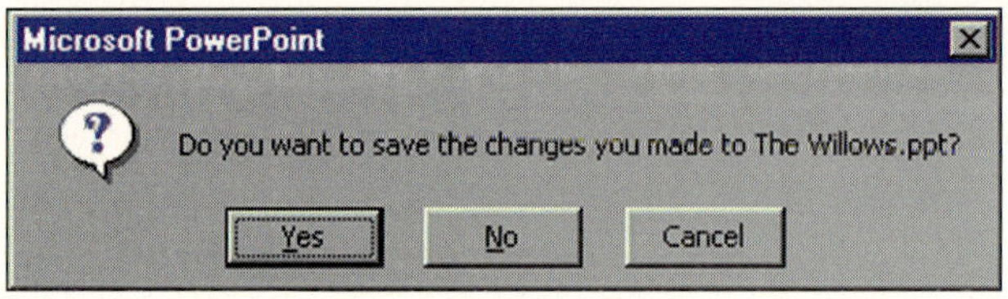

Summary and Exercises

Summary

- Microsoft PowerPoint is a presentation graphics program designed to prepare slide shows.
- Presentations may include handouts, speaker notes, slides, and outlines.
- PowerPoint displays presentations in four different views: Slide View, Outline View, Slide Sorter View, and Notes Pages View. Each view is designed to help you accomplish specific tasks.
- Each presentation may contain numerous slides, each designed to focus on a particular aspect of the broad-based presentation theme.
- Toolbars containing tools needed to accomplish specific tasks appear automatically.
- PowerPoint offers a variety of resources from which you can get online help.
- PowerPoint reminds you to save your changes before you exit the program.

Key Terms and Operations

Key Terms	Operations
AutoLayout	create a blank PowerPoint presentation
master	exit Microsoft PowerPoint
menu bar	get help with Office Assistant
Office Assistant	launch Microsoft PowerPoint
online help	retrieve help from the Web
placeholder	
ScreenTip	
status bar	
template	
title bar	
toolbar	
view	

Study Questions

Multiple Choice

1. To display the Help dialog box,
   a. choose Help, Contents, and Index.
   b. click the Office Assistant button.
   c. press Shift+F1.
   d. choose Help, About Microsoft PowerPoint.

2. To start PowerPoint,
   a. double-click the Outlook icon on the desktop.
   b. click Start and choose Microsoft PowerPoint.
   c. start Windows 95 and then press Alt+W.
   d. open My Computer.

3. PowerPoint presentations can be used to generate all of the following except
   a. slides.
   b. handouts.
   c. outlines.
   d. Masters.

4. The PowerPoint view that displays a small slide image at the top of a page and provides space for speaker notes is
   a. Slide view.
   b. Outline view.
   c. Slide Sorter view.
   d. Notes Pages view.

5. When you launch Microsoft PowerPoint,
   a. a new presentation appears.
   b. the Open dialog box appears.
   c. the PowerPoint dialog box appears so that you can tell PowerPoint whether you want to create a presentation or open an existing presentation.
   d. a blank slide appears so that you can enter your title slide.

6. The PowerPoint view that displays only title and body placeholder text is
   a. Slide view.
   b. Outline view.
   c. Slide Sorter view.
   d. Notes Pages view.

7. The PowerPoint view that makes rearranging slides easier is
   a. Slide view.
   b. Outline view.
   c. Slide Sorter view.
   d. Notes Pages view.

8. The term that refers to the layout of objects on slides is
   a. AutoLayout.
   b. Master.
   c. template.
   d. slide.

9. Professional designs that contain graphics and background color schemes you can use to dress up a presentation are called
   a. AutoLayouts.
   b. Masters.
   c. templates.
   d. slides.

10. The basic unit of a presentation is a
   a. slide.
   b. placeholder.
   c. picture.
   d. template.

Short Answer

1. What are the three default toolbars displayed in the Slide view of a presentation?
2. What's the basic object of a presentation?
3. What supporting materials can you generate from a presentation?
4. How many views are available in PowerPoint?
5. Which view allows you to type text into placeholders, create drawings on a slide, and insert other objects on the slide?
6. What toolbar is displayed in Outline view that doesn't appear in Slide View?
7. What are AutoLayouts?
8. What six things should you consider as you plan your presentation?
9. What does a grayed menu command indicate?
10. What features are available on the World Wide Web to help you as you work with PowerPoint?

For Discussion

1. How does the procedure for launching Microsoft PowerPoint differ from the procedure for launching other Windows 95 applications?
2. Why is planning your presentation important?
3. What's the difference between AutoLayout formats, templates, and Masters?
4. How does the phrase "Less is more" relate to presentations?

Review Exercises

1. Designing a New Presentation

The Willows Marketing department needs a presentation about the sports facilities at the resort. Marketing representatives will use the presentation during sales conferences and trade shows to provide an overview of the resort to prospective guests and convention planners. The Willows sporting facilities are listed in Table 0.2 on the next page. Use this list to develop a plan for the Marketing department presentation.

Table 0.2 The Willows Sporting Facilities

Facility	Features
Golf	Three 18-hole PGA courses Two driving ranges Five practice putting greens
Tennis	Ten asphalt courts Two clay courts Two grass courts
Exercise/Aerobic Center	Three saunas Four whirlpools Three massage beds scheduled by appointment Personal trainers Step aerobic classes twice daily Low impact aerobic classes daily
Miniature golf	Two 18-hole courses (Bye Bye Birdie and The Eagle's Nest)
Little Tree Playground	Heavy duty playground equipment for young children
Willow Pond Riding Stables	Fifteen horses One-, two-, and three-hour bridle paths Bicycle rentals
Willows Water Park	Wave pool Water slides Olympic-size swimming pool
The Willows Beach Front	Five miles of Atlantic Coast beach with lifeguards, a boardwalk, jet-ski rentals, surfing, etc.

2. Getting Help

Because PowerPoint comes with professionally designed templates you can use to dress up your presentation, you need to know how to apply the templates to presentations you develop. Ask the Office Assistant to locate information about applying a template to an existing presentation.

1. Click the Office Assistant button on the toolbar.
2. Type **How do I apply a template to a presentation?** in the question box of the Office Assistant window and press ENTER.
3. Click Apply a different design to a presentation in the list of items the Office Assistant displays.
4. Review the information in the Help window.
5. Click the Show me button at the top of the Help window and watch as PowerPoint identifies the Apply Design button on the toolbar.
6. Click the Apply Design button twice to display the Apply Design dialog box.
7. Click a template name in the list of templates to display a sample of the template in the view area of the dialog box.

Tip If the view area isn't displayed in the Apply Design dialog box, click the Preview button on the Apply Design toolbar to display the view area.

Assignments

1. Designing a Personal Presentation

The Willows posted a notice in the newspaper, advertising the position of design specialist in the Marketing department. As a response to the advertisement, develop a presentation outline on paper, based on your résumé, to accompany your official résumé and letter of application. Design the presentation so that it adequately relates your skills and talents.

2. Searching the Internet for Images

The Willows would like to vary the graphics included in its presentations and publications to better reflect the topics presented. Search the World Wide Web for pictures that relate to sports that you might want to include in the Sports Facilities presentation you designed earlier. Download these images to a floppy disk and make a list of filenames for the images you find.

Do not download copyrighted images.

1

PROJECT

Building a Presentation

To be effective, each presentation you create should be designed to achieve an objective. Whether the objective of the presentation is to sell a product or provide information, you can sketch out the presentation plan on paper and then create the presentation on the computer using PowerPoint. In this project, you create a blank presentation and begin building the presentation using both the Slide view and the Outline view.

Objectives

After completing this project, you will be able to:

- **Create a blank presentation and a title slide**
- **Save and close a presentation**
- **Open a presentation and add slides**
- **Navigate a presentation**
- **Apply a template**
- **Switch views**
- **Add text in Outline view**
- **Print slides as handouts and presentation outlines**

The Challenge

The managers at The Willows decided at a recent meeting that they would like to have someone develop a graphic presentation describing some of the features available at The Willows. The presentation should identify each of the facilities and give a brief description of them.

The Solution

As the graphic artist employed by The Willows, you have been asked to put your creative talents to work designing an effective presentation. Use PowerPoint to create a new presentation, add text to the slides, and format and save your presentation by following the steps presented in the tasks that follow. Figure 1.1 shows the first five slides one of the managers sketched for the presentation.

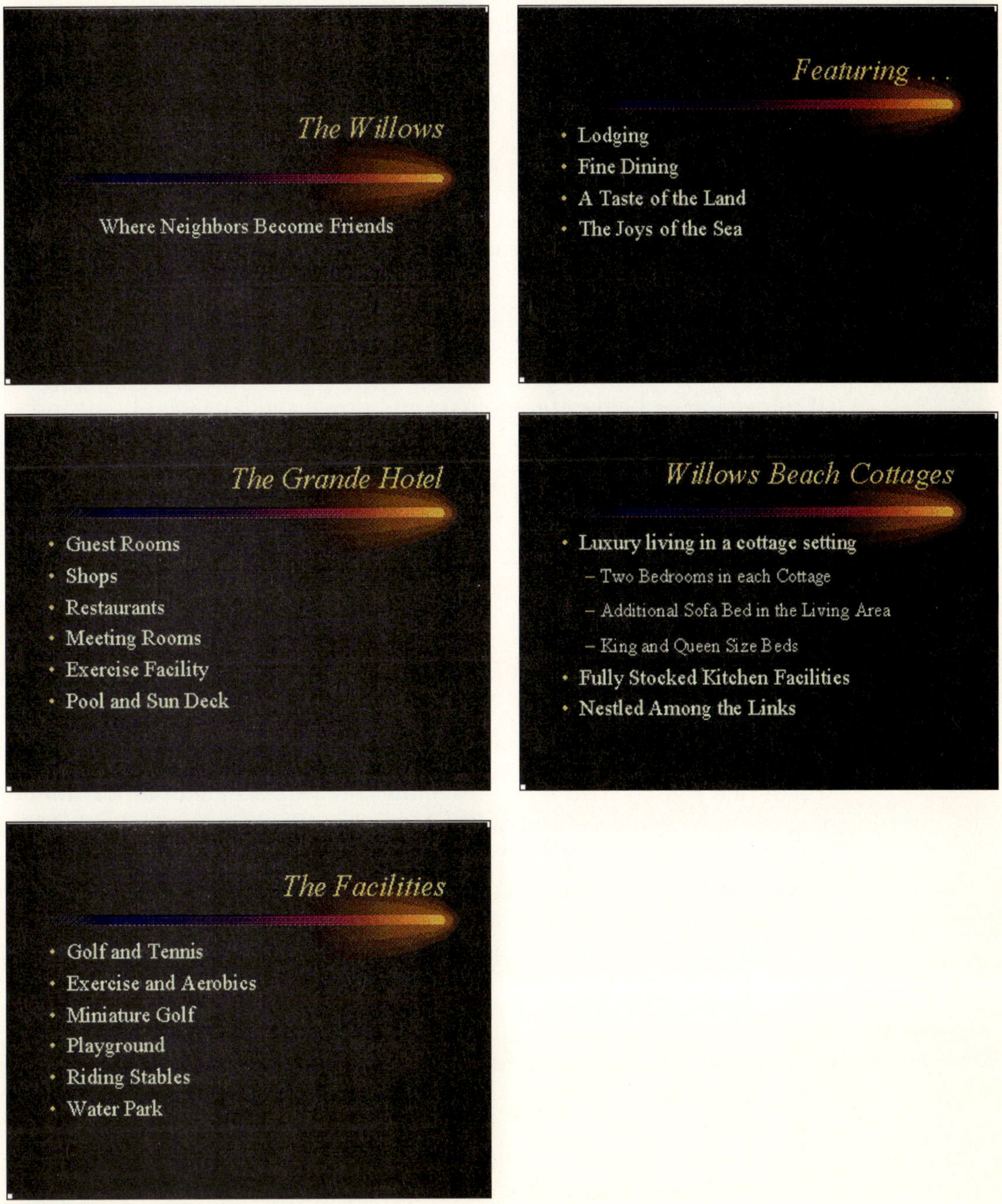

Figure 1.1

The Setup

Just to make sure that you're on the same screen as your book, you may want to check some of the settings before you get started. This book assumes that the default settings were in place when the lab guru installed PowerPoint on the machine. However, because some students nose around where they shouldn't, some of the settings may have changed.

If you don't see the default toolbars on the screen when you open a blank presentation, choose View, Toolbars. Then click Standard, Formatting, and Common Tasks and/or Drawing to display the missing toolbar(s). If you see extra toolbars, close them. PowerPoint automatically displays appropriate toolbars as you work with different views and features in the presentation, so don't be surprised when something new pops up.

If you don't see a status bar, choose Tools, Options. When the Options dialog box displays, click the View page tab and then click the check box beside Status Bar at the top of the page. While you're in the Options dialog box, check to make sure that all options on the View page tab of the dialog box are checked except the last one—end with black slide.

If rulers appear below the toolbars and down the left side of your presentation window, you can hide them, if desired, by choosing View, Ruler. You can close the Office Assistant, or leave it active. Most of the illustrations and figures don't show the Office Assistant, but you know it's there when you need it.

Creating a Blank Presentation and a Title Slide

The Blank presentation option in the opening PowerPoint dialog box lets you create a "plain vanilla" presentation with standard text format, no color, and no graphics.

Each time you create a new presentation or add a slide to an existing presentation, PowerPoint displays the New Slide dialog box, which contains 24 ***AutoLayout*** formats. Each AutoLayout format contains placeholders that outline the areas of the slide set aside to contain text and graphic ***objects*** you can include on the slide. The first slide in a presentation is generally formatted with the Title AutoLayout format.

TASK 1: TO CREATE A NEW BLANK PRESENTATION WITH A TITLE SLIDE:

1 Launch PowerPoint.

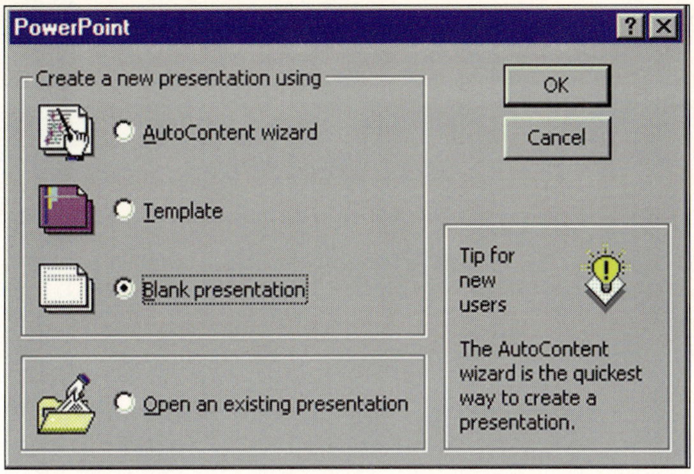

2 Click the Blank presentation option in the PowerPoint dialog box and then click OK.

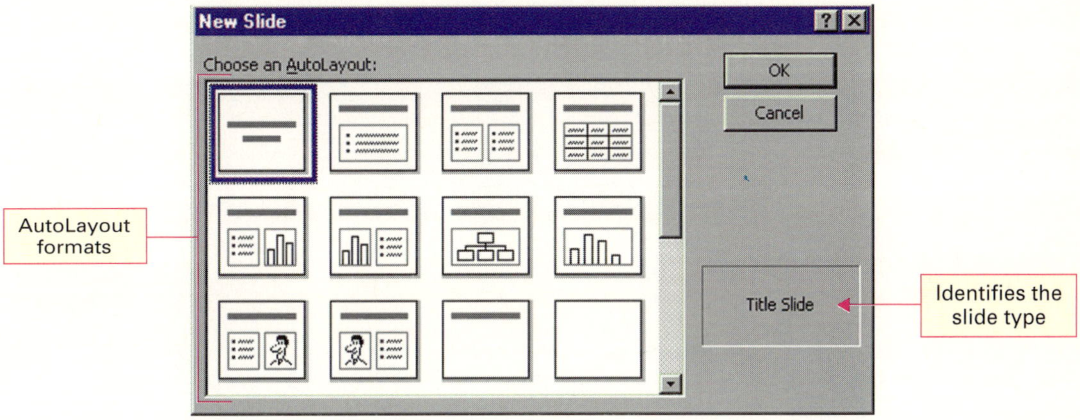

3 Click OK to accept the Title Slide AutoLayout format for the first slide.

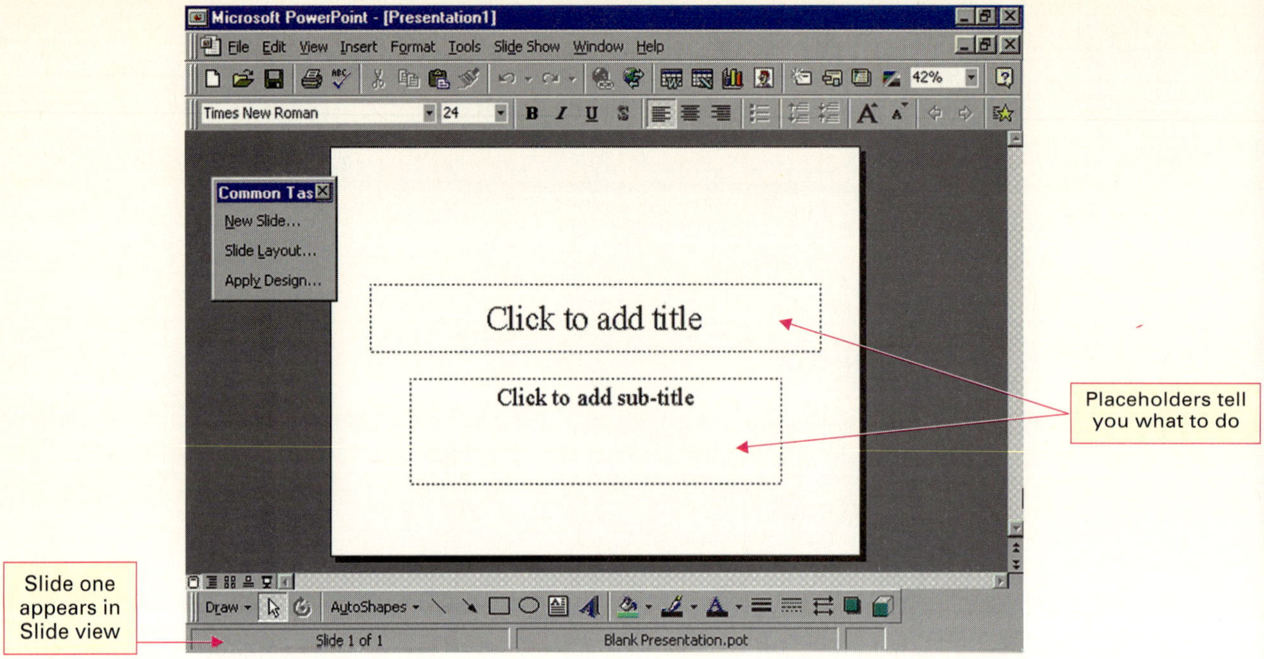

4 Click the title placeholder.
The placeholder border is selected and the insertion point appears at the center, replacing the instruction text.

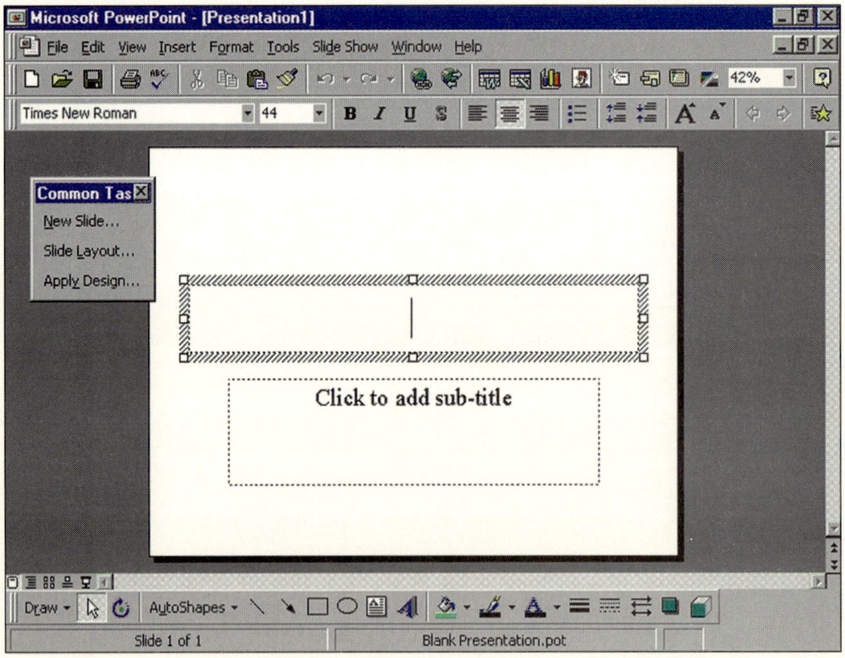

5 Type **The Willows** in the title placeholder.

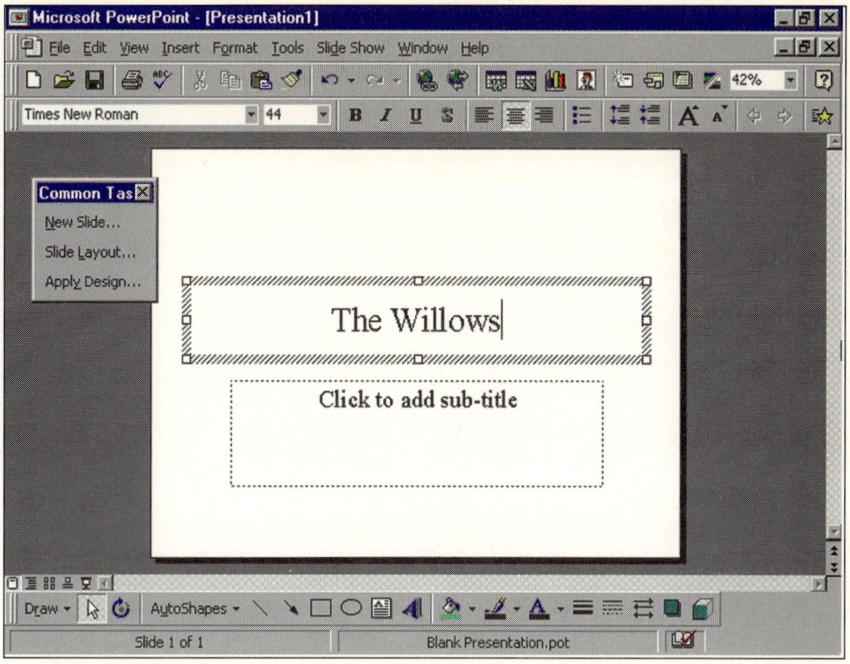

6 Press (CTRL)+(ENTER) to move to the subtitle placeholder. This area is selected and the instruction text is replaced by the insertion point.

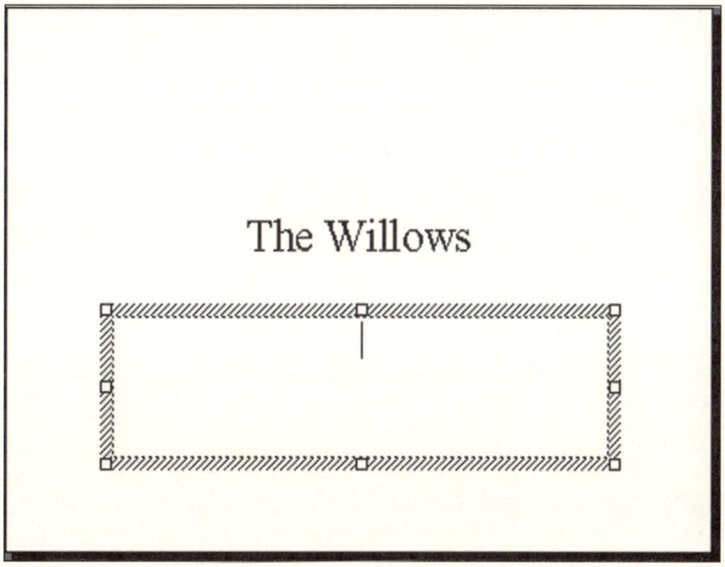

7 Type **Where Neighbors Become Friends**.

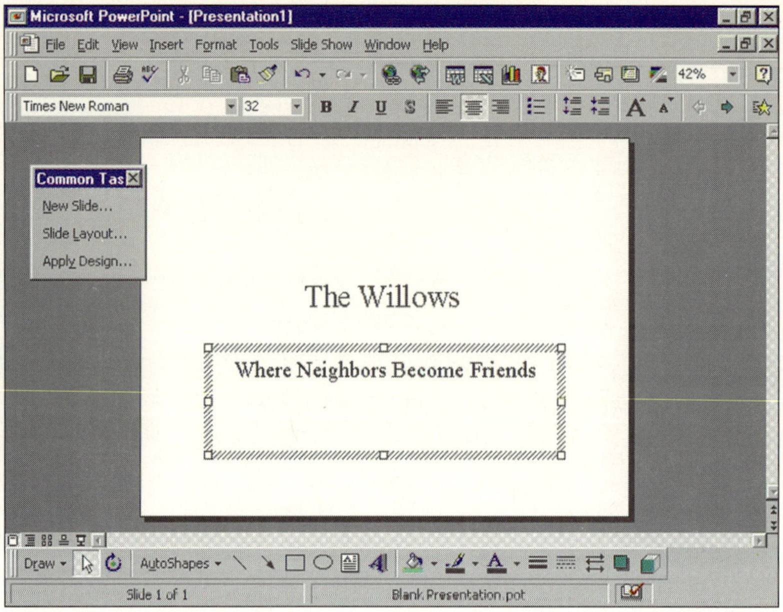

Saving and Closing a Presentation

You can use the same procedures to save a presentation in PowerPoint that you use to save files in other Windows 95 applications. All slides in the presentation are stored in one file. When you save a presentation for the first time, the Save dialog box opens the *My Documents* folder unless someone told PowerPoint to store files somewhere else. If you want to store your presentation in a different folder or on a different disk, you need to open the disk and folder before saving.

TASK 2: TO SAVE AND CLOSE A PRESENTATION:

1 Click the Save button on the Standard toolbar.

2 Select a folder to store the presentation.
The folder you choose to store your document should appear in the Save in text box at the top of the Save window.

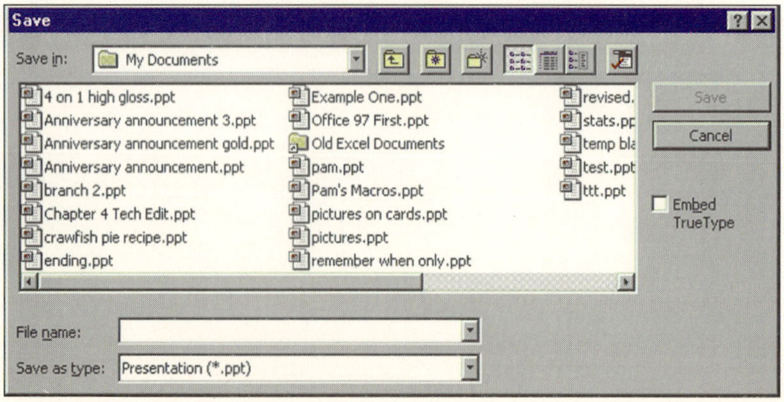

3. Type **The Willows** in the file name box and press (ENTER) or click the Save button.

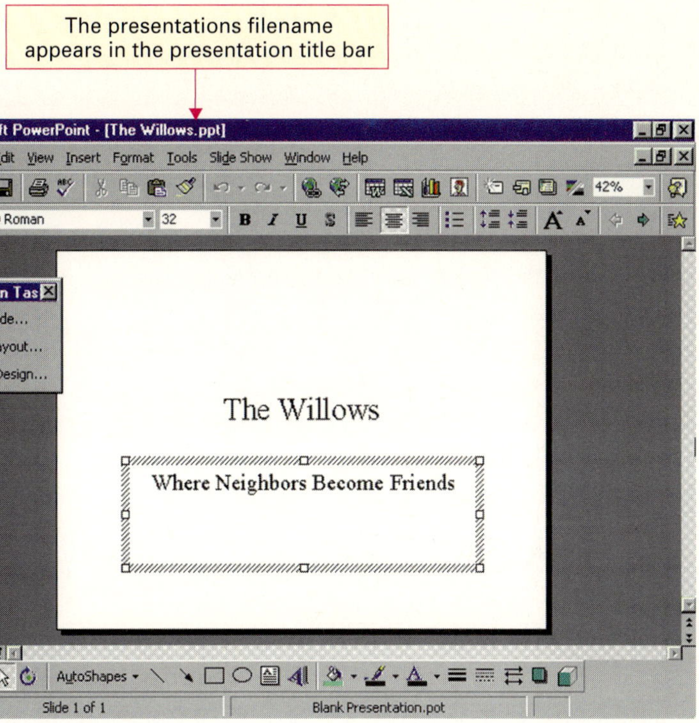

4. Click the Close [X] button for the presentation window to close the presentation.

> **Note** To create a new blank presentation after closing a presentation, click the New button on the Standard toolbar.

Opening a Presentation and Adding Slides

Most presentations consist of a series of slides, each devoted to a particular topic you want to cover in the presentation. Behind each topic slide you often need to add slides to provide explanatory information about the topic, or supporting documentation. When you want to add slides to an existing presentation, you need to open the presentation and display the slide that the new slide(s) will follow.

The procedures you use to open a presentation when PowerPoint is running are the same procedures you use to open files in most Windows 95 applications. You can also select the Open an existing presentation option from the PowerPoint dialog box when you launch PowerPoint.

TASK 3: TO OPEN A PRESENTATION AND ADD SLIDES:

1 Click the Open button.

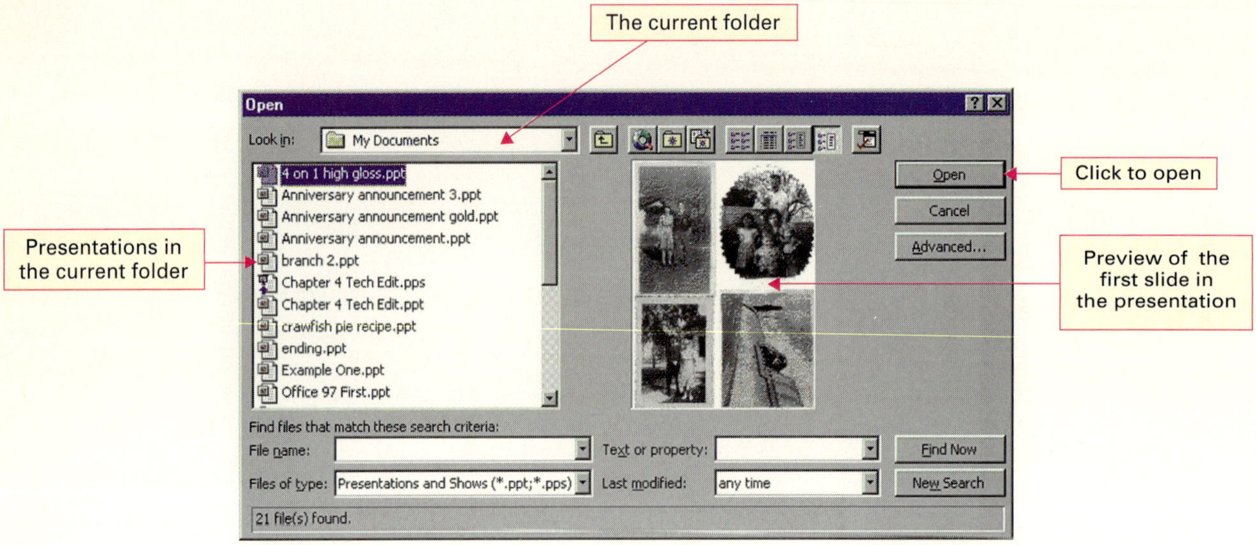

2 Select the folder containing your presentation from the Look in drop-down list and double-click the presentation called *The Willows*.

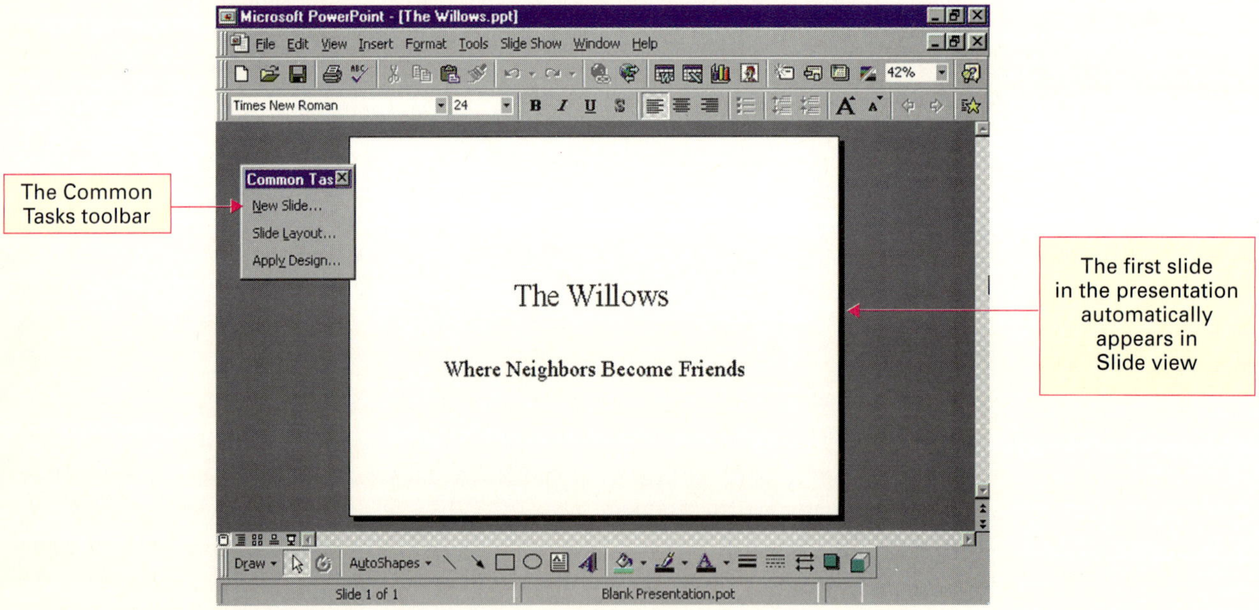

3 Click New Slide in the Common Tasks toolbar.

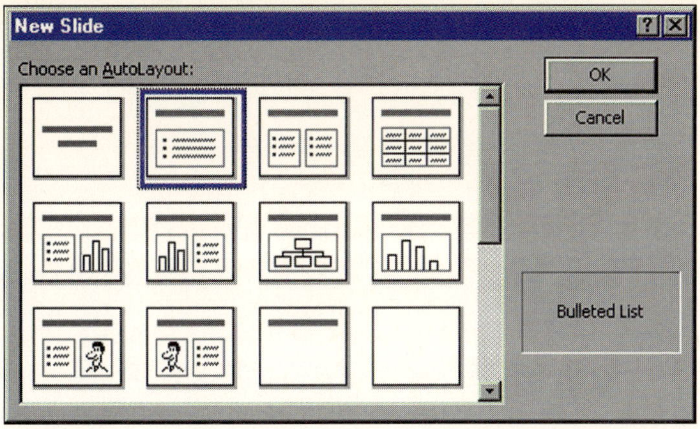

4 Click the Bulleted List AutoLayout format, if necessary, and click OK.

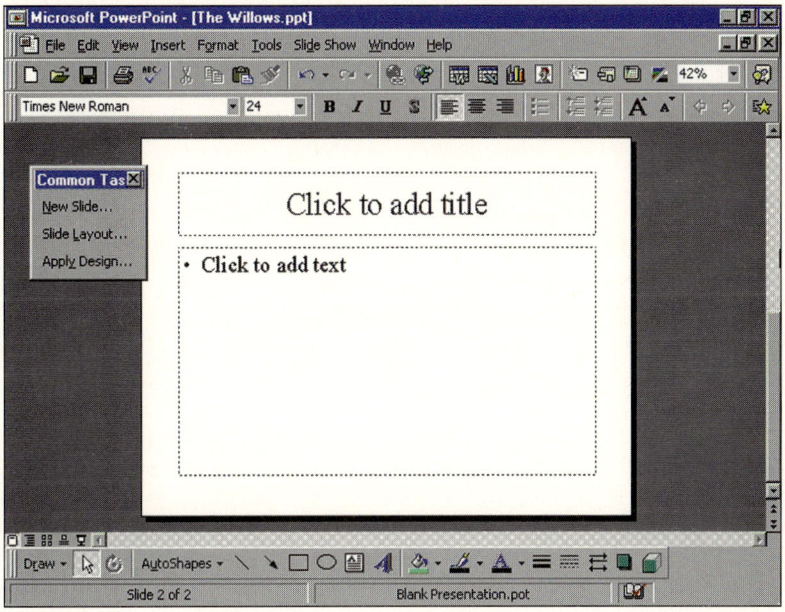

5 Click the title placeholder and type **Featuring . . .**

6 Click the bulleted list placeholder; then type **Lodging** and press (ENTER).

7 Type **Fine Dining** and press (ENTER).

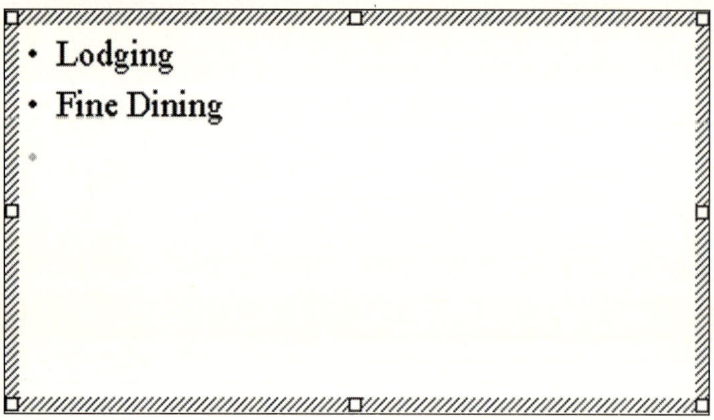

8 Repeat step 7, substituting the text shown below for the last two bulleted items:

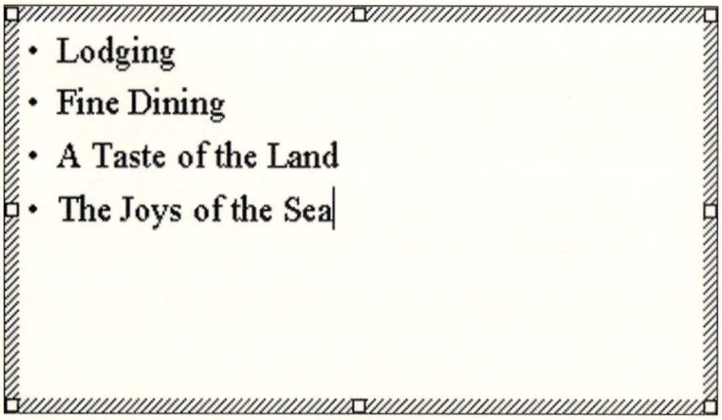

9 Press (CTRL)+(ENTER) to create another new bulleted list slide.

> **Note** Pressing Ctrl+Enter from any other placeholder activates the next placeholder on the slide instead of creating a new slide.

Navigating a Presentation

As you build your presentation and your presentation begins to grow, you need to be able to navigate among the slides to display the slides you need to edit or review. You can use both the mouse and keyboard to display different slides in Slide view. Figure 1.2 identifies techniques for navigating slides using the mouse.

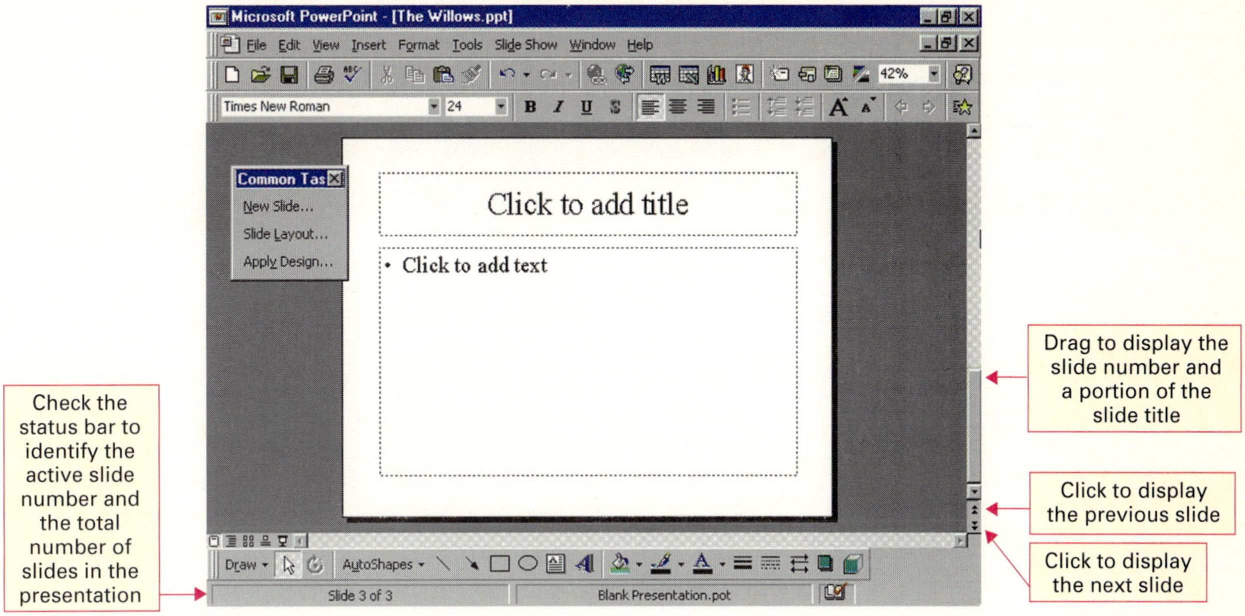

Figure 1.2

TASK 4: TO NAVIGATE SLIDES IN A PRESENTATION:

1. Press (PGUP) to display Slide 2 of the presentation *The Willows.*
2. Press (CTRL)+(HOME) to display the first slide in the presentation.
3. Press (PGDN) to display Slide 2 of the presentation.
4. Press (CTRL)+(END) to display the last slide in the presentation.
5. Click the Show Previous Slide button to display Slide 2.
6. Click the scroll box and drag it to the top of the scroll bar to display Slide 1.

Applying a Template

PowerPoint provides a number of ***templates*** that you can use to enhance the look of your presentation. Templates provide the style, color, and pizzazz your presentation needs to attract the attention of your audience. Templates hold special font formats and text alignments, background color, and bullet formats for text contained in placeholders of the presentation. Applying a template to a presentation helps maintain consistency among the slides in your presentation.

Templates are stored in a special *Templates* folder that automatically opens when you choose a template command from the menu or toolbars. When you apply a template, all slides in the presentation are automatically formatted with the template design.

TASK 5: TO APPLY A TEMPLATE TO A PRESENTATION:

1. Click Apply Design in the Common Tasks toolbar.

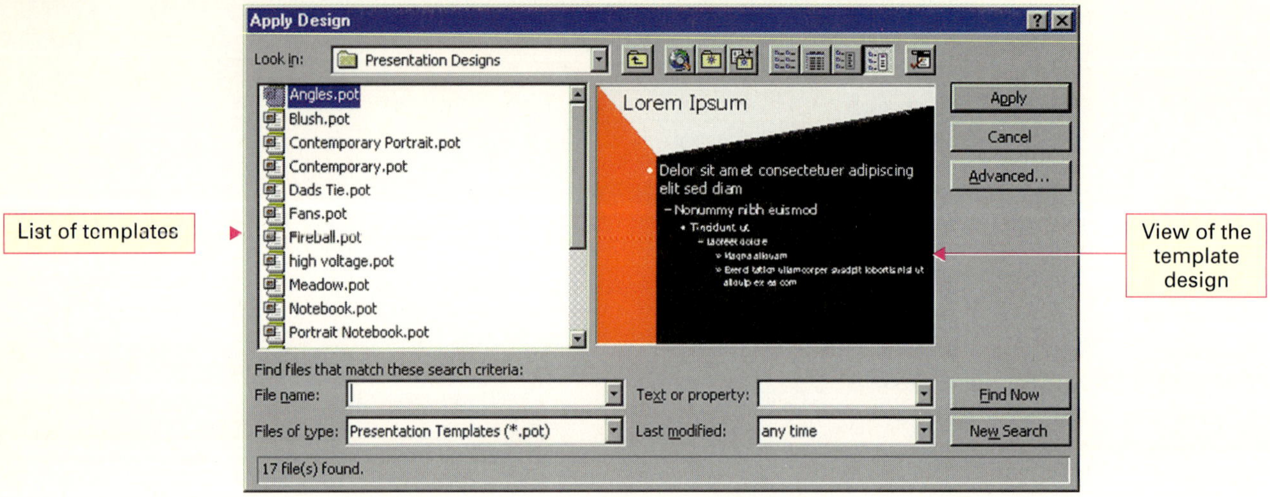

2. Click Fireball.pot and view the template design.

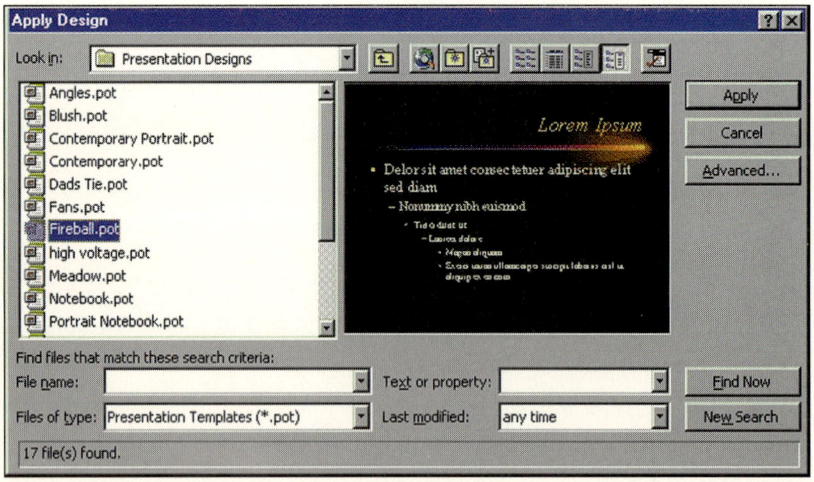

3 Click Apply to apply the template to the presentation.

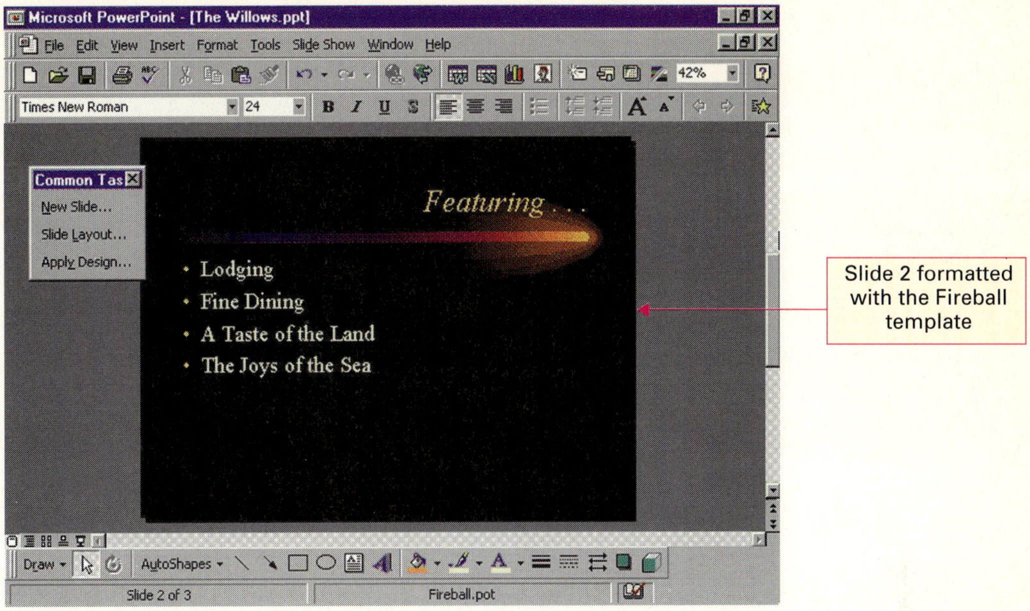

Switching Views

When you want to review the flow of a presentation or view all slides after applying a new slide format or design, you can display your presentation using a different view. The default view, the view you have been working in, is called slide view. Slide Sorter view displays small images (often called ***thumbnail images***) of each slide in the presentation so that you can review the effects of applying a template design to all the slides in the presentation. Outline view displays the title and body text you add to placeholders in a notebook-like format so you can review the content of the presentation.

TASK 6: TO SWITCH VIEWS:

1 Position the mouse pointer on the third view button at the bottom of the presentation window.

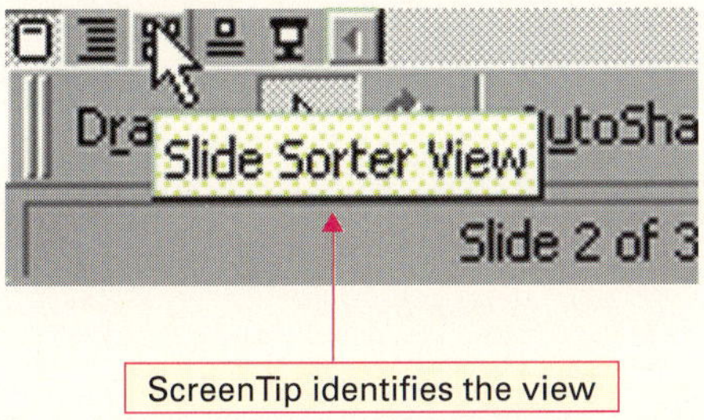

2 Click the Slide Sorter View button.

Each slide in the presentation is formatted with the template

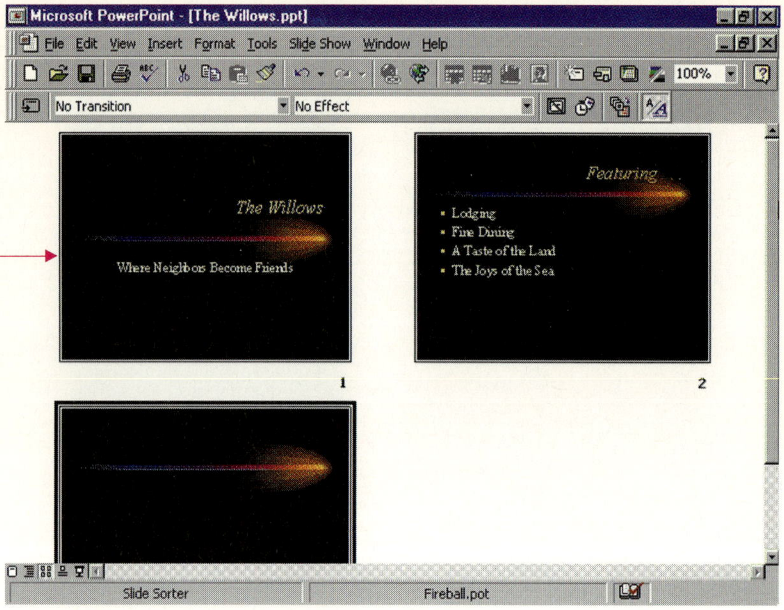

Tip If the Common Tasks toolbar gets in your way, point to the toolbar's title bar and drag it out of the way.

3 Click Slide 3 and then click the Outline View button.
Title and body placeholder text shows the slide content.

Click to promote the text to title or higher level

Click to demote the text to bulleted list points or subtitle text

Type the title for the next slide here

Slide icons and numbers show where new slides start

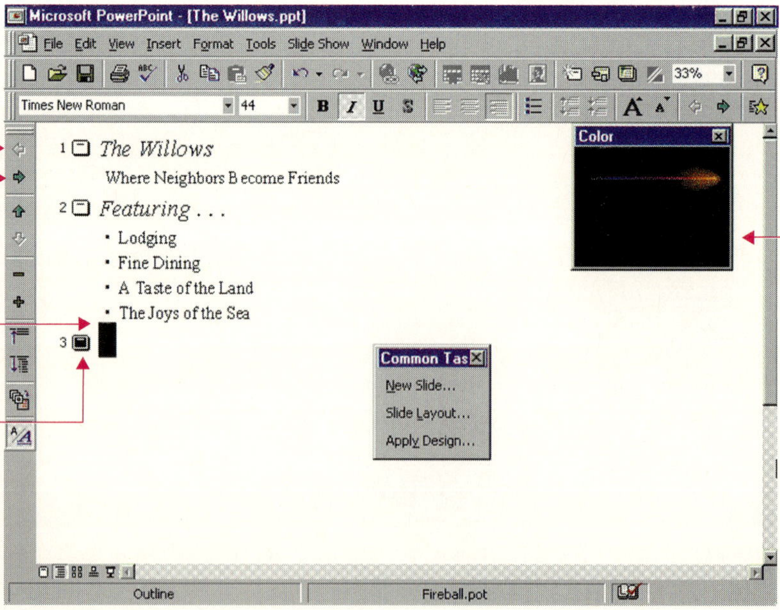

View of the slide in the Color box

Adding Text in Outline View

When you have developed an outline of text and information you want to include in a presentation, you'll find that Outline view enables you to type the title and body text for your slides more quickly. PowerPoint provides formatting for five levels of text plus the title text on a slide. You can move to the next text level by pressing Tab and return to a higher text level by pressing Shift+Tab. When you finish typing the outline text, you can view the slides in Slide view and add graphics and other enhancements to individual slides or apply a presentation design to all slides.

TASK 7: TO ADD TEXT IN OUTLINE VIEW:

1 Type **The Grande Hotel** as the title for Slide 3 and press (ENTER).

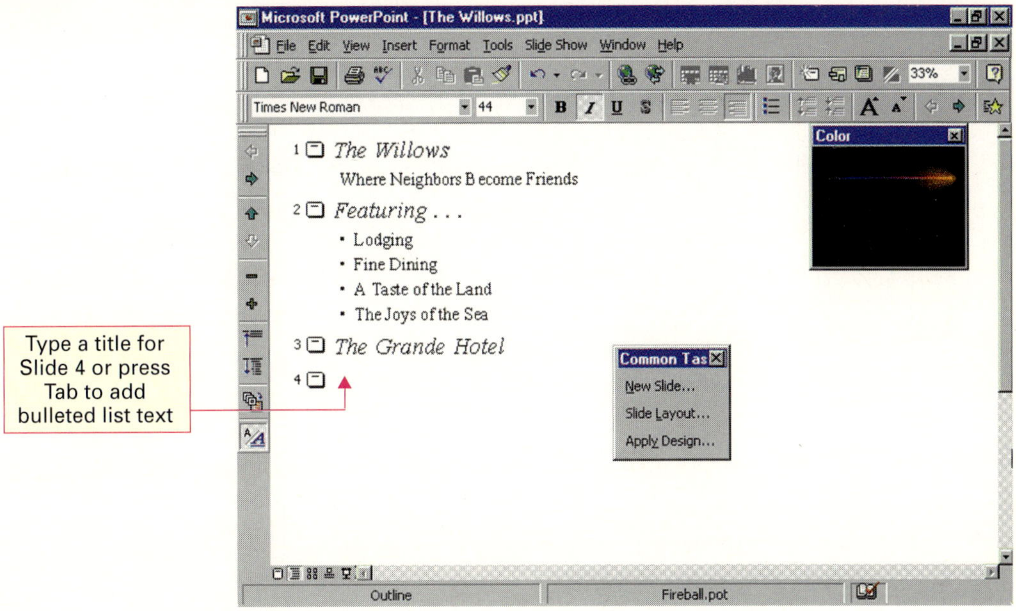

2 Press (TAB) to add the bulleted list text and then type:

Guest Rooms
Shops
Restaurants
Meeting Rooms
Exercise Facility
Pool and Sun Deck

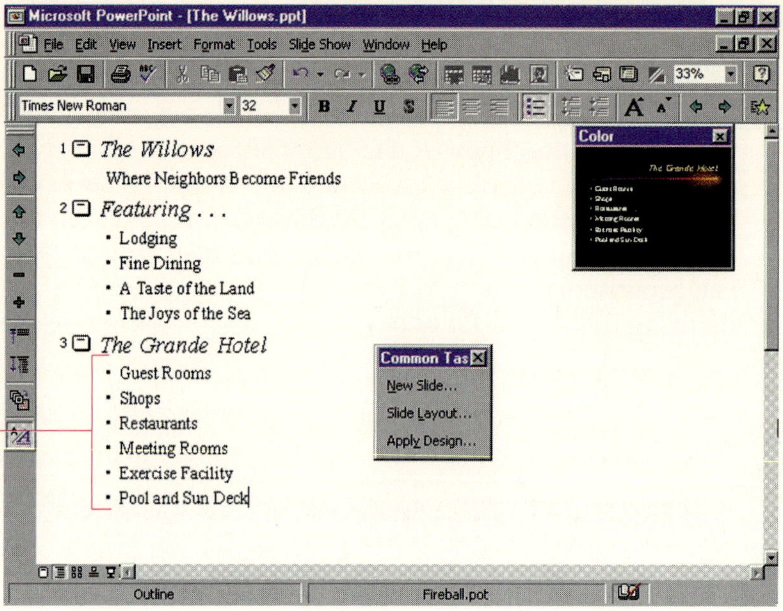

Bulleted list for Slide 3

3 Press (ENTER) after typing the last bullet point and then press (CTRL) + (ENTER) to start a new slide. Continue typing to create the following slides:

4 *Willows Beach Cottages*
- Luxury living in a cottage setting
  - – Two Bedrooms in each Cottage
  - – Additional Sofa Bed in Living Area
  - – King and Queen Size Beds
- Fully Stocked Kitchen Facilities
- Nestled Among the Links

5 *The Facilities*
- Golf and Tennis
- Exercise and Aerobics
- Miniature Golf
- Playground
- Riding Stables
- Water Park

Press Tab to indent to a second level of bulleted list

Press Shift+Tab to return to the first level of bullets

Press Ctrl+Enter to create the new slides

4 Save the changes to the presentation.

Printing Slides, Handouts, and Presentation Outlines

Because PowerPoint is primarily a graphically oriented program and can print your presentation in a variety of formats, the Print dialog box contains features and options unique to PowerPoint. For example, you can print each slide individually on a sheet of paper, print multiple slides on the same page in a format called ***handouts***, or print the Outline view of your presentation. Figure 1.3 identifies additional print options that you can set to control the quality of the print for different types of printers.

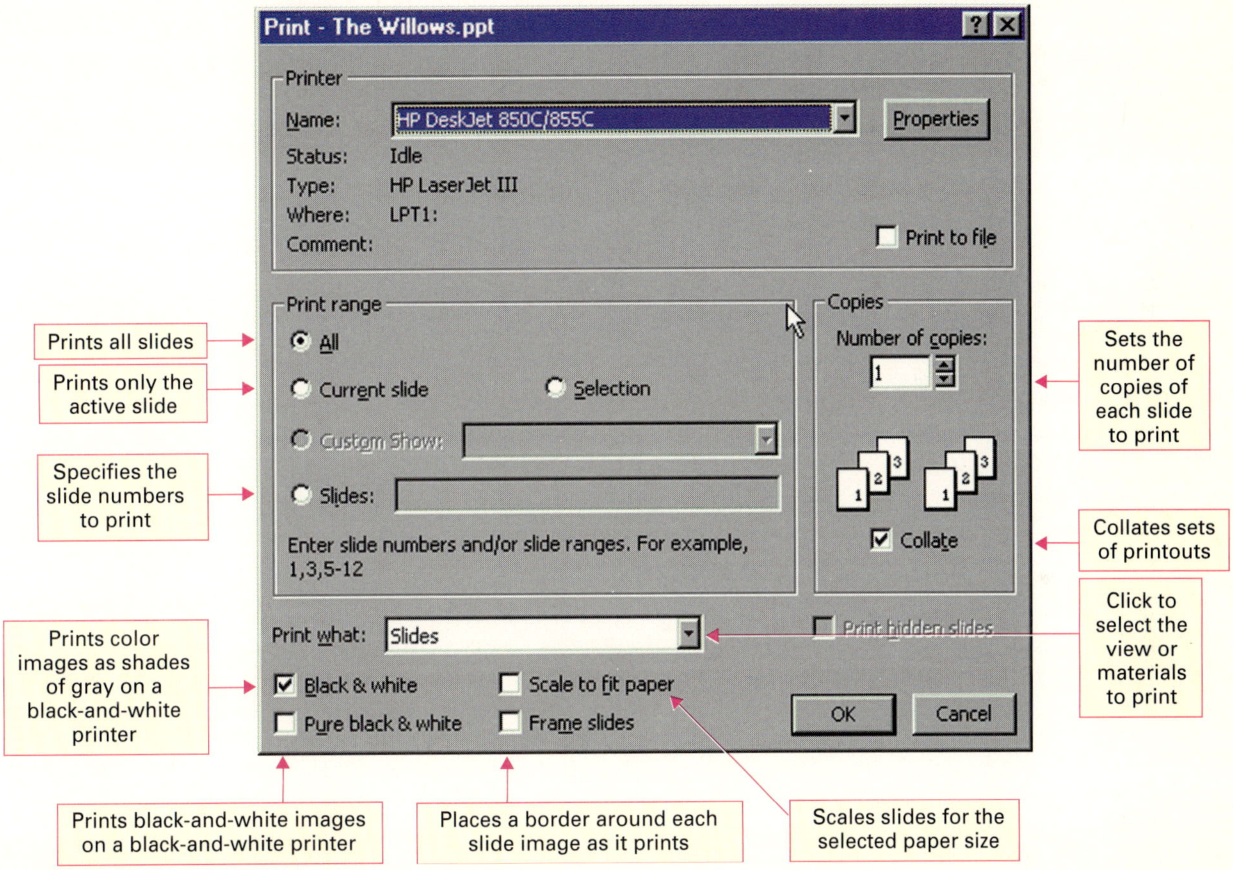

Figure 1.3

TASK 8: TO PRINT SLIDES AND OUTLINES:

1. Choose File, Print to display the Print dialog box shown in Figure 1.3.

> **Tip** To bypass the Print dialog box and print the complete presentation using the print settings last set, click the Print button on the Standard toolbar. Each time you launch PowerPoint, the print settings return to the default settings.

2. Click the drop-down arrow at the end of the Print What text box.

3 Click Handouts (Six Slides per Page).

4 Click the Black & White check box, if necessary, and click OK. PowerPoint compiles the slides, sizes them for printing together on one page, and then prints the slides (see Figure 1.4).

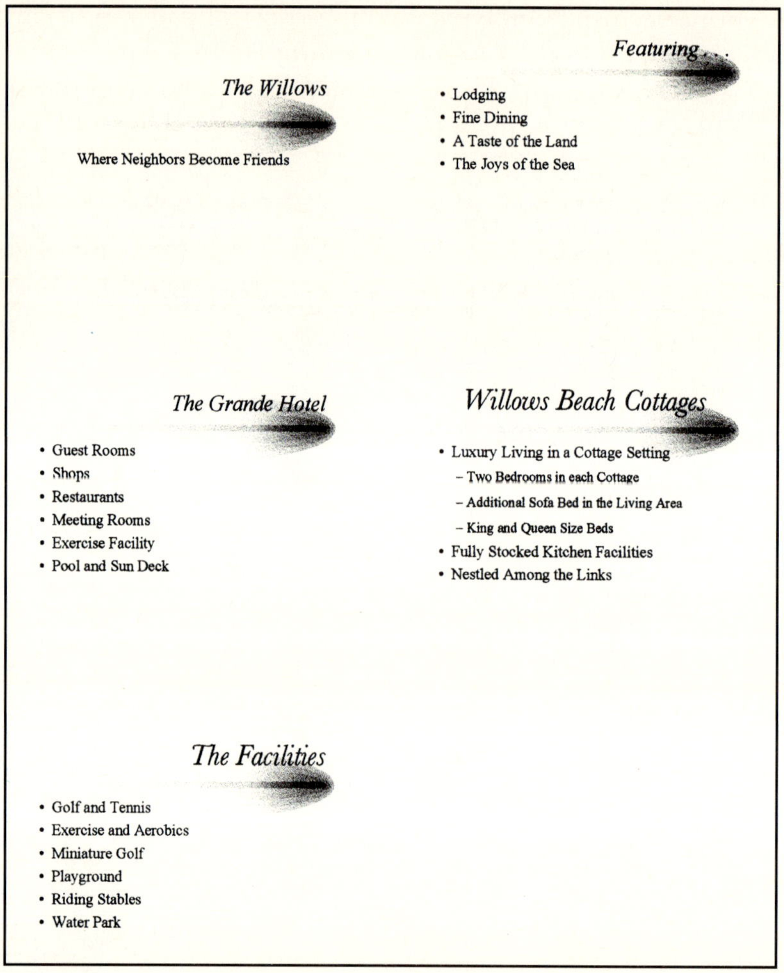

Figure 1.4

5 Choose File, Print again, select Outline View from the Print What drop-down list, and click OK (see Figure 1.5).

1 *The Willows*
Where Neighbors Become Friends

2 *Featuring . . .*
- Lodging
- Fine Dining
- A Taste of the Land
- The Joys of the Sea

3 *The Grande Hotel*
- Guest Rooms
- Shops
- Restaurants
- Meeting Rooms
- Exercise Facility
- Pool and Sun Deck

4 *Willows Beach Cottages*
- Luxury Living in a Cottage Setting
  - Two Bedrooms in each Cottage
  - Additional Sofa Bed in the Living Area
  - King and Queen Size Beds
- Fully Stocked Kitchen Facilities
- Nestled Among the Links

5 *The Facilities*
- Golf and Tennis
- Exercise and Aerobics
- Miniature Golf
- Playground
- Riding Stables
- Water Park

Figure 1.5

The Conclusion

If time permits, practice printing different materials and setting different options in the Print dialog box to see the effects they have on the way your slides print. When you're done, save changes to the presentation and close the presentation. If you've completed your work in PowerPoint, exit the program and shut down your computer as instructed.

Summary and Exercises

Summary

- PowerPoint enables you to create blank presentations formatted with no special design as well as presentations formatted using special designs called templates. You can change the look of slides in a presentation by selecting a different template design.
- AutoLayout formats make creating slides with preformatted text easier.
- You can add, delete, format, and select presentation text using many of the same techniques used in other Windows-based programs.
- PowerPoint displays presentation slides using four different views: Slide view, Slide Sorter view, Notes Pages view, and Outline view. Each view is designed to help you accomplish specific tasks.
- Presentations normally contain numerous slides; you can add slides and move from slide to slide in a presentation using a variety of different mouse and keyboard techniques.
- You save, open, close, and print presentations using many of the same procedures used in other Windows applications; you can print a variety of different presentation materials by selecting the desired format from the Print dialog box.

Key Terms and Operations

Key Terms	Operations
AutoLayout	add slides to a presentation
handouts	create, save, open, and close a presentation
Outline view	move around a presentation
Notes Pages view	print slides and handouts
Slide Sorter view	switch presentation views
template	use templates to change the look of a presentation

Study Questions

Multiple Choice

1. To create a new, blank presentation,
   a. simply launch PowerPoint—a new presentation automatically appears.
   b. choose New Presentation from the PowerPoint dialog box.
   c. select Blank presentation from the PowerPoint dialog box and press Enter.
   d. select Template from the PowerPoint dialog box and press Enter.

2. Slides added to a presentation are formatted using
   a. an AutoLayout format.
   b. text and title boxes.
   c. blank slides that resemble blank pieces of paper.
   d. outlines.

3. New slide layouts contain
   a. fields.
   b. placeholders.
   c. tables.
   d. templates.

4. Placeholders identify
   a. slide names.
   b. slide fields.
   c. slide titles.
   d. slide objects.

5. To add a new slide to a presentation, use any of the following techniques *except*
   a. double-clicking the active slide.
   b. clicking the New Slide button on the toolbar.
   c. clicking the New Slide command on the Common Tasks toolbar.
   d. choosing Insert, New Slide from the menu.

6. Most slides contain
   a. slide tables.
   b. pictures.
   c. slide titles.
   d. slide names.

7. Outline view displays
   a. all slide objects.
   b. slide title and body text only.
   c. small slide images.
   d. slide images and notes about the slide.

8. Slide Sorter view displays
   a. all slide objects.
   b. slide title and body text only.
   c. small slide images.
   d. slide images and notes about the slide.

9. Notes Pages view displays
   a. all slide objects.
   b. slide title and body text only.
   c. small slide images.
   d. slide images and notes about the slide.

10. Slide view displays
   a. all slide objects.
   b. slide title and body text only.
   c. small slide images.
   d. slide images and notes about the slide.

Short Answer

1. How do you create a new presentation if PowerPoint is already running?
2. What's a template?
3. What are AutoLayout formats and what do they contain?
4. What are the four presentation views and when should you use each view?
5. How do you switch views?
6. How do you print handouts?
7. How can you use the vertical scroll bar to display a specific slide?

8. How do you apply a template?
9. How do you open a presentation when you launch PowerPoint?
10. How do you move from one placeholder on a slide to another without using the mouse?

For Discussion

1. What are the four options in the PowerPoint dialog box when you launch PowerPoint and what does each option enable you to do?
2. How do you identify the material you want to print, and what options should you check if you're using a black-and-white printer?
3. What are the advantages of formatting a presentation by using a template?
4. What kind of presentations could you create with PowerPoint for your other classes?

Review Exercises

1. Creating, Saving, and Adding Slides and Text to Presentations

Ruth Lindsey, Manager of The Willows Shops, has been asked to display the diversity of gift items available in different shops at The Willows. She has developed the preliminary outline shown in Figure 1.6 and asks you to create a presentation using the outline.

1 The Willows Shops
  Where Exploring Becomes an Adventure
2 The Newsstand
  - Newspapers
  - Magazines
  - Recent Publications
  - The Willows Post Office
3 Sindy's Sun Closet
  - Swimsuits
  - Bathing Accessories
  - Lotions
  - Towels
  - Flippers
4 Weeping Willow Gallery
  - Paintings
  - Sculpture
  - Iron Works
  - Local Artists
5 Live Oak Gifts
6 Creative Cutlery
  - A Wide Assortment of Kitchen Wares
7 Cherry Street Market
  - Home Grown Produce
  - Natural Flora from the Carolinas
8 Victorian Tea Room
  - Victorian gifts and clothing
  - Victorian High Tea Served Daily
9 Ken's Kids
  - Children's games and toys
  - Children's clothing
10 Appalachian Crafts
  - Treasures from the Hills
  - Displays of local artists

Figure 1.6

Using PowerPoint, create a new blank presentation named *The Willows Shops*. Follow these instructions to complete the presentation:

1. Launch PowerPoint and create a new blank presentation that contains a title slide.

2. Switch to Outline view and add the text shown in Figure 1.6.
3. Save the presentation using the filename *The Willows Shops*.
4. Close the presentation and exit PowerPoint when you have completed your work.

2. Switching Views, Navigating Presentation Slides, Applying a Template, and Printing Handouts

Ms. Lindsey would like a copy of the slides in the presentation *The Willows Shops* for her assistant managers to review before she makes the presentation. She would like to have the presentation slides formatted using the template shown in Figure 1.7.

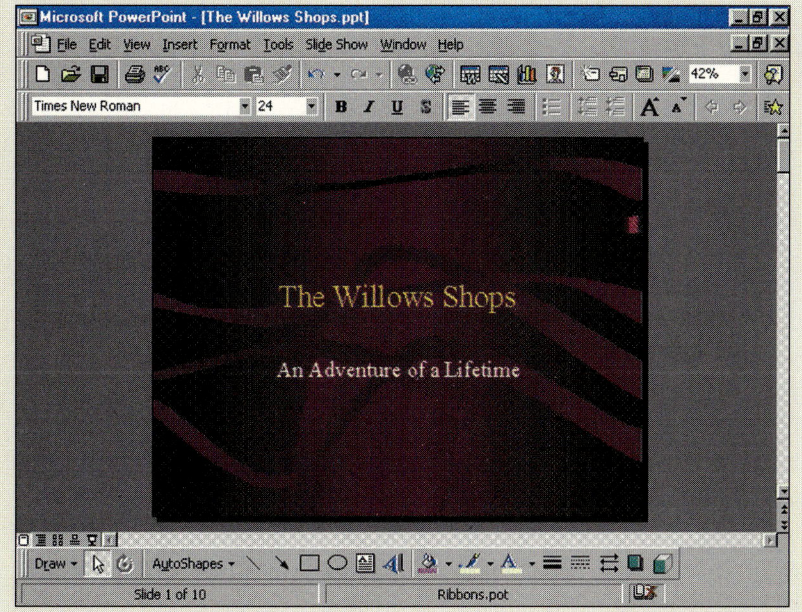

Figure 1.7

She asks you to reformat the presentation with the template and print copies for her assistant managers. Follow these instructions to meet Ms. Lindsey's request:

1. Open the presentation *The Willows Shops* and review the presentation in Outline view.
2. Display Slide 1 in Slide view and apply the Ribbons template to the presentation.
3. Review each slide on-screen using different navigation tools.
4. Save changes to the presentation and print a copy of the presentation as black-and-white handouts with six slides per page.
5. Close the presentation and exit PowerPoint when you have completed your work.

Assignments

1. Creating, Formatting, and Saving a Multi-Slide Presentation

The Willows area of South Carolina features a number of festivals and attractions. Create a presentation named *Festivals and Attractions* that contains the slides pictured in Figure 1.8.

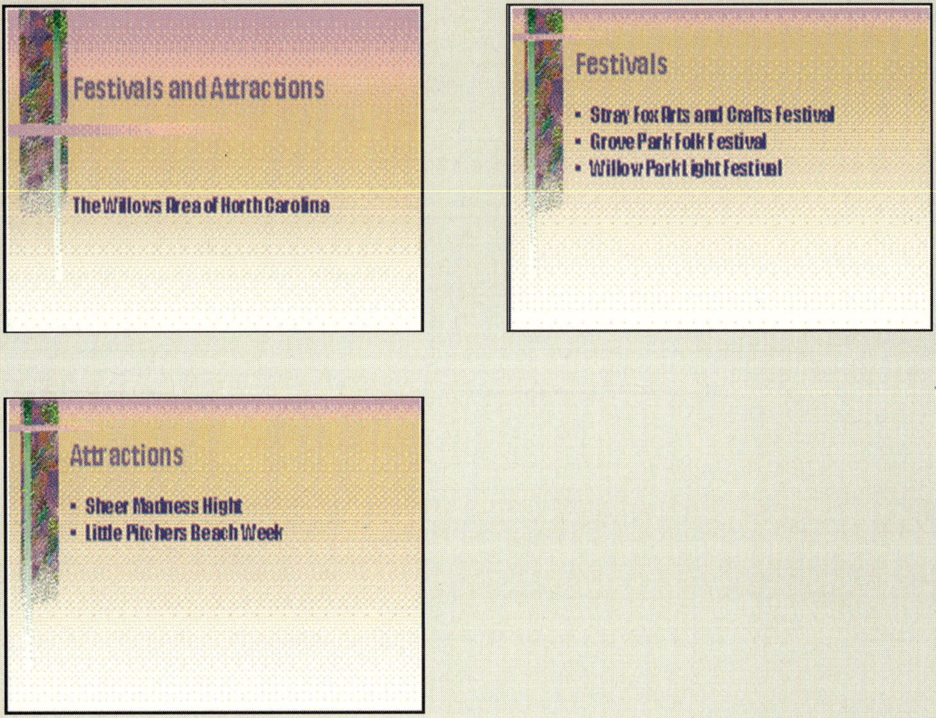

Figure 1.8

Apply the Blush template and view the presentation in all four views. Save the presentation and print a copy of the presentation as black-and-white handouts with three slides per page. Close the presentation and exit PowerPoint when you have completed your work.

2. Finding Templates on the Internet

Search the PowerPoint Internet site and locate additional templates that you can use to format presentations. (Go to Microsoft's home page at WWW.Microsoft.com and then click on Products.) Download a template and apply it to the Festivals and Attractions presentation created in the preceding assignment. Save the presentation and print a copy of the title slide.

PROJECT 2

Editing Slide Text

PowerPoint contains a variety of tools that you can use to edit text you add to slides. The techniques you use to edit text are similar to the techniques you use to edit text in other Windows 95 applications. In this project, you apply different techniques to edit and enhance text, format text placeholders, and change the setup of your slide page.

Objectives

After completing this project, you will be able to:

- **Select and edit placeholder text**
- **Change the appearance of text**
- **Find and replace text**
- **Check the style and spelling of text**
- **Format text placeholders**
- **Change the page setup**
- **Create a presentation using a wizard**

The Challenge

Francesca Savoy has been hired to coordinate a marketing campaign designed to promote The Willows resort. She has reviewed the presentation slides you created in Project 1 and has made changes to the slide text. In addition, she has recommended changes to the text format and text placeholder positions to improve the display of information on slides in the presentation. Slides in the presentation should appear as shown in Figure 2.1 after you complete your edits.

Figure 2.1

In addition, Ms. Savoy would like you to create the structure of a new presentation designed to be used as a marketing tool for the resort. She plans to use the presentation as a guide and will provide the text she wants to include in the new presentation from the presentation outline that you prepare. Your completed presentation outline appears in Figure 2.2.

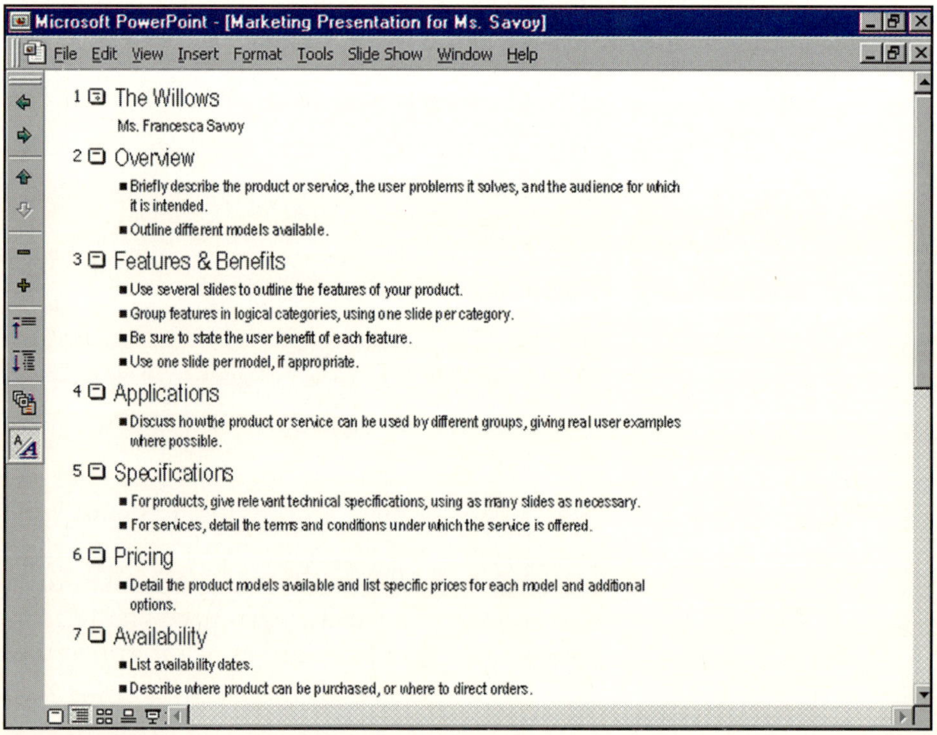

Figure 2.2

The Solution

As the graphic artist at The Willows, it's your responsibility to edit text on each slide in the presentation for The Willows, format text and text placeholders on the slides, and ensure that there are no spelling or formatting errors on the slides. Follow the steps in the tasks in this project to make the edits required by Ms. Savoy. When you complete the edits, you can create the outline for Ms. Savoy's marketing presentation using the PowerPoint AutoContent Wizard.

The Setup

Before starting this project, you may want to make sure that the following settings are active so that your presentations display in a format that matches the pictures in this book. Figures and illustrations use the default settings installed automatically with the PowerPoint program. If someone has fiddled with these settings, you may find that your screen looks different from those pictured here. Here are a few things to check:

- Do you see the four default toolbars—Standard, Formatting, Common Tasks, and Drawing? If not, choose View, Toolbars and then select the ones that are missing. Close any extra toolbars displayed.
- Display the status bar, if you don't see it, by choosing Tools, Options, and then checking the options on the View page tab. Make sure that all options on the View page tab of the dialog box are checked except the last one.
- If rulers appear, hide them by choosing View, Ruler.
- Make sure that your presentation window is maximized by clicking the Maximize button on the presentation window.

Selecting and Editing Placeholder Text

To edit text or to change the appearance of text, you must first ***select*** the text. PowerPoint offers a variety of techniques to select text. You can edit the text in slide placeholders using either Slide view or Outline view.

TASK 1: TO SELECT AND EDIT PLACEHOLDER TEXT:

1 Open the presentation *The Willows* and display the first slide in Slide view.

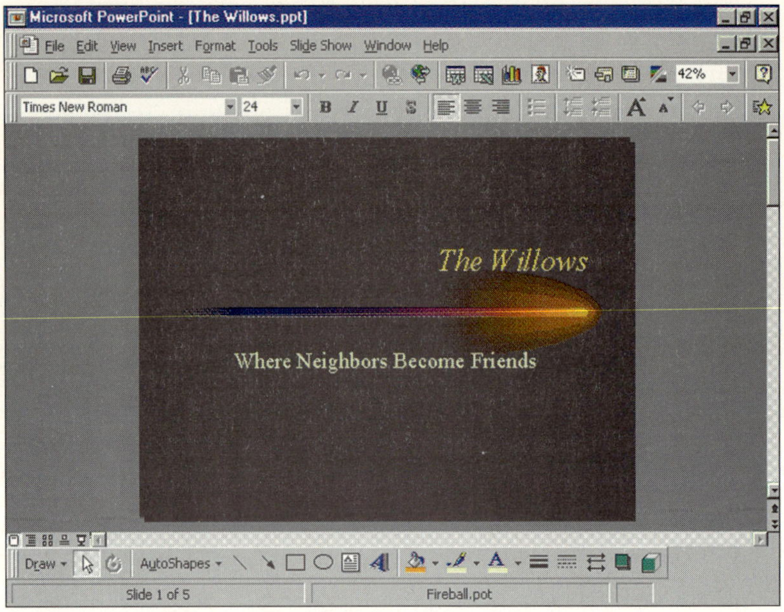

2 Double-click the word "Neighbors" and press (DELETE) to remove the word. The text appears as "Where Become Friends."

3 Position the insertion point between "Where" and "Become" and type **Guests.**

4 Display Slide 2, double-click the word "Lodging," and type **Luxury Accommodations**.

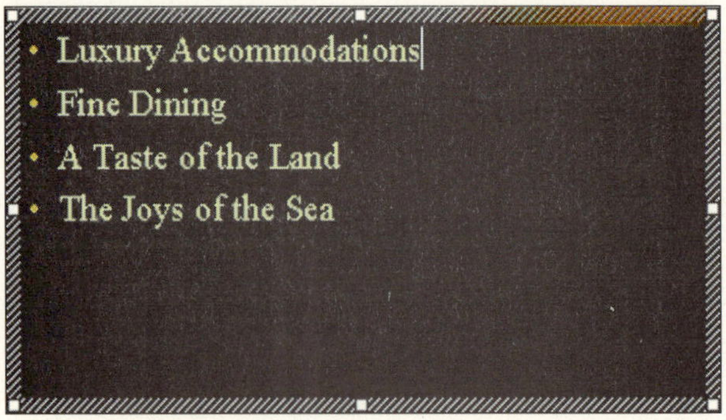

5 Select the text for the second bullet point and type **Four-Star Restaurants.**

6 Switch to Outline view and click the bullet beside the third bulleted item in Slide 2.

7 Drag the bullet to the bottom of the Slide 2 bulleted list and drop it.

8 Click the slide icon beside Slide 4.

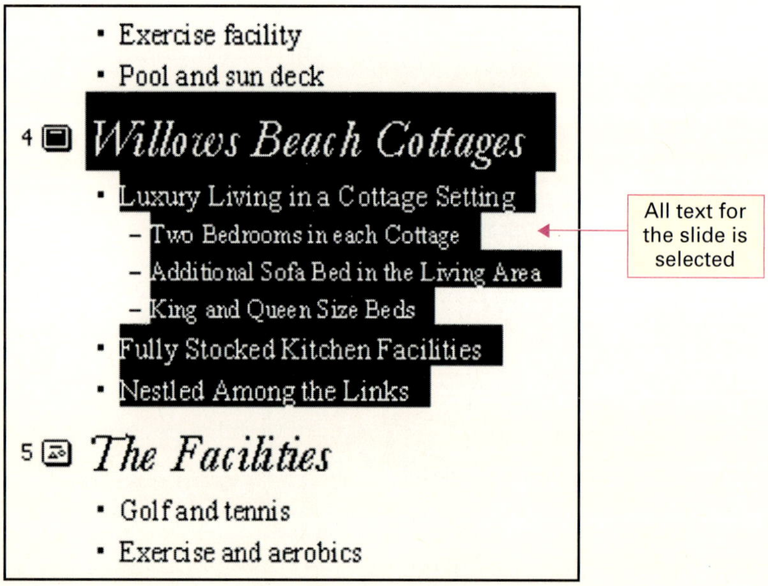

9 Position the mouse pointer on the selected slide icon, click, and drag the text to the bottom of the outline.

The slides renumber automatically

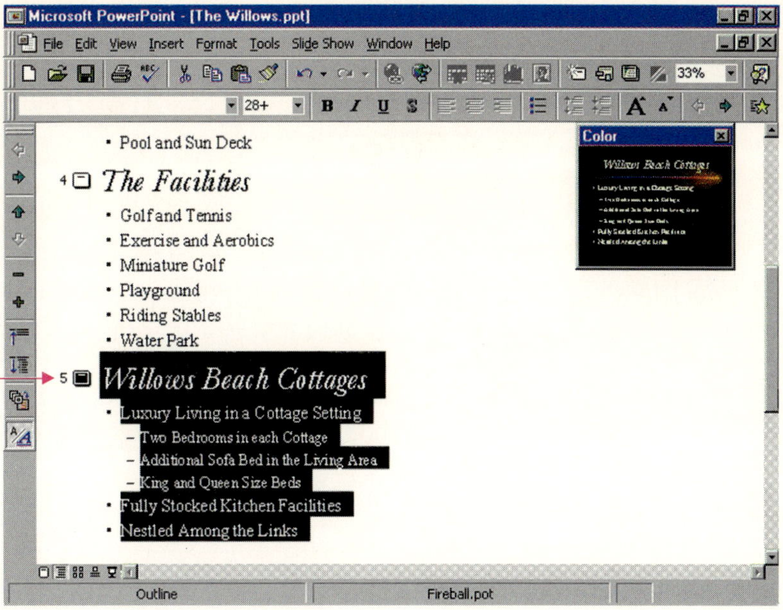

10 Return to Slide view, display Slide 1, and triple-click the title placeholder.

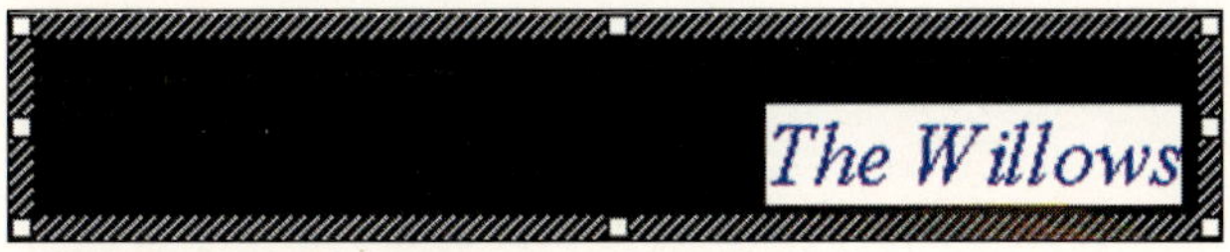

11 Click the Copy button on the Standard toolbar.

12 Display Slide 5 and add a new bulleted list slide at the end of the presentation.
A new slide appears, formatted with a title placeholder and bulleted list placeholder.

13 Click the title placeholder and then click the Paste button on the Standard toolbar.

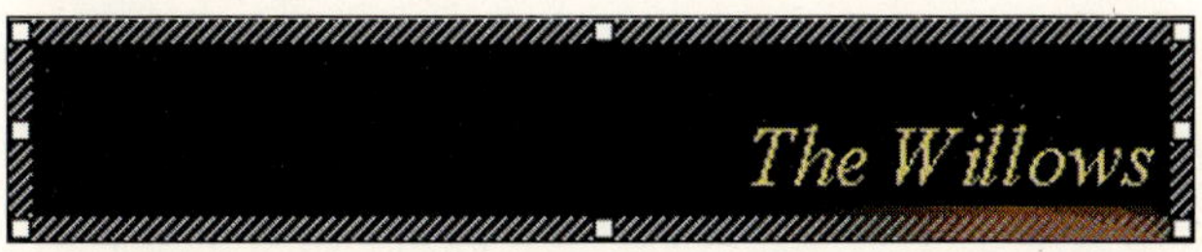

Changing the Appearance of Text

To make the changes to the appearance of the text that Ms. Savoy requested, you need to change the font, change the font size, apply enhancements, and change the color of the text. You can apply many of these features using tools on the Formatting toolbar, as shown in Figure 2.3.

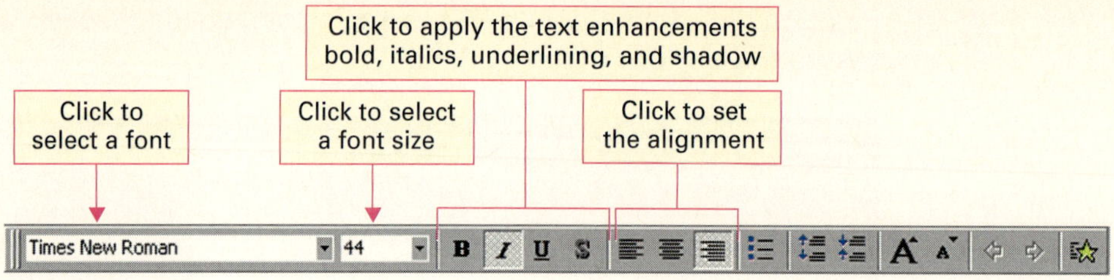

Figure 2.3

Enhancements and changes you make to slide text affect only text you select before making the change. If an enhancement you want to apply doesn't have a button on the toolbar, you can open the Font dialog box and select additional options. You can then copy the text format and apply it to text on other slides by using the Format Painter to ensure consistency.

TASK 2: TO CHANGE THE APPEARANCE OF TEXT IN A PRESENTATION:

1. Display Slide 1 of the presentation *The Willows* in Slide view and select the slide title text.

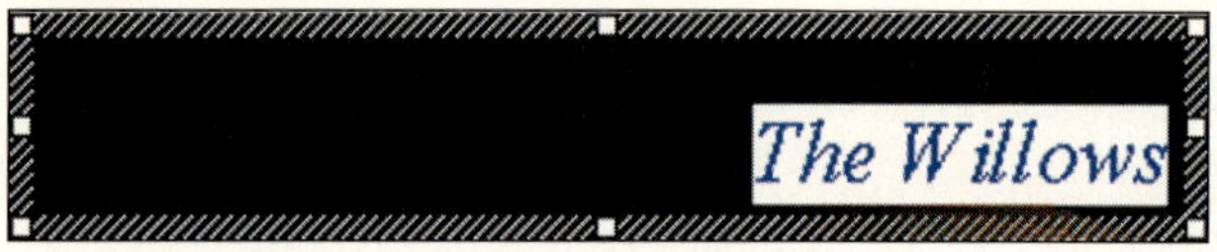

2. Click the arrow button beside the Font box on the Formatting toolbar to open the drop-down list.

3. Select Baskerville from the Font list.

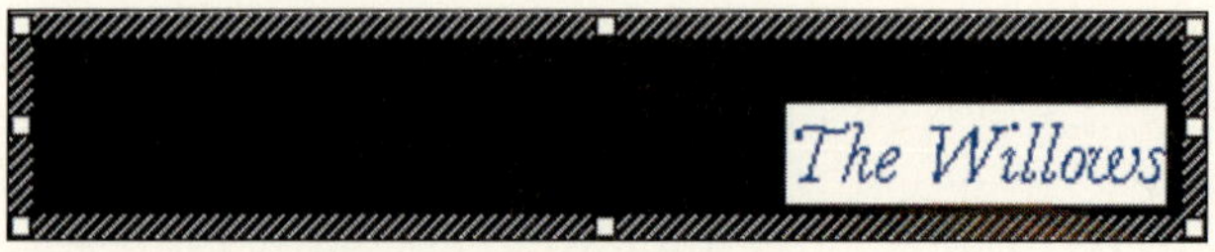

4 Click the arrow button beside the Font Size box on the Formatting toolbar to open the drop-down list.

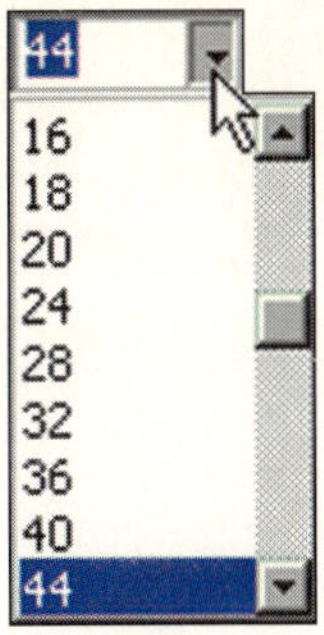

5 Scroll as necessary and select 60 from the font size list and then click the Bold **B** button on the Formatting toolbar.

6 Choose Format, Font to display the Font dialog box.

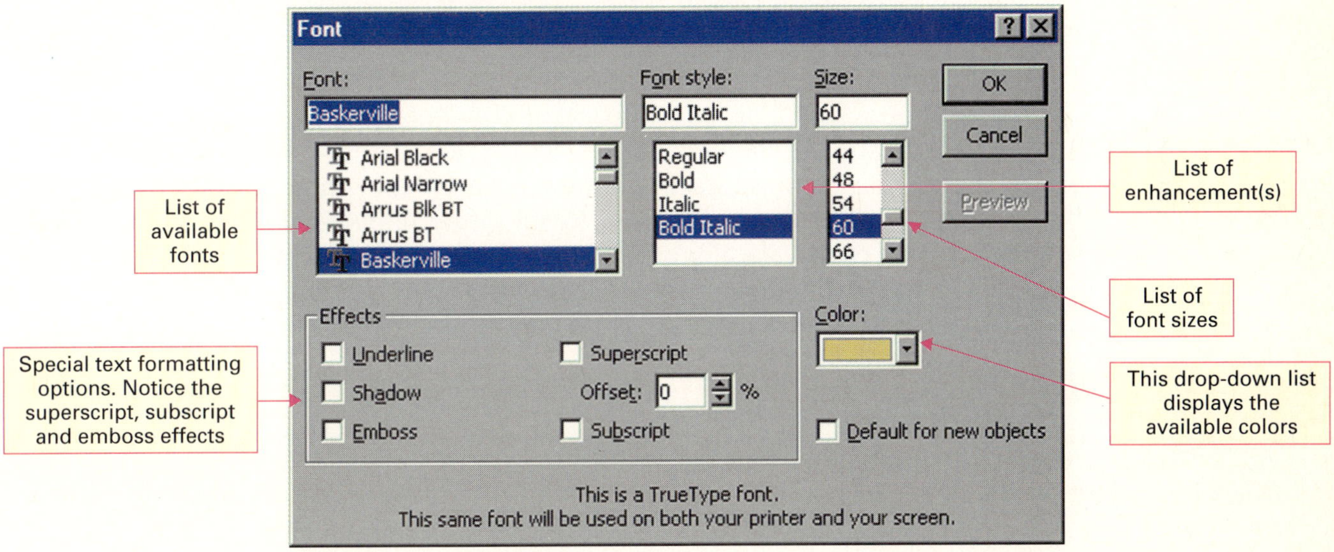

7 Click the arrow button beside the Color box, click the lighter yellow color, and press ENTER.

8 Click B to remove the bold and then double-click the Format Painter button.

The mouse pointer carries a paintbrush to paint other text with the text format of the selected text

9 Display Slide 2 and select the slide title.
The title text appears reformatted.

10 Repeat step 9 to change the format of title text for all slides in the presentation.

11 Press ESC to drop the paintbrush.

12 Save the changes to the presentation.

Finding and Replacing Text

The Find feature in PowerPoint enables you to search for text contained in text placeholders on slides, in outlines, or in the notes area of notes pages. The Replace feature enables you to substitute different text for the text PowerPoint finds. Take, for example, a presentation that contains the company name that you've misspelled throughout the presentation. Using the Replace feature, you can quickly change all occurrences of the misspelled name to the correct spelling.

TASK 3: TO FIND AND REPLACE TEXT:

1 Press CTRL+HOME to display the first slide in the presentation.
You can start the Find and Replace feature from any location in the presentation; starting at the first slide in this task ensures that your screen will resemble the figures shown here.

> **Note** If a placeholder is active when you press Ctrl+Home, PowerPoint places the insertion point at the top of the active placeholder. Click outside all placeholders and then press Ctrl+Home to display the first slide.

2 Choose Edit, Find.

3 Type **Joys** in the Find what textbox, click the Match case check box, and press ENTER.

First slide containing the text you want to find

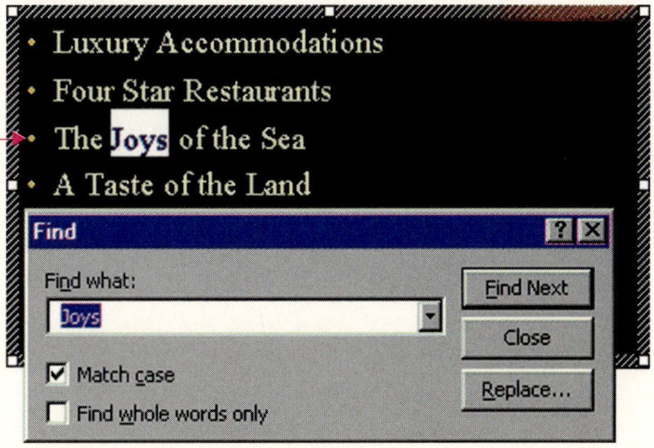

Tip Drag the Find dialog box out of the way to view the text behind it.

4 Press (ESC) to close the Find dialog box and type **Bounty** to replace the word *Joys*.

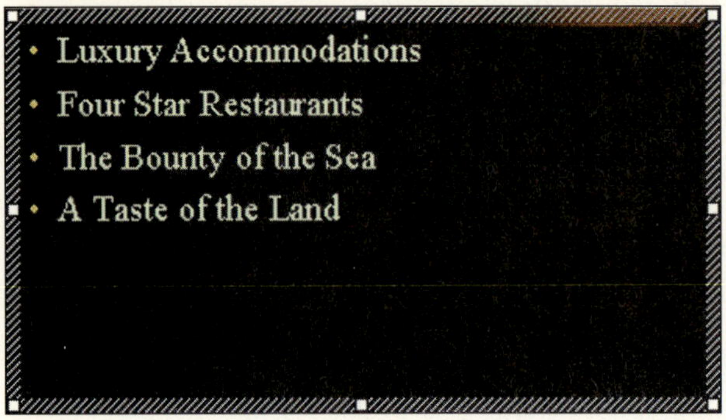

5 Choose Edit, Replace.

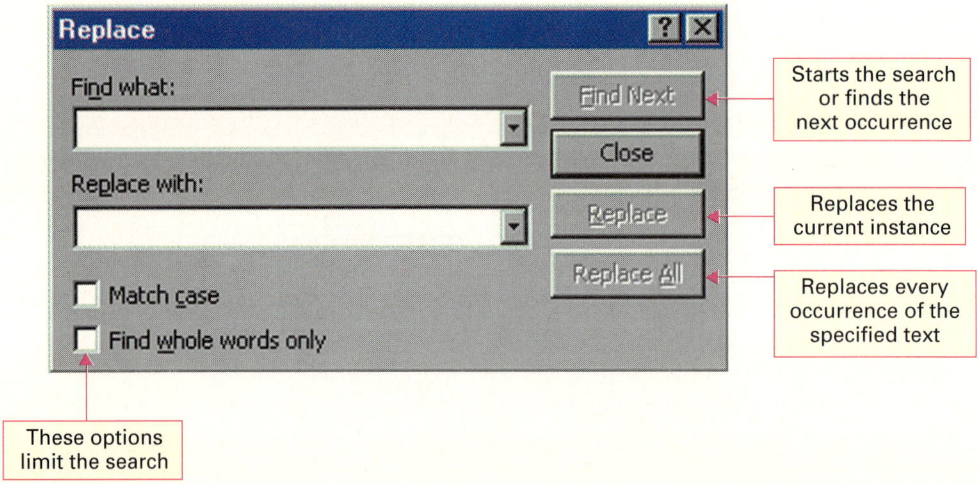

6 Type **Shops** in the Find what text box, press TAB, type **Boutiques** in the Replace with text box, and press ENTER.

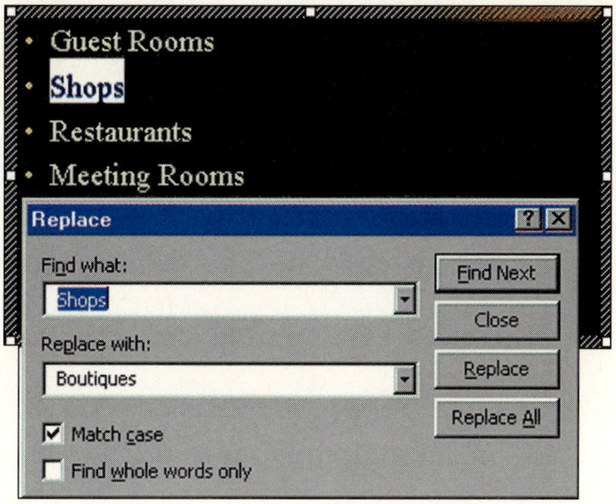

7 Click Replace.
"Shops" changes to "Boutiques."

8 Click Find Next, if necessary.

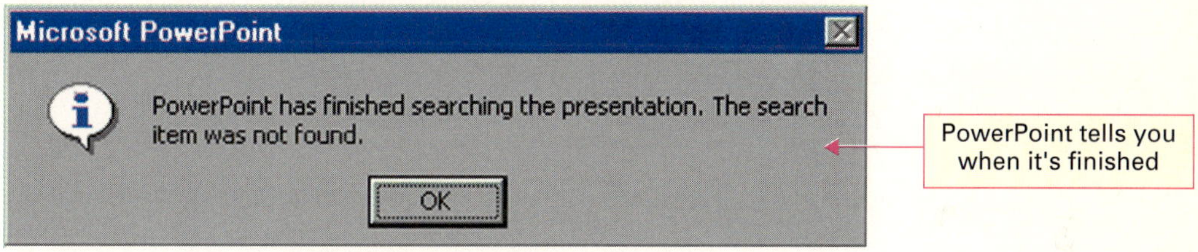

9 Click OK to acknowledge the message, press ESC to close the Replace dialog box, and click the Save button to save the changes to the presentation.

Checking the Style and Spelling of Text

The PowerPoint Spelling feature proofs all the materials in your presentation and locates words in text placeholders that it doesn't recognize.

The PowerPoint Style Checker checks placeholder text on presentation slides for consistency in end punctuation, capitalization, and spelling. When you use the Style Checker to check capitalization, PowerPoint automatically formats all words except the first word in each bulleted item in lowercase. Checking the Spelling option in the Style Checker dialog box eliminates the need to run the Spelling feature separately.

TASK 4: TO CHECK A PRESENTATION FOR STYLE AND SPELLING:

1 Press (CTRL)+(HOME) to display the first slide in the presentation. You can start the Style Checker from any location in the presentation; starting at the first slide in this activity ensures that your screen will resemble the figures shown here.

2 Choose Tools, Style Checker.

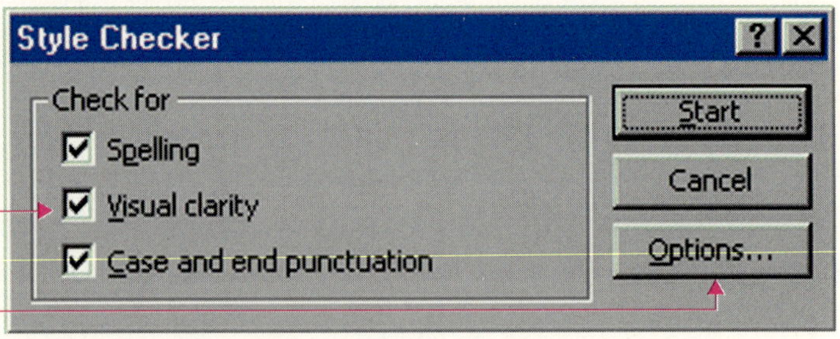

3 Select the check boxes for Spelling, Visual Clarity, and Case and End Punctuation, and click Options.

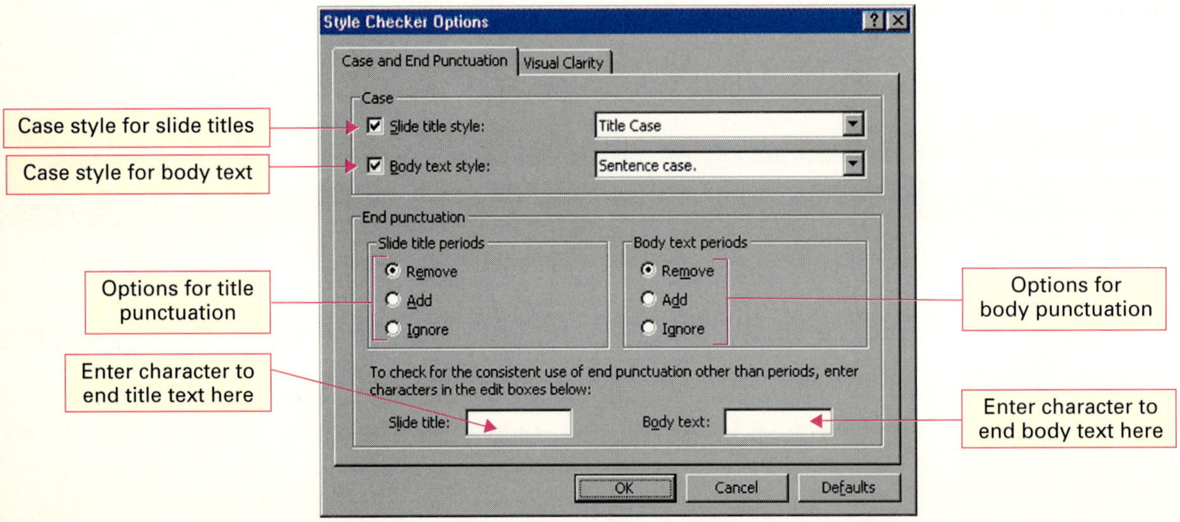

4 Set the options shown above on the Case and End punctuation page of the style checker options dialog box and then click the Visual Clarity page tab.

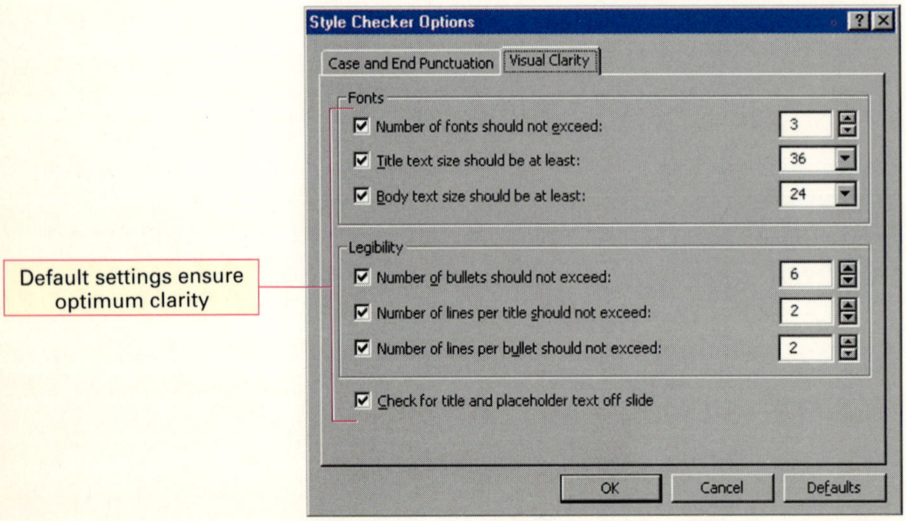

5 Select each option on the Visual Clarity page and change option values to those shown earlier, if necessary. Then press (ENTER) and click the Start button.

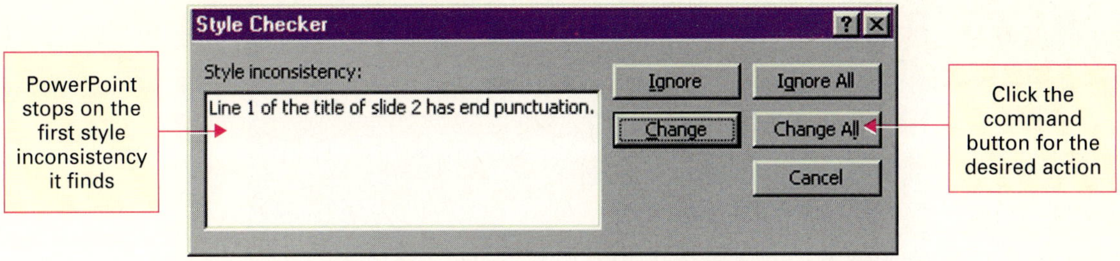

Tip To see the slide text identified, drag the dialog box out of the way.

6 Click the command button for the action you want to take. PowerPoint locates the next style error and displays a message identifying the error.

7 Repeat step 6 until you've reviewed all style errors.

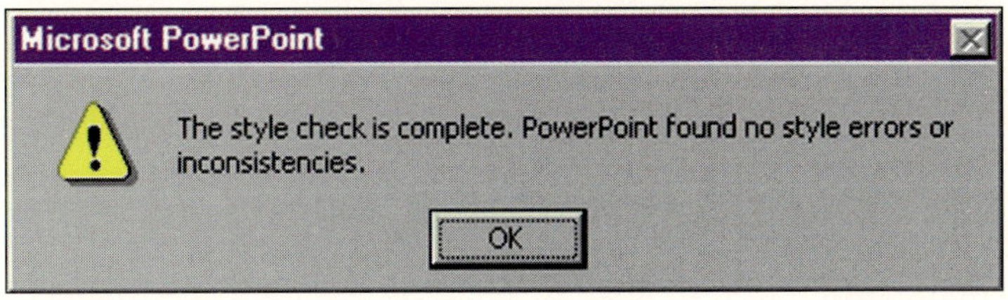

8 Click OK to close the message box and then click [Save] to save changes to the presentation.

Formatting Text Placeholders

Placeholder objects contained on slides in your presentation can be selected, sized, and moved using the same techniques you use to size other objects. Changing the size of the text placeholder makes it possible to adjust the position of slide text and can be compared to setting margins on word processing documents. In addition, you can change the alignment and ***line spacing*** of all text in a placeholder by first selecting the placeholder and then adjusting the setting. Selected placeholders display ***handles*** on their corners and sides, as shown in Figure 2.4.

Tip Displaying the ruler helps to position and size placeholders more precisely. To display the ruler, choose View, Ruler.

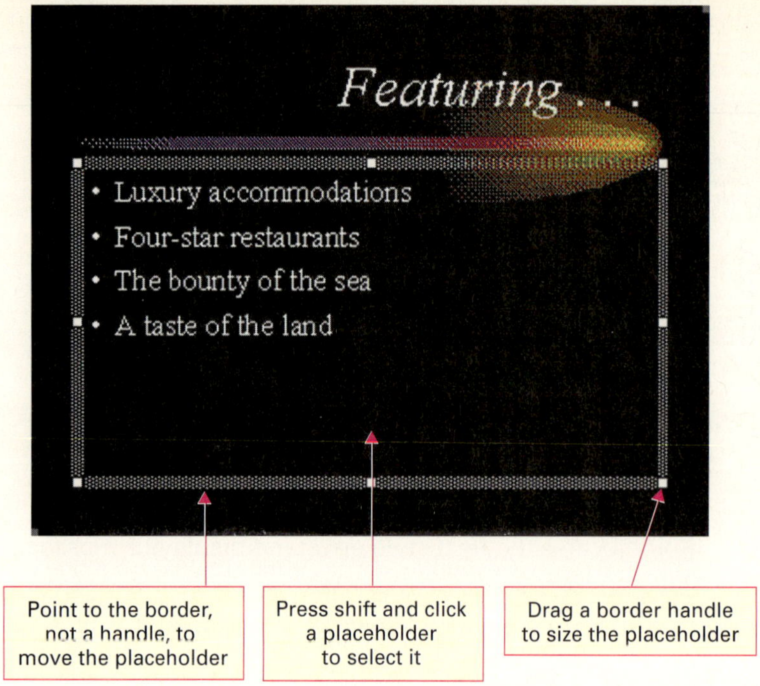

Figure 2.4

TASK 5: TO FORMAT TEXT PLACEHOLDERS:

1 Display Slide 5 of the presentation *The Willows*, press (SHIFT), and click the title placeholder.

2 Click the Center button on the Formatting toolbar.

3 Display Slide 2 and select the bulleted list placeholder.

4 Drag the lower-right corner handle diagonally toward the placeholder text.

The mouse changes shape and the placeholder size is outlined as you drag

5 Position the mouse pointer on a border of the placeholder away from a handle and drag the placeholder diagonally down and right.

The pointer changes shape and the placeholder is outlined as you drag; when you release the mouse button, the placeholder is repositioned on the slide

6 Display Slide 5 and select the three second-level bulleted items following "Luxury living in a cottage setting."

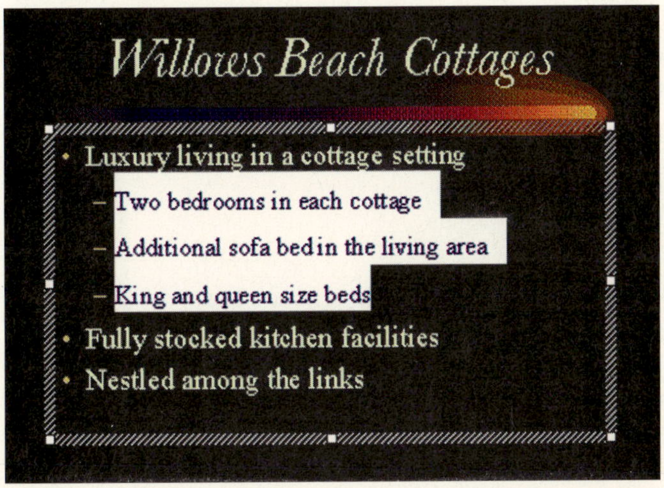

7 Choose Format, Line Spacing.

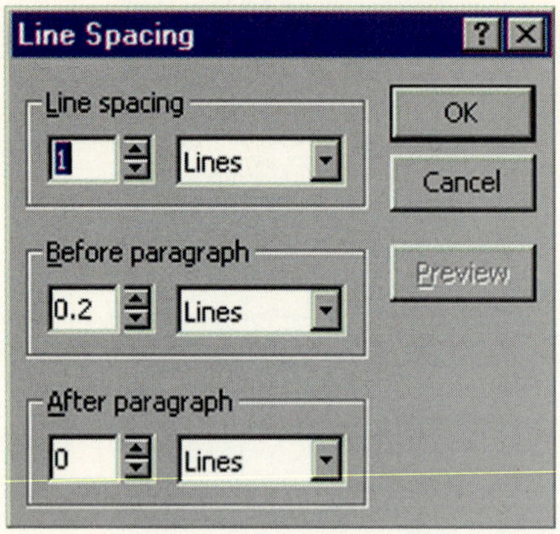

8 Click the spin buttons to increase the Line spacing to 1.5 and to decrease the Before paragraph spacing to 0; then click OK.

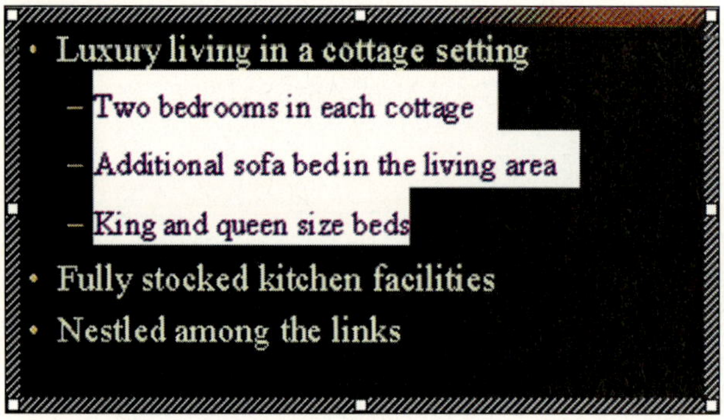

9 Save changes to the presentation.

Changing the Page Setup

To change the size and ***orientation*** (direction) of paper you want to use to print slides and other materials, you need to change the ***page setup***. The Page Setup dialog box presents a set of options for setting the orientation of text on slides and a separate set of options for setting the page orientation for outlines, handouts, and notes pages, as shown in Figure 2.5. You can also format slides to print on different size paper by selecting the paper size from the Slides Sized For drop-down list, enter values in the Width and Height value boxes, and set the page number for the first slide in the presentation.

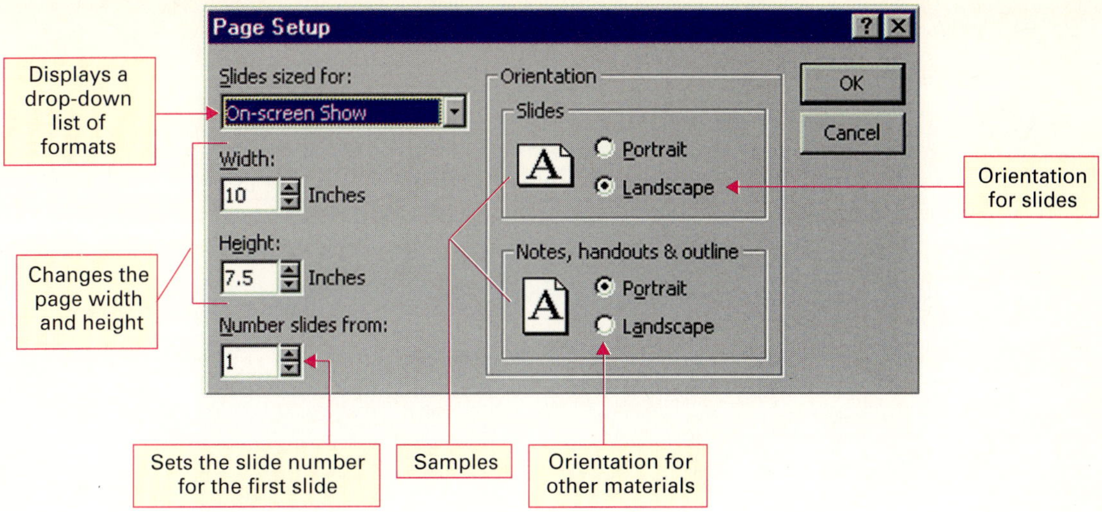

Figure 2.5

TASK 6: TO CHANGE THE PAGE SETUP FOR MATERIALS IN A PRESENTATION:

1. Choose File, Page Setup.
   The dialog box in Figure 2.8 displays.

2. Change the settings in the Page Setup dialog box as in:

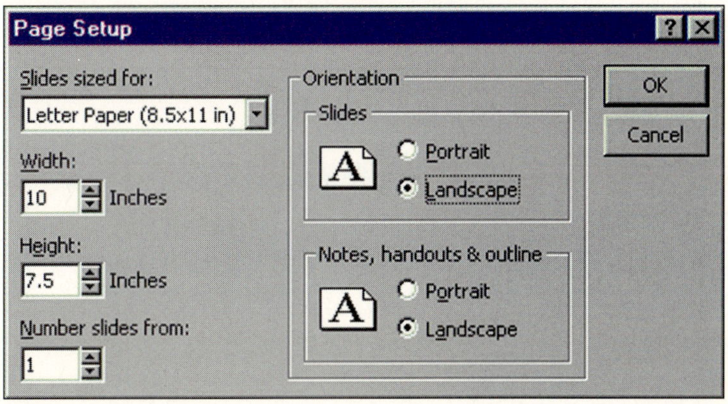

3. Click OK, save the changes to the presentation, and close the presentation.

Creating a Presentation Using a Wizard

The PowerPoint AutoContent Wizard helps you build an outline for specific types of presentations by presenting options for you to choose and enabling you to fill in specific pieces of information about the presentation. You can choose the AutoContent Wizard from the PowerPoint dialog box when you launch PowerPoint, or select the AutoContent Wizard from the New Presentation dialog box.

Using the Wizard, you can quickly and easily create the presentation outline for the marketing presentation Ms. Savoy requested.

TASK 7: TO CREATE A PRESENTATION USING THE AUTOCONTENT WIZARD:

1. Close all open presentations.
   You don't have to close all presentations to use the wizard; doing so now ensures that your screen resembles those shown in this section.

2. Choose File, New, and click the Presentations tab.

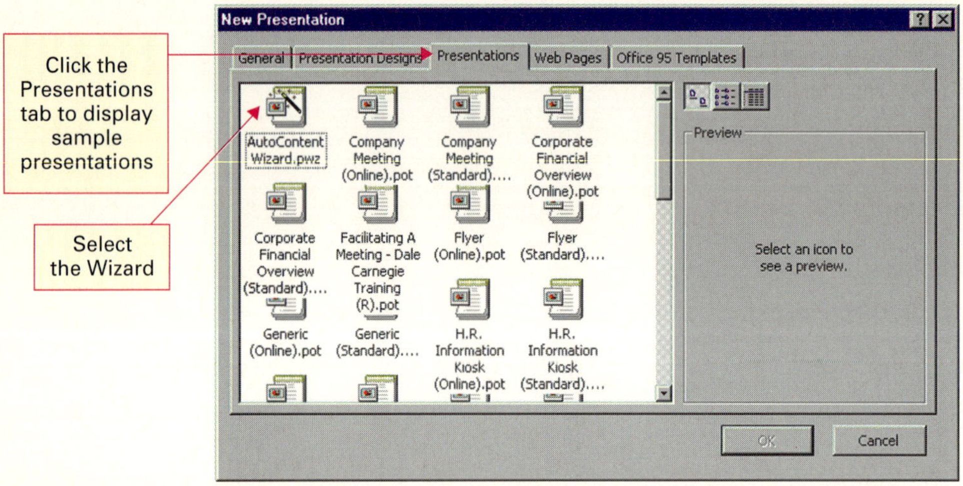

Note: Files listed on the Presentations page that have a .pot extension are sample presentation templates.

3. Doubleclick the *AutoContent Wizard.pwz.*

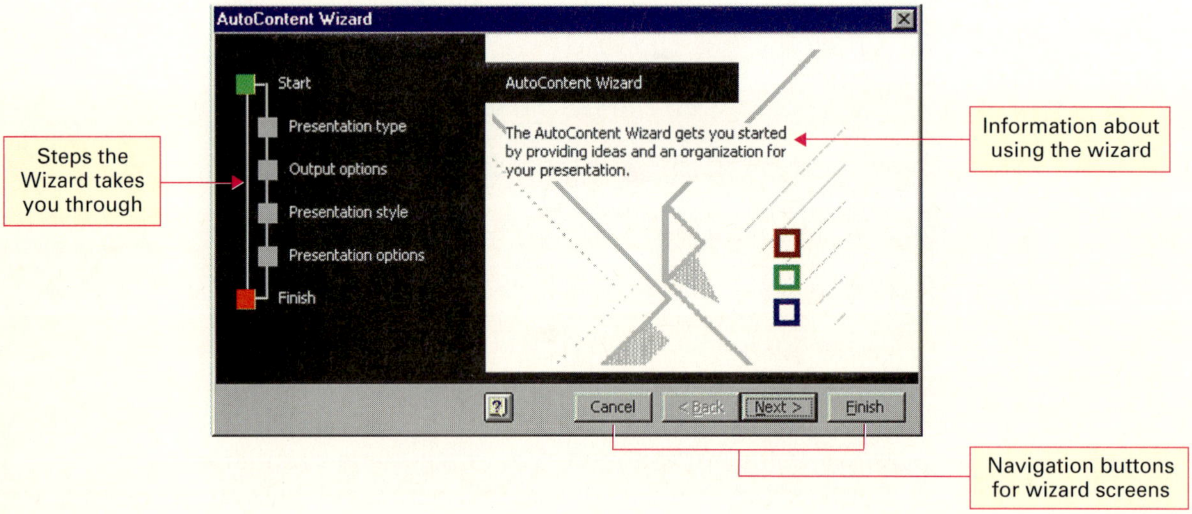

4 Click Next.

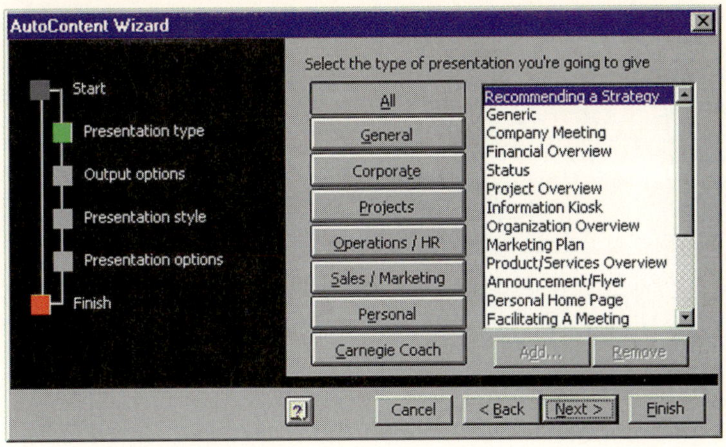

5 Click the Sales/Marketing button, select Product/Services Overview, and then click Next.

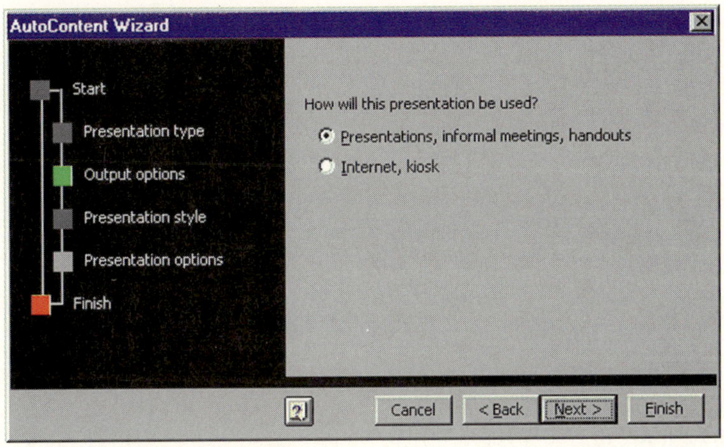

6 Select Presentations, informal meetings, handouts and then click Next.

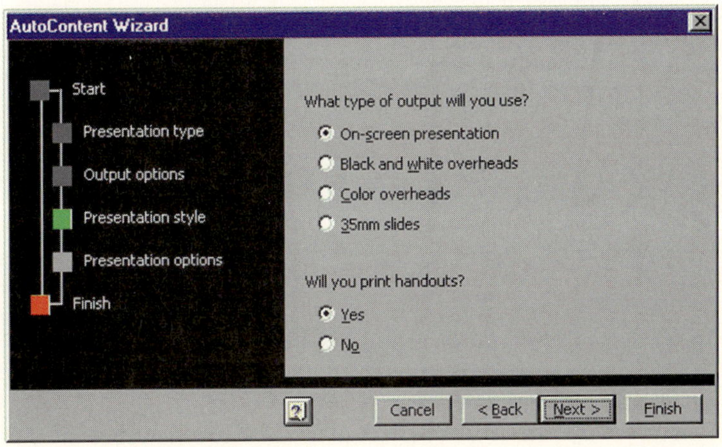

7 Click Next to accept the default presentation style options.

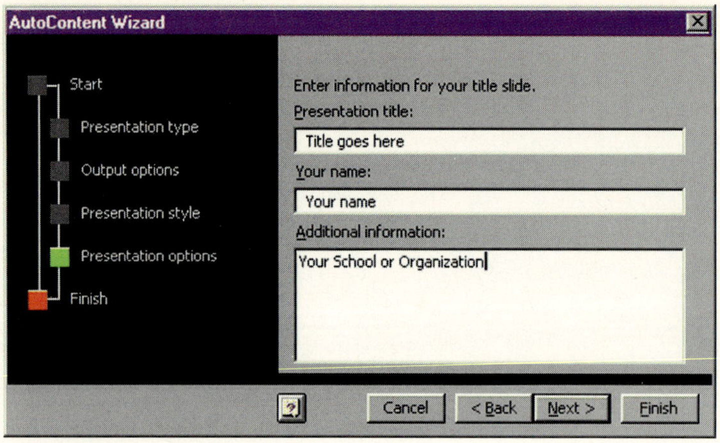

8 Type **The Willows** in the Presentation title text box, **Ms. Francesca Savoy** in the Your name text box, delete the text in the Additional information box, and then click Next.
The last screen the wizard presents instructs you to click Finish to continue. If you need to make changes to previous wizard screens, click the Back button until the screen appears, make the changes, and then click Finish from any screen.

9 Click Finish.

Sample text in Outline view

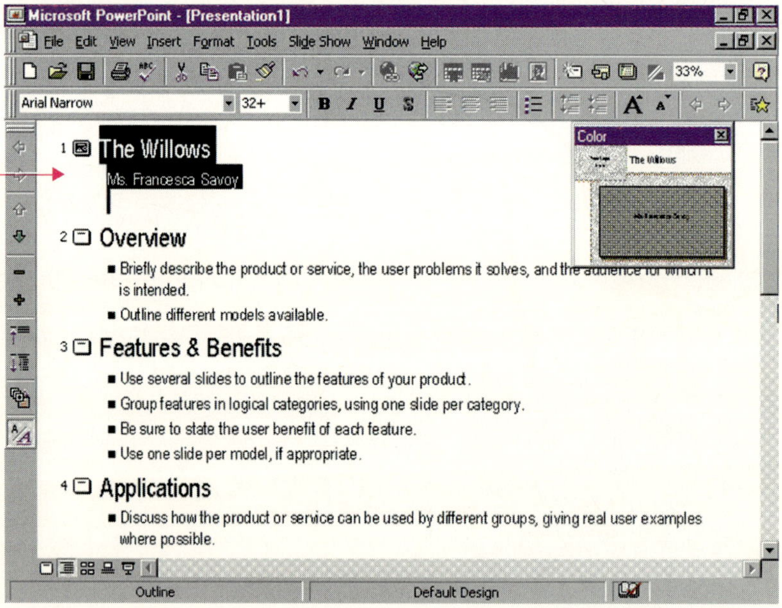

10 Save the presentation using the filename *Marketing Presentation for Ms. Savoy* and close the presentation.

The Conclusion

Print copies of Slides 1, 2, 4, and 5 in the presentation *The Willows* as black-and-white slides. Print a copy of the marketing presentation in Outline view for Ms. Savoy. When you're done, save changes to both presentations and close the presentations.

Summary and Exercises

Summary

- Many of the techniques used to select, insert, delete, enhance, move, and copy text used in other Windows applications can be used to work with text in PowerPoint as well.
- You can use the Find and Replace commands to automatically substitute new text for existing text in a presentation.
- PowerPoint comes complete with features that enable you to check the spelling and style of slide text.
- You can change the size of object placeholders on slides by selecting the placeholder and dragging a handle; you can move the object placeholder on a slide by selecting the placeholder and dragging it to a new location.
- The Page Setup dialog box enables you to change the orientation of slides and other presentation materials and to set different dimensions for slides and presentation materials.
- Wizards enable you to create a new presentation based on the purpose of a presentation, and to format the presentation using a template appropriate to the presentation type. Presentations created using wizards include sample and instructive text that you can replace with specific text to complete your presentation.

Key Terms and Operations

Key Terms	Operations
AutoContent Wizard	change the size and orientation of slides and presentation materials
font	create a presentation using the AutoContent Wizard
handles	edit placeholder format
line spacing	select and edit text
orientation	use PowerPoint tools to check a presentation
page setup	

Study Questions

Multiple Choice

1. To select text,
   - **a.** you must use the keyboard.
   - **b.** you must use the mouse.
   - **c.** you can use either the mouse or keyboard.
   - **d.** position the insertion point on a word and press Enter.

2. To insert a word between existing words in a bulleted list,
   - **a.** position the insertion point where you want the new word and type the word.
   - **b.** delete existing text and retype all text, adding the new word where you want it.
   - **c.** create a new blank line to contain the new word.
   - **d.** you must use Outline view.

3. Text enhancements in PowerPoint include all the following *except*
   a. bold.
   b. strikethrough.
   c. italics.
   d. superscripts.

4. The easiest way to copy text formatting is to use
   a. copy/paste.
   b. drag and drop.
   c. menu commands.
   d. the Format Painter.

5. To copy the font for selected text in a presentation to different text, use
   a. the Format Painter.
   b. the Replace Fonts command.
   c. copy/paste commands.
   d. drag and drop techniques.

6. To ensure consistency for end punctuation among bulleted lists, use the
   a. Spell Checker.
   b. Find command.
   c. Style Checker.
   d. Format Painter.

7. To ensure that capitalization of specific terms remains consistent throughout a presentation, use the
   a. Spell Checker only.
   b. Spell Checker or Style Checker.
   c. Style Checker only.
   d. Format Painter.

8. To place extra space between bulleted list items in a placeholder,
   a. change the font.
   b. make the placeholder larger.
   c. change the line spacing for text within the placeholder.
   d. press Enter two times between list items.

9. Instead of setting margins for text on slides,
   a. click the placeholder border.
   b. use the ruler.
   c. use a dialog box.
   d. size the text placeholder.

10. The Page Setup dialog box enables you to set
    a. the orientation for slides separately from that of other presentation materials.
    b. one orientation for all materials.
    c. the size of body text placeholders.
    d. one paper size for all materials.

Short Answer

1. How do you select all text for a bulleted list item?
2. What features are copied when you use the Format Painter?

3. What's the easiest way to apply the most frequently used text enhancements?
4. What text formatting features are found on the Formatting toolbar in PowerPoint that aren't usually found on the Formatting toolbar in other Windows applications?
5. What options can you set to limit the instances of text found using the Find feature in PowerPoint?
6. How do you change the size of paper you plan to use to print a presentation?
7. What are the two basic alignment settings you can apply to a placeholder?
8. How do you move a placeholder?
9. What settings can you change using the Page Setup dialog box?
10. What's the advantage of using the AutoContent Wizard to create a new presentation?

For Discussion

1. How do you choose a wizard to use for creating a presentation?
2. What's the difference between sizing a placeholder and sizing objects in other Windows applications?
3. What features does PowerPoint check when you use the Style Checker?
4. Which of PowerPoint's wizards will be most helpful to you in your area of study?

Review Exercises

1. Editing Text in an Existing Presentation

Based on the response received from her assistant managers, Ruth Lindsey, Manager of The Willows Shops, would like you to edit text contained on some of the slides in the presentation *The Willows Shops*. Revisions to slide text appear in the outline shown in Figure 2.6.

1 The Willows Shops
Where Exploring Becomes an Adventure

2 Sindy's Sun Closet
- Swimsuits and Accessories
- Sun Cosmetics
- Beach and Pool Toys

3 Weeping Willow Gallery
- Paintings
- Sculpture
- Iron Works
- Local Artisans

4 Live Oak Gifts

5 Creative Cutlery
- A Large Assortment of Kitchen Wares

6 Cherry Street Market
- Home Grown Produce
- Natural Flora from the Carolinas

7 Victorian Tea Room
- Victorian gifts and clothing
- Victorian High Tea Served Daily

8 Ken's Kids
- Children's games and toys
- Children's clothing

9 Appalachian Crafts
- Treasures from the Hills
- Displays of local Artisans

10 The Newsstand
- Newspapers
- Magazines
- Recent Publications
- The Willows Post Office

Figure 2.6

Use the techniques explored in this project to edit the slides. Follow these instructions to complete the presentation:

1. Launch PowerPoint, if necessary, and open the presentation *The Willows Shops.*
2. Display the presentation in Outline view; select, edit, and enhance text on each slide as indicated in Figure 2.10.
3. Use the Find and Replace feature to change each occurrence of "Artists" in the presentation to "Artisans."
4. Move Slide 2 to the end of the outline.
5. Use the Spelling feature to check the spelling of your presentation.
6. Save changes to the presentation and print a copy of the presentation in Outline view.
7. Close the presentation and exit PowerPoint when you've completed your work.

2. Formatting Placeholders, Changing the Page Setup, and Checking the Style of Slides in a Presentation

Ms. Lindsey requests the format changes shown in Figure 2.7 for slides in the presentation *The Willows Shops.*

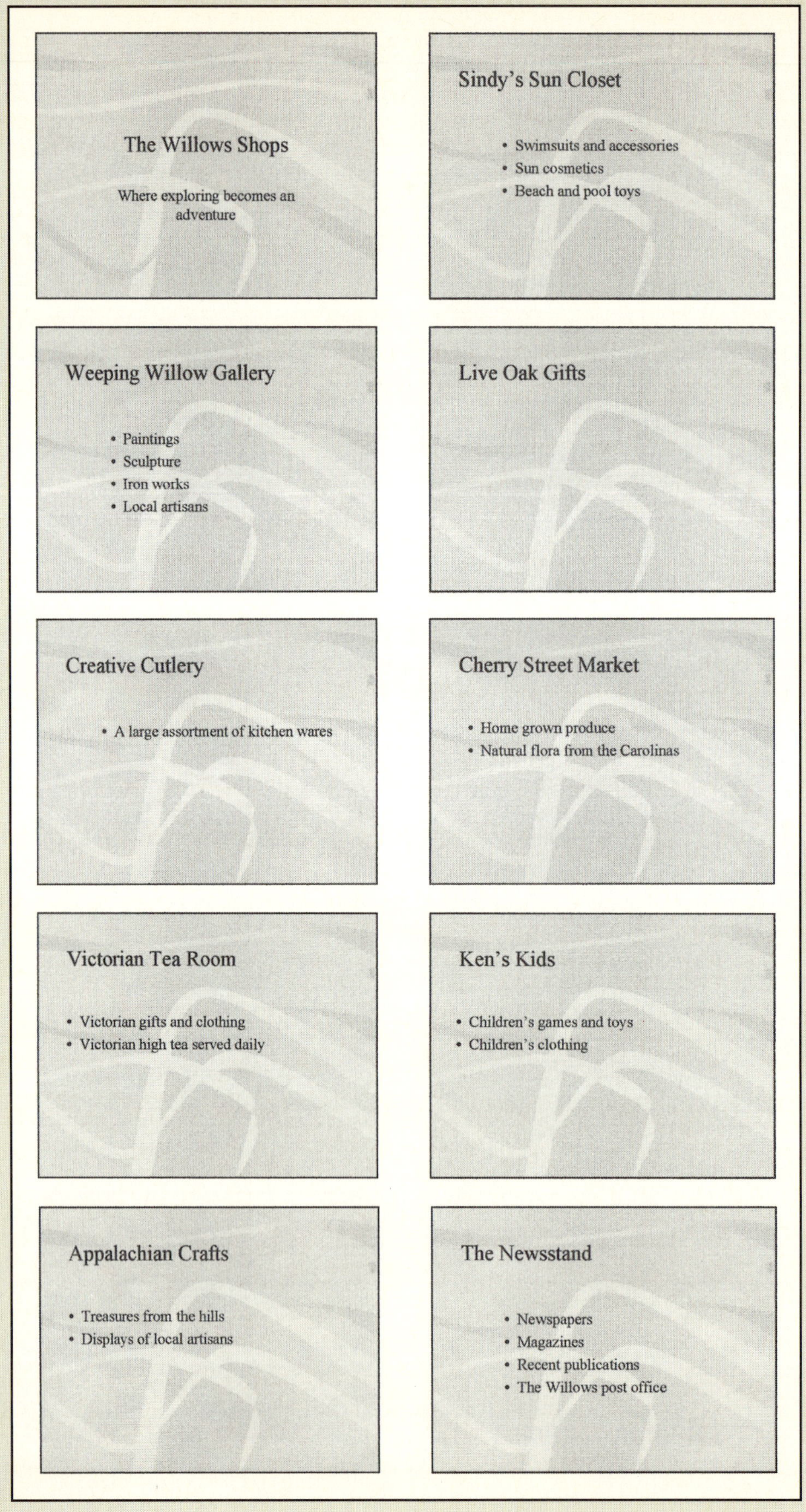
The Willows Shops
Where exploring becomes an adventure
Sindy's Sun Closet
• Swimsuits and accessories
• Sun cosmetics
• Beach and pool toys
Weeping Willow Gallery
• Paintings
• Sculpture
• Iron works
• Local artisans
Live Oak Gifts
Creative Cutlery
• A large assortment of kitchen wares
Cherry Street Market
• Home grown produce
• Natural flora from the Carolinas
Victorian Tea Room
• Victorian gifts and clothing
• Victorian high tea served daily
Ken's Kids
• Children's games and toys
• Children's clothing
Appalachian Crafts
• Treasures from the hills
• Displays of local artisans
The Newsstand
• Newspapers
• Magazines
• Recent publications
• The Willows post office

Figure 2.7

Follow these steps to complete the formatting:

1. Launch PowerPoint, if necessary, and open the presentation *The Willows Shops*.
2. Display Slide 5 in Slide view, select the bulleted list placeholder, and set the alignment of text to center horizontally in the placeholder.
3. Size placeholders to better fit the text each bulleted list placeholder contains. Position the placeholder on Slides 2, 3, and 10 so that the left edge of the placeholder aligns at the 3″ mark on the horizontal ruler and the top of the placeholder aligns at the 1″ mark above center on the vertical ruler.
4. Position the bulleted list placeholders for Slides 5–9 so that the top edge of the placeholder aligns with the 1″ mark above center on the vertical ruler.
5. Left-align text in the title placeholder of Slide 2. Select the placeholder (not the text) and use the Format Painter to copy the alignment to title placeholders of all slides except Slide 1.
6. Use the Style Checker to check the style of text on slides in the presentation.
7. Save changes to the presentation and print slides as black-and-white handouts with six framed slides per page.
8. Close the presentation when you've completed your work.

Assignments

1. Editing and Formatting Slide Text and Placeholders

The revised *Festivals and Attractions* presentation slides appear in Figure 2.8.

Figure 2.8

Use tools presented in this project to edit your presentation. Size, position, and format the text placeholders using the double-spaced, bold Modern font. Change the page setup of the presentation to format slides in portrait orientation. Check the spelling and style of the presentation. Because most of the features and attractions are proper names, however, don't check the presentation style for case. Save changes to the presentation and print black-and-white handouts with three framed slides per page. Close the presentation and exit PowerPoint when you've completed your work.

2. Creating a Presentation Using the Wizard

Ask your instructor how to obtain a presentation named *Resume.ppt.* The presentation contains an outline structure of information you should include in a résumé. Compare the sample résumé presentation to the one you designed in the Overview of PowerPoint to ensure that you've included all the necessary information. Then use the sample presentation and your own personal résumé to create a new presentation about yourself. Check the spelling and style of your presentation and format text and placeholders as desired. Apply a template to dress up the presentation. Save your presentation using your first and last names as the filename. Print a copy of your presentation as black-and-white handouts with three framed slides per page.

Close the presentation when you have completed your work.

3

PROJECT

Adding Art to a Presentation

PowerPoint makes dressing up your presentation with pictures quick and easy. Not only can you apply your own artistic talents to design powerful creations, but you can pull designs from the Clip Gallery or download them from the Internet. You can also use the PowerPoint WordArt module to change text into "words of art." In this project, you learn how to add graphics to your presentation slides and how to change the appearance of graphics to better fit your presentation needs.

Objectives

After completing this project, you will be able to:

- **Insert clip art into a slide**
- **Move and size clip art**
- **Download and insert clip art from the PowerPoint Web site**
- **Create WordArt**
- **Format WordArt**
- **Create drawings**
- **Manipulate art on a slide**

The Challenge

The template you applied to your presentations in Project 2 dressed up the design of your presentation but did nothing to fill in the blank space on presentation slides. Ms. Savoy would like for you to add appropriate graphics to slides in the presentation *The Willows*.

The Solution

As the graphics artist at The Willows, you get to add art to the slides in the presentation *The Willows*. Your dressed-up slides will appear as shown in Figure 3.1.

Figure 3.1

The Setup

So that your screen will match the illustrations shown in this project, make sure that the PowerPoint settings in the following table are selected on your computer:

Setting	Description
View menu	Choose Toolbars and then click the toolbar name for the one(s) you want to display. The four default toolbars and other toolbars that pop up automatically are displayed in this project.
Screen settings	Click the Maximize button to maximize the presentation window.
Tools menu	If you don't see the status bar, choose Options and then click the View tab. Select the check box beside Status Bar at the top of the page.

Inserting Clip Art

PowerPoint comes with a gallery of ***clip art*** images that you can use to enhance your presentation. You can use an AutoLayout that contains a clip art placeholder to add an image to a slide, or add an image to a slide that contains other types of placeholders. When you add a clip art image to a slide that contains a clip art placeholder, PowerPoint places the image in the placeholder and sizes it to fill the placeholder. When you add an image to a slide that doesn't contain a clip art placeholder, PowerPoint places the image in the middle of the slide and sizes it according to the default size of the clip art image.

The first time you access the Clip Gallery, PowerPoint takes a few moments to build the gallery and then presents thumbnail images of pictures.

TASK 1: TO INSERT CLIP ART IMAGES FROM THE CLIP GALLERY:

1 Open the presentation *The Willows* and display Slide 3 in Slide view.

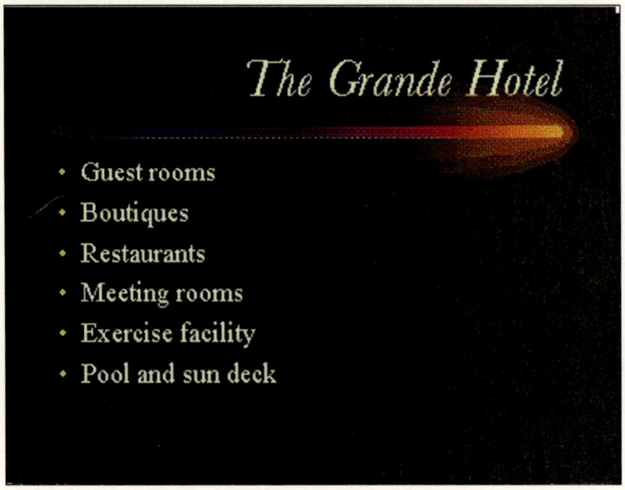

2 Choose Insert, Picture.

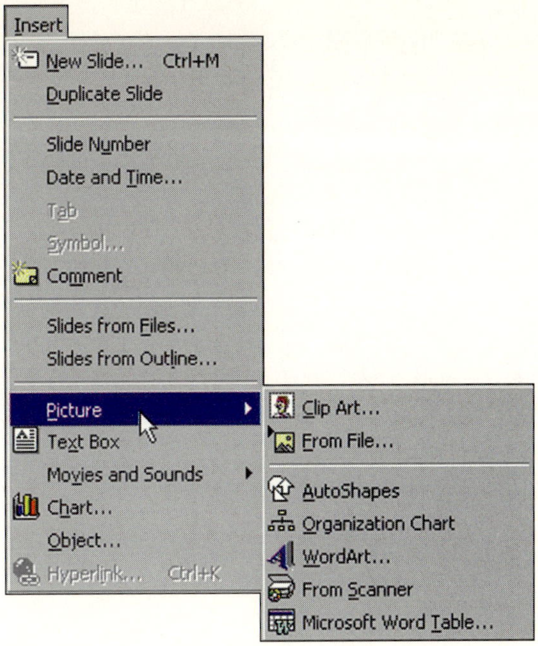

3 Choose Clip Art.

Note You may see a message box telling you where you can find additional clips on the CD-ROM. Click OK to acknowledge the message.

4 Click the Screen Beans category and then scroll until you see the Strong Powerful Invincible Superior Human image.

Note If you don't see the image in your Clip Gallery, select a different image as directed by your instructor.

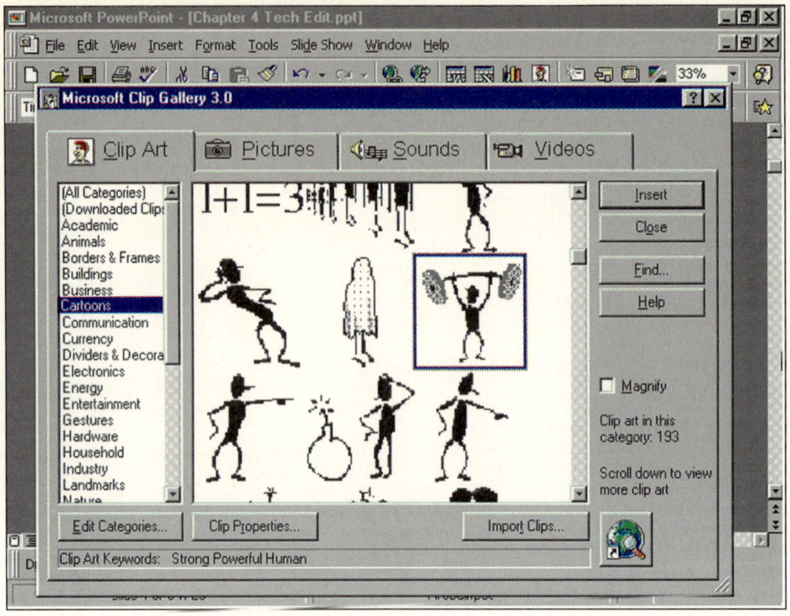

5 Click Insert.

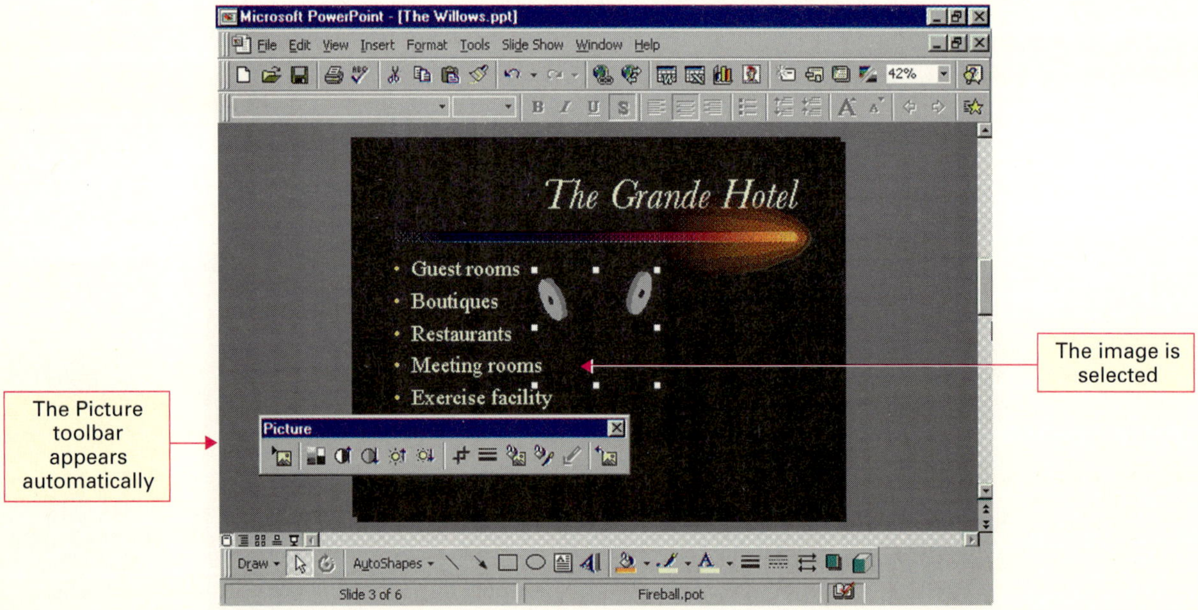

6. Click the Black and White View button on the Standard toolbar.

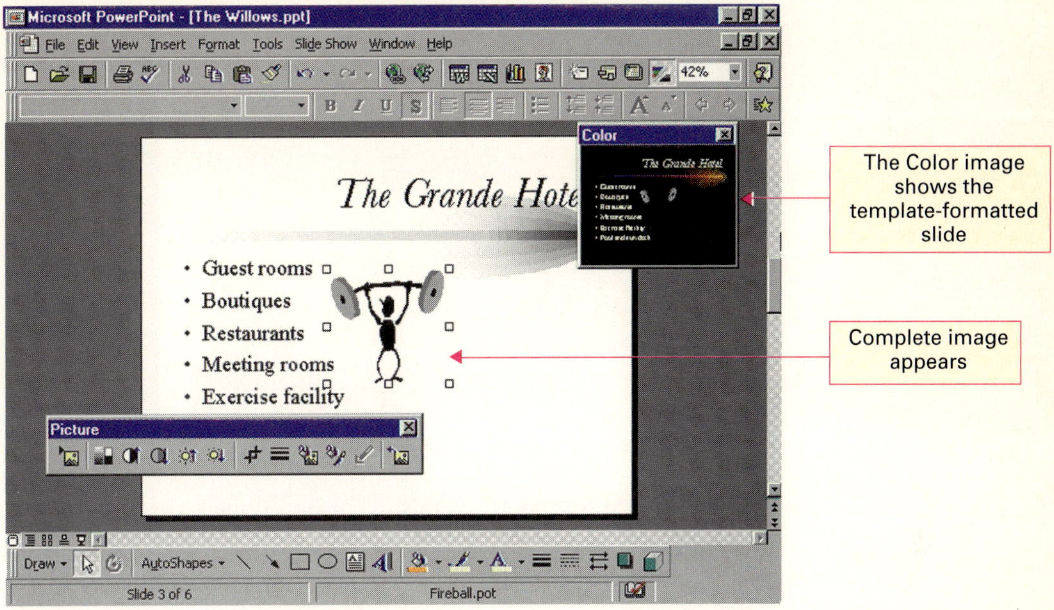

7. Save the changes to the presentation.

Moving and Sizing Clip Art

Clip art images that you add to slides often need to be positioned and sized so that they don't interfere with the text on the slide. When you add a clip art image to a slide, the image remains selected until you select another object or display a different slide. Selected images display handles on the corners and sides that you can use to size the image. To get a full-screen view of your slides as you work with the graphics, close the Color view box and the Picture toolbar.

TASK 2: TO MOVE AND SIZE A CLIP ART IMAGE:

1. Position the pointer on the selected image added to Slide 3.

2 Click and drag the image to the lower-right corner of the slide.

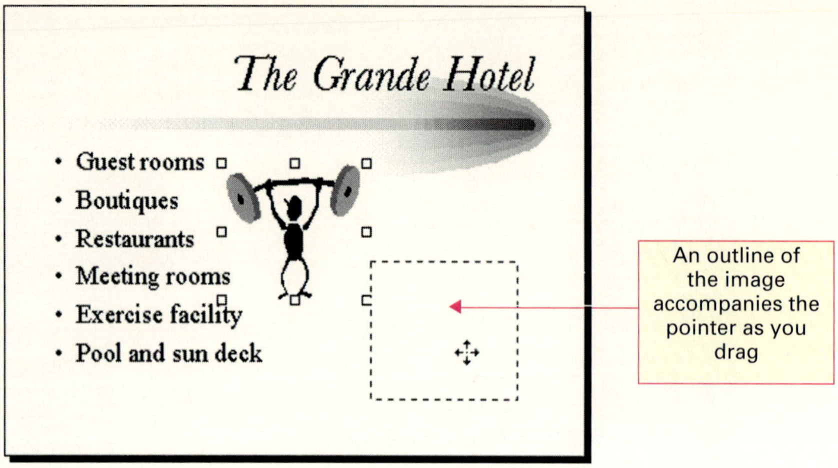

3 Release the mouse button to drop the image.

4 Position the pointer on the handle in the upper-left corner.

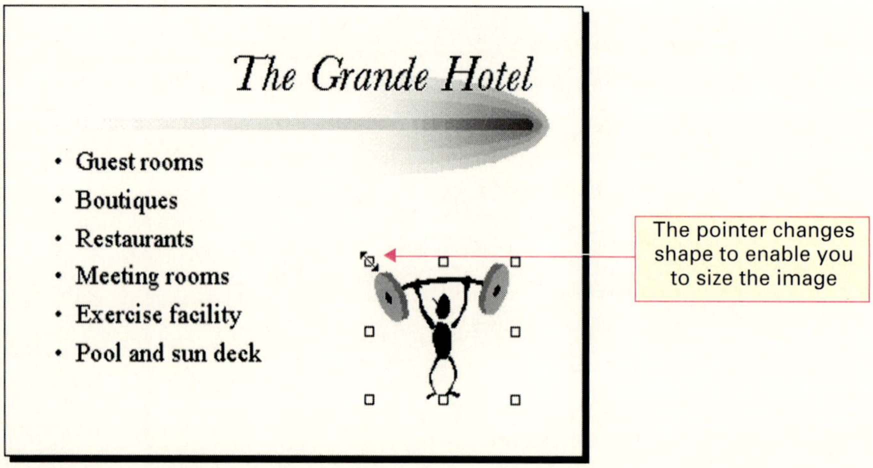

5 Click and drag the corner handle to size the image.

6 Save the changes to the presentation.

Downloading and Inserting Clip Art from the PowerPoint Web Site

When the Clip Gallery that comes with PowerPoint doesn't contain the pictures you need, you can search the PowerPoint Web site for additional graphics.

TASK 3: TO DOWNLOAD CLIP ART FROM THE POWERPOINT WEB SITE:

1 Display Slide 4 of the presentation *The Willows* in Slide view.

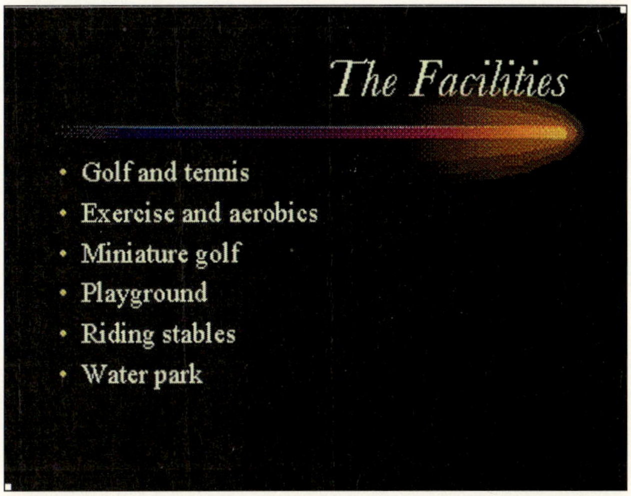

2 Choose Insert, Picture, Clip Art to open the Clip Gallery. The Clip Gallery window opens.

3 Click the globe icon representing a shortcut to the Web.

> **Note** Depending on how your computer is set up, you may see the following message box. Simply click OK to acknowledge the message.

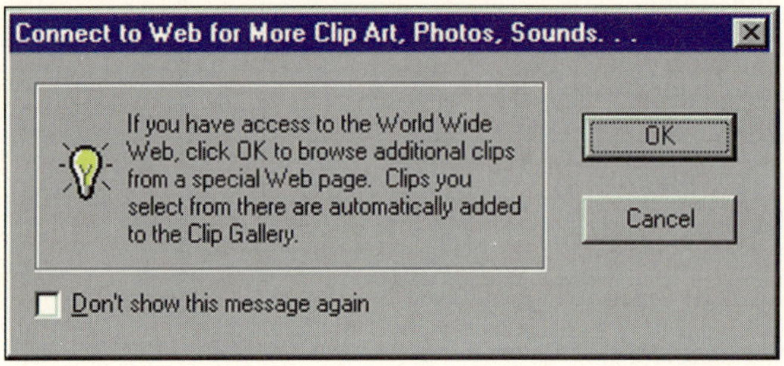

4 Log on to the Internet, using standard logon procedures.

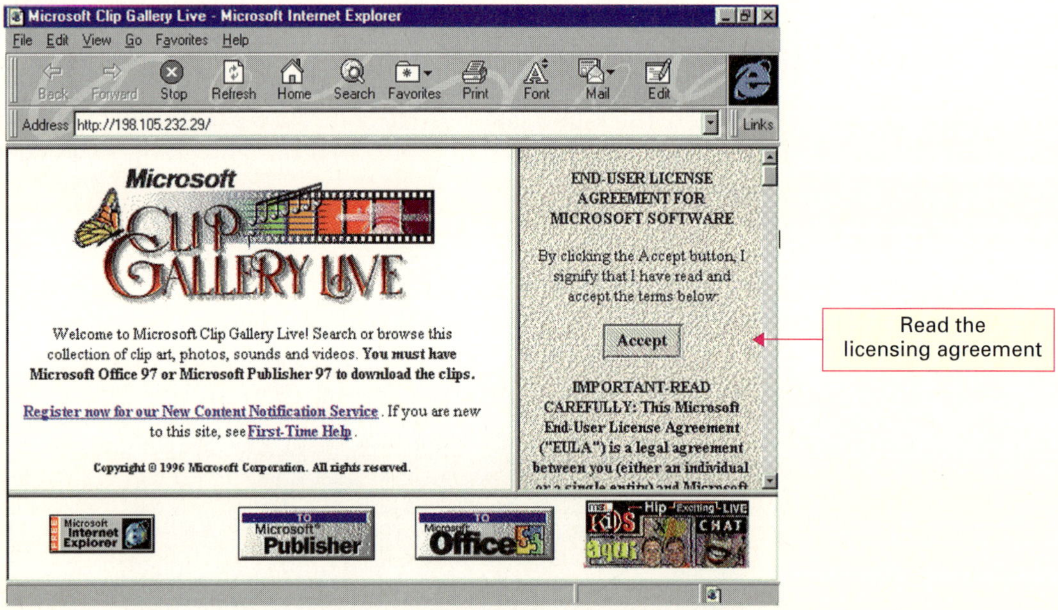

5 Read the license agreement and then click the Accept button.

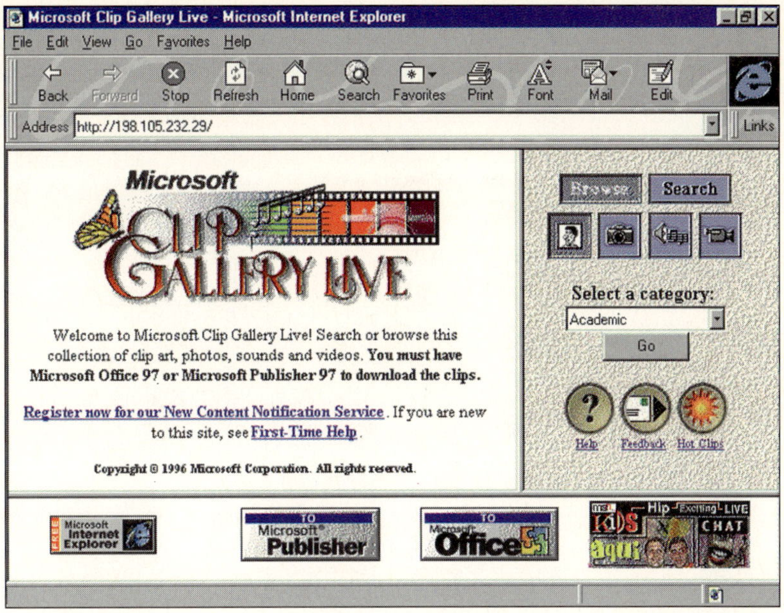

> **Note** The Web page you see may differ from the one pictured here. Microsoft changes Web pages regularly to reflect updates to software and to add new clips.

6 Click the arrow button beside the Select a category list box, select Animals, and click Go.

7 Click the Search button.

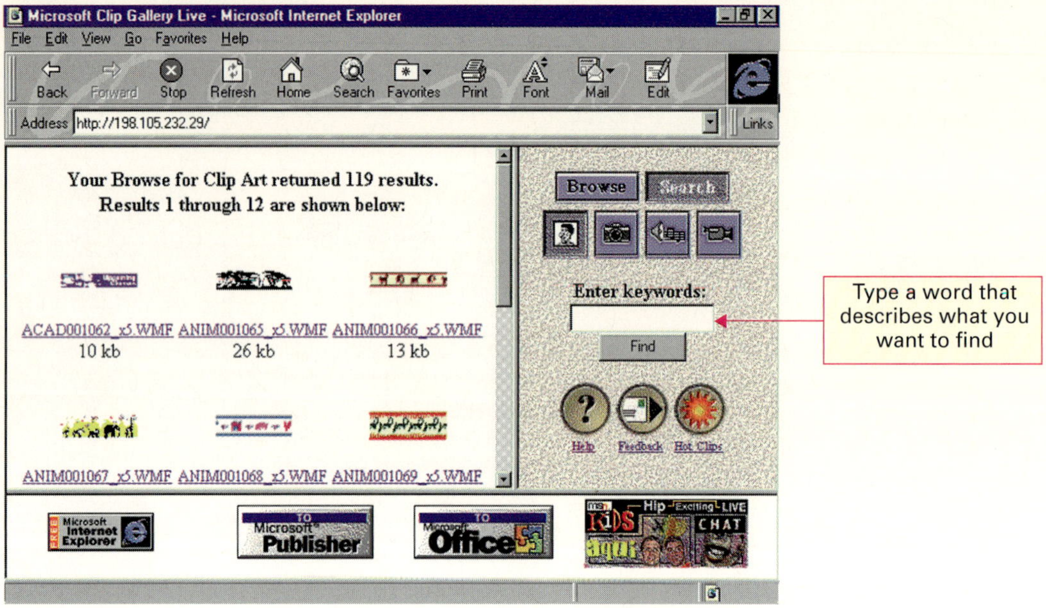

8 Type **Golf** in the Enter keywords text box and then click the Find button.

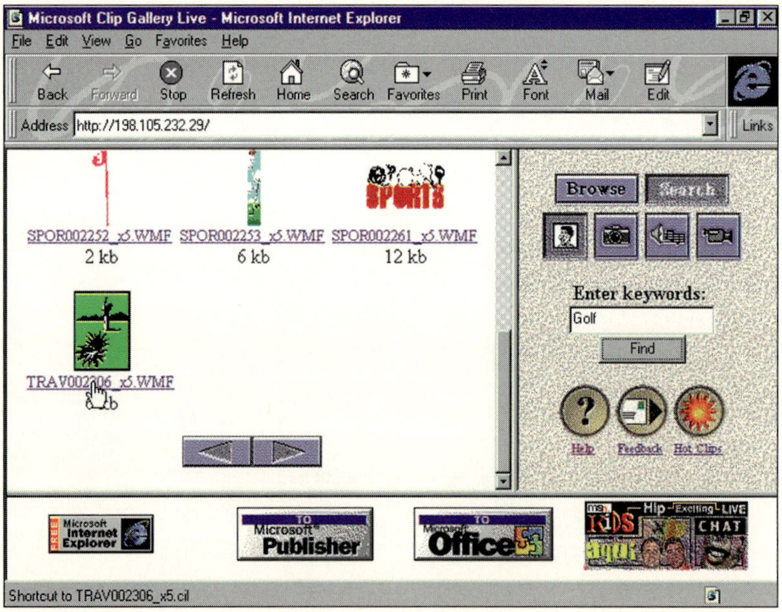

9 Scroll until you see the filename *TRAV002306_x5.wmf* and then click the filename to select the image.

Select an option to store the file

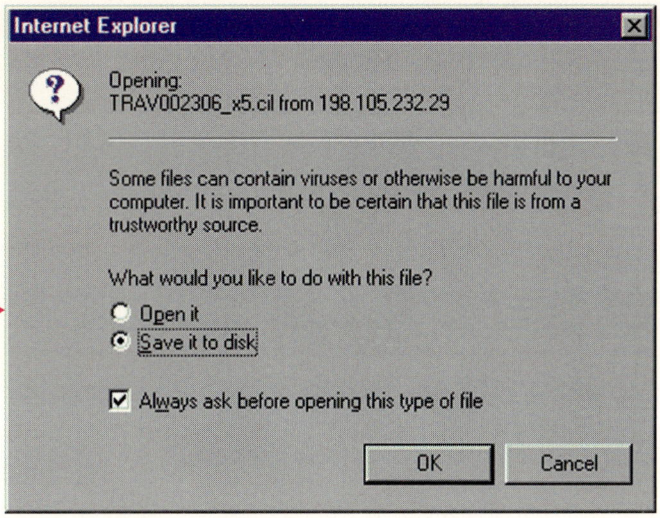

10 Click the Open it option and then click OK.
PowerPoint adds the image to the Downloaded Clips category of the Clip Gallery 3.0 window.

11 Select the downloaded image and click Insert.
PowerPoint places the image on the slide that was active when you launched the Web site.

12 Log off the Internet and display Slide 4 in PowerPoint Slide view.

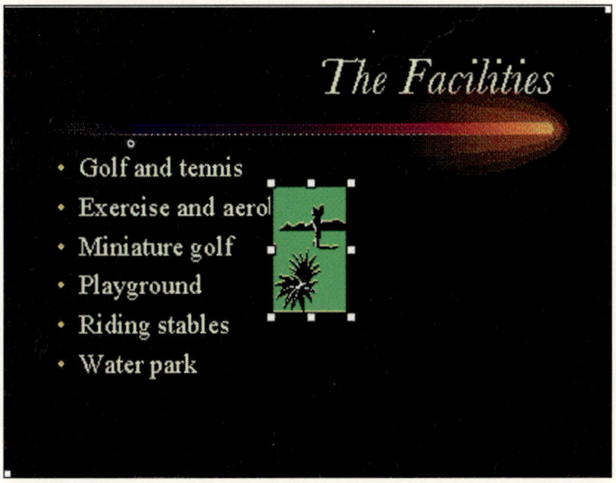

13 Size and position the graphic as shown and then save the changes to the presentation.

Creating WordArt

The ***WordArt*** module available in PowerPoint is the same module you may have used in other Microsoft applications. WordArt enables you to type text, curve, skew, or mold the text into a shape that better fits the area of the slide you want it to occupy. It's a great way to grab someone's attention.

TASK 4: TO CREATE WORDART:

1 Display Slide 6 in Slide view.

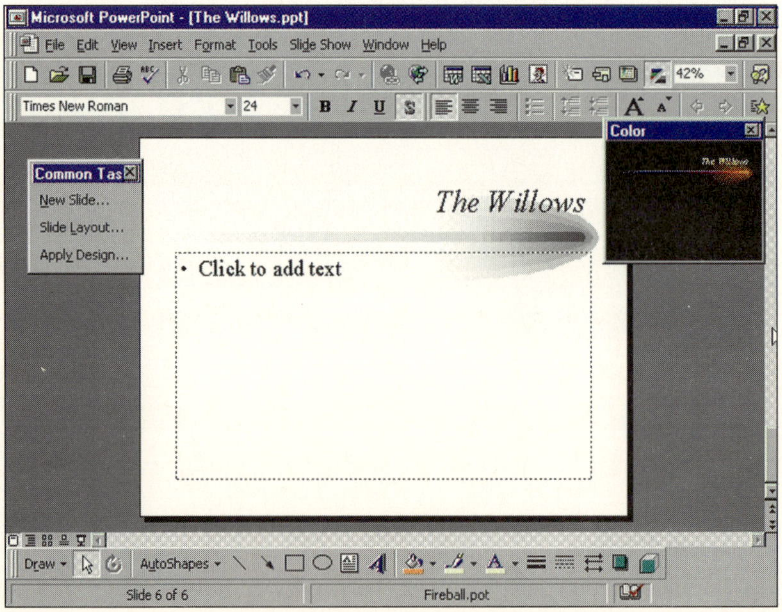

2 Press (SHIFT) and click the bulleted list placeholder; then press (DEL). The title placeholder is now the only object on the slide.

3 Choose Insert, Picture, WordArt.

4 Select the fifth style in the top row and press (ENTER).

5 Type **A Symbol of Genteel Quality** and click OK.

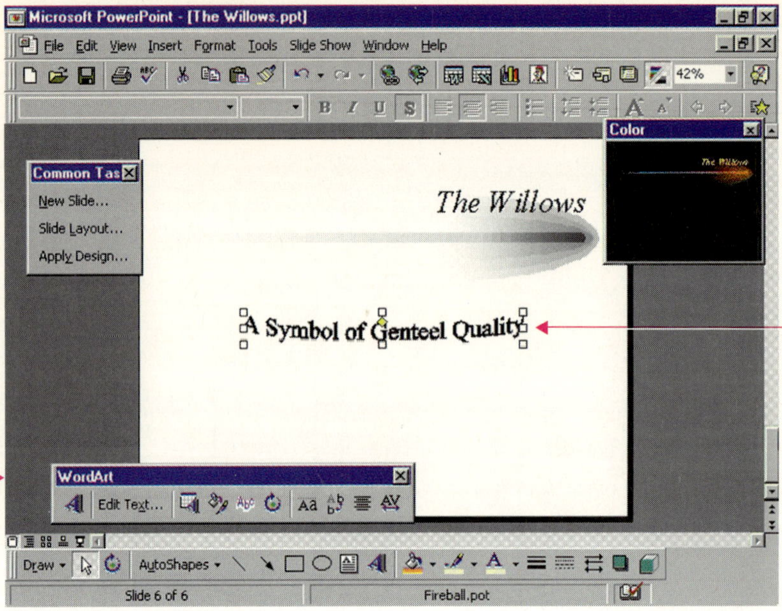

The selected WordArt object

The WordArt toolbar appears automatically

6 Drag the WordArt object to a position at the bottom of the slide.

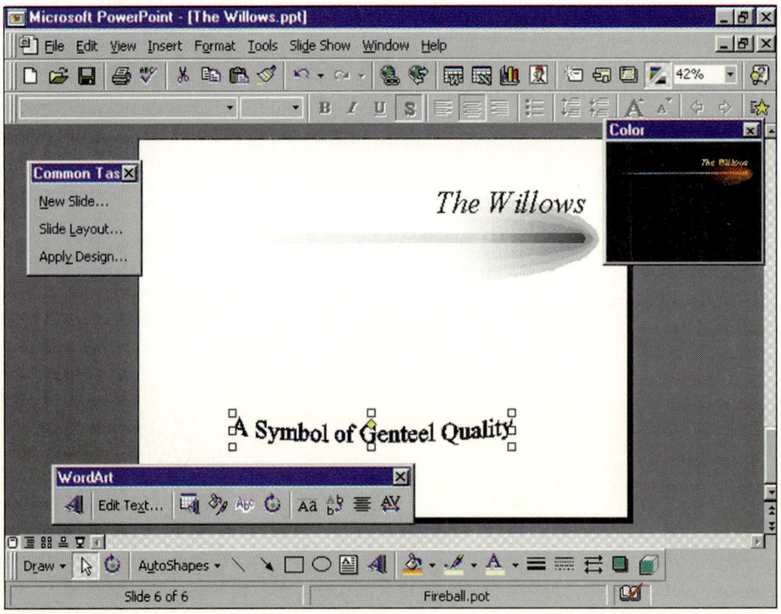

7 Save the changes to the presentation.

Formatting WordArt

After you get the WordArt object on the slide, you need to format the WordArt so that it appears the way you want it. You can use the WordArt toolbar to edit WordArt text as well as to change the shape, format, and angle of the WordArt object.

TASK 5: TO FORMAT WORDART OBJECTS:

1. Click the WordArt object on Slide 6, if necessary, to select it.
The WordArt object displays handles on the corners and sides.

2. Click the Format WordArt button on the WordArt toolbar.

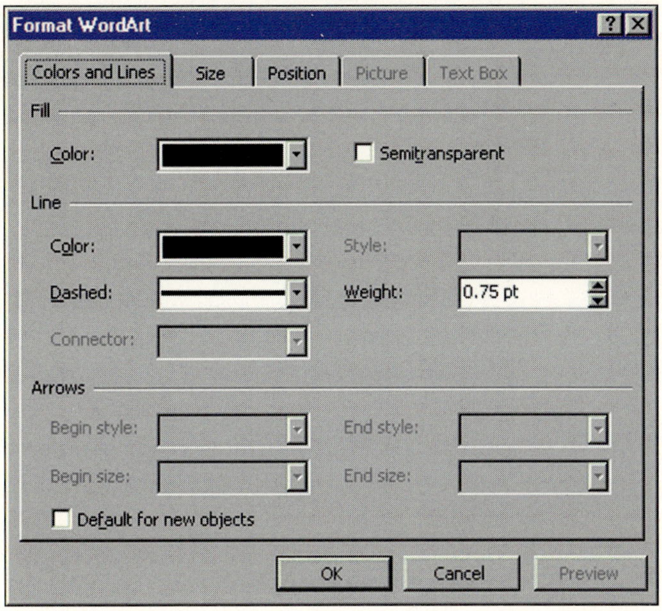

3. Click the arrow button for the Fill Color option.

> **Note** The color you select from the Fill palette controls the color of the WordArt text.

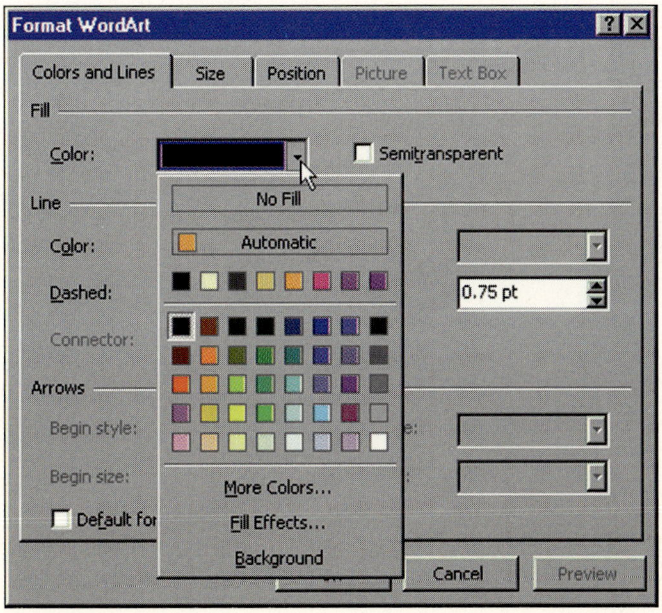

4 Click the second color box on the bottom row of the color palette and then click the arrow button to open the Line Color option.

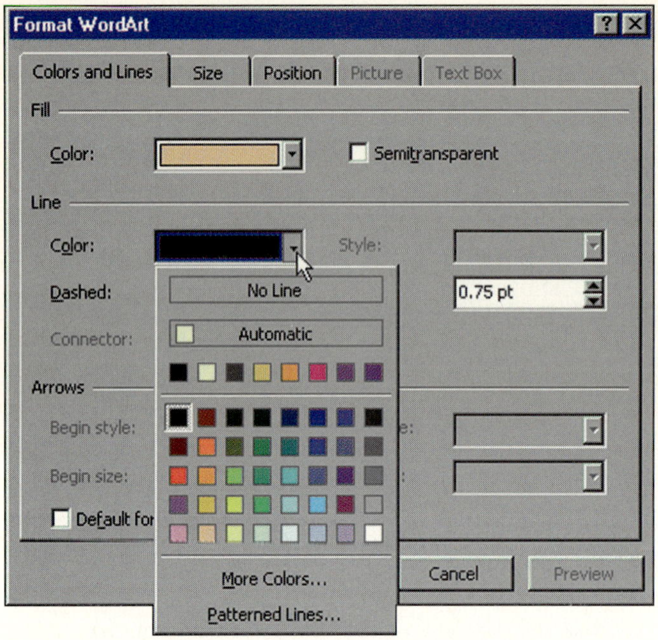

5 Click the second color box on the bottom row of the color palette and then click OK.

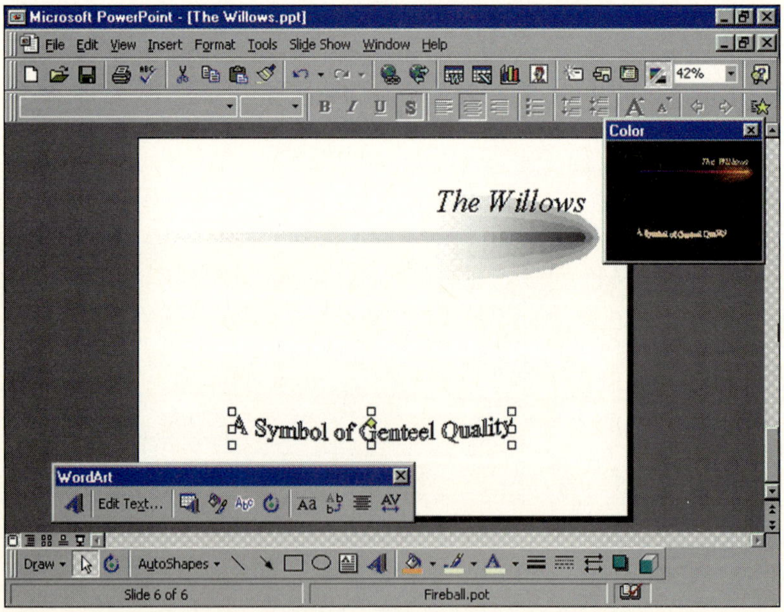

6 Click [icon] to display the slide in color.

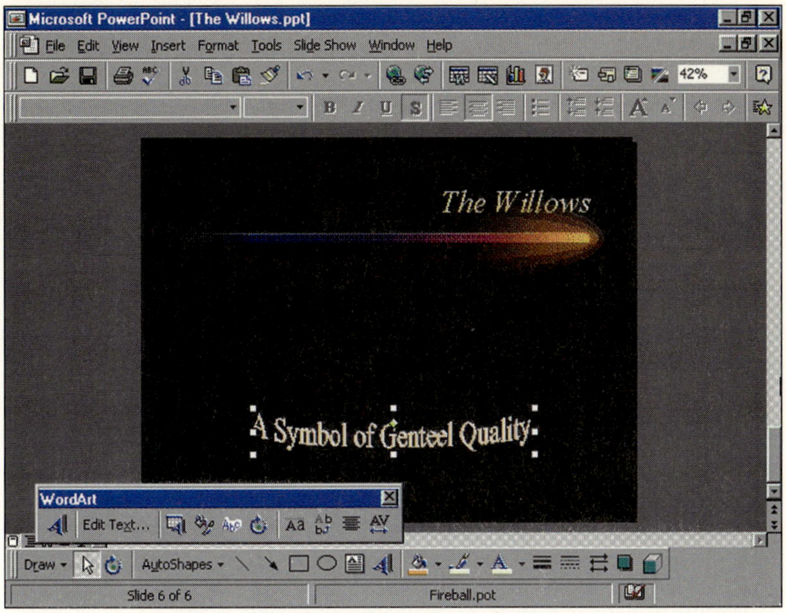

7 Drag the top center handle of the WordArt object to expand the size of the object.

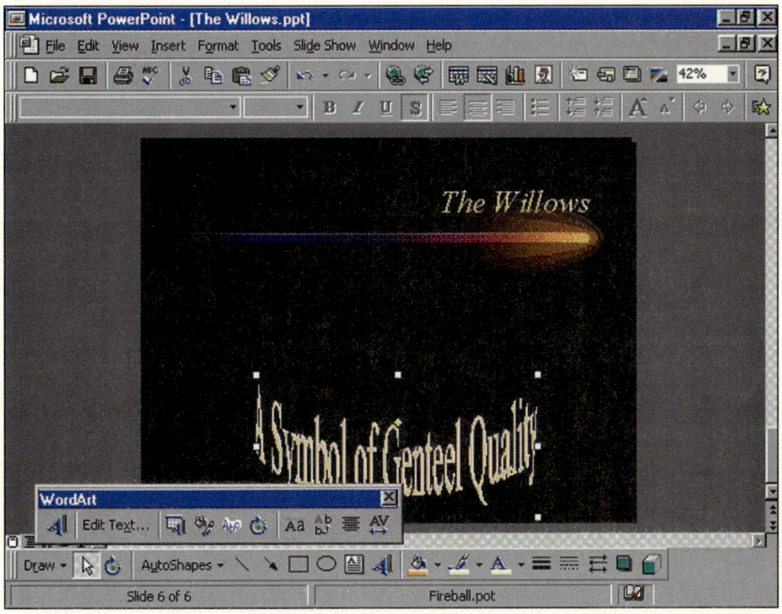

8 Save the changes to the presentation.

Creating Drawings

In addition to the special features such as WordArt, you'll also find quite a sophisticated drawing module that enables you to enhance your slides with original ***freehand*** creations. Even if you're no artist, you'll find the tools on the Drawing toolbar easy to use. Simply select the tool that represents the shape you want to draw, position the pointer where you want to start the drawing, click, and drag the pointer to the point where you want the shape to end.

TASK 6: TO CREATE DRAWINGS USING THE DRAWING TOOLBAR:

1. Display Slide 2 in Slide view.

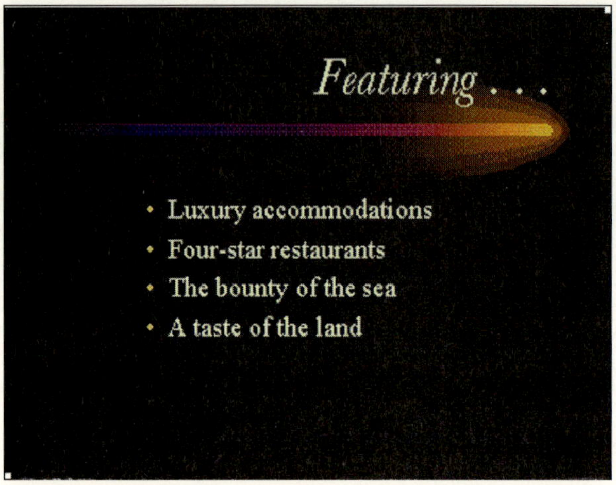

> **Note** If you don't see the Drawing toolbar on your screen, position the pointer on any active toolbar, right-click, and then select the Drawing toolbar.

2. Click the AutoShapes button on the Drawing toolbar and select Stars and Banners.

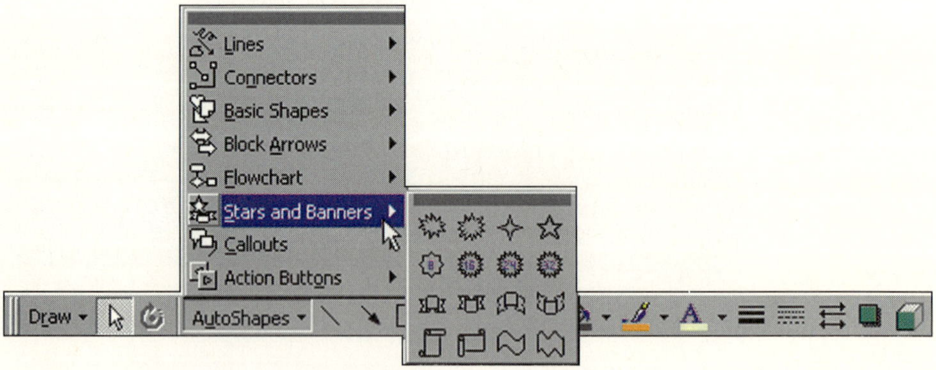

3. Click the 5-Point Star shape on the first row of the palette.
   The mouse pointer changes shape and looks like a plus (+) sign.

4. Position the pointer below and to the left of the last bulleted item, click, and drag diagonally to draw the shape.

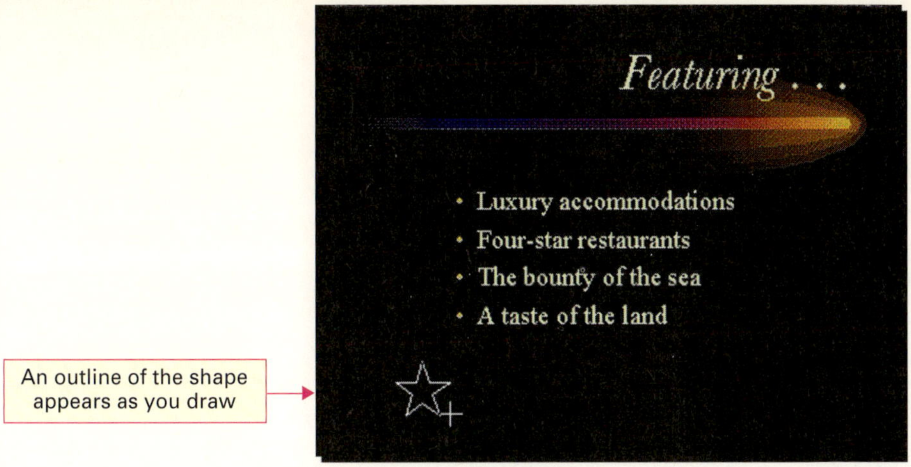

5 Click the Arrow button on the Drawing toolbar, press (SHIFT), and draw an arrow below the second bulleted item.

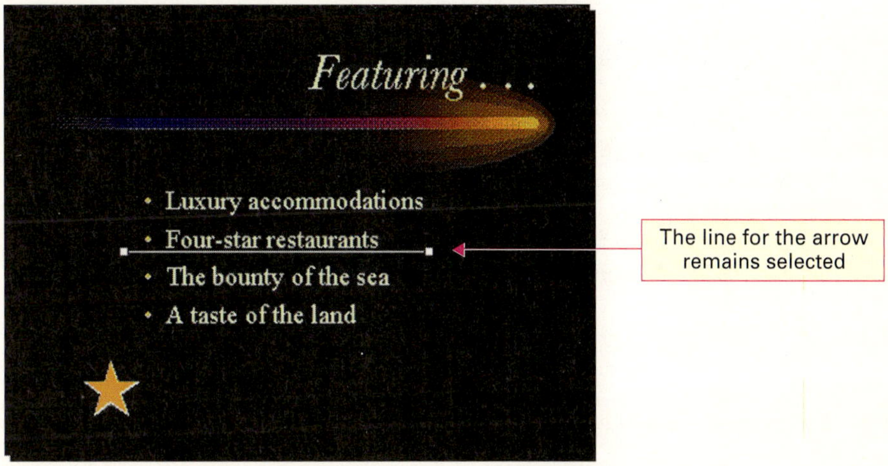

6 Click the Arrow Style button on the Drawing toolbar.

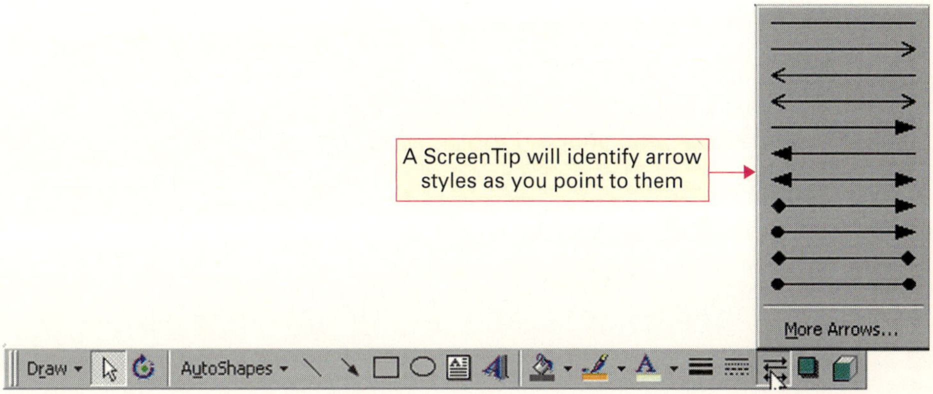

7 Select Arrow Style 10 and then double-click the line for the arrow you just drew.

8 Click the spin buttons beside the Line Weight text box to increase the weight to 2 pt, if necessary; then click OK.

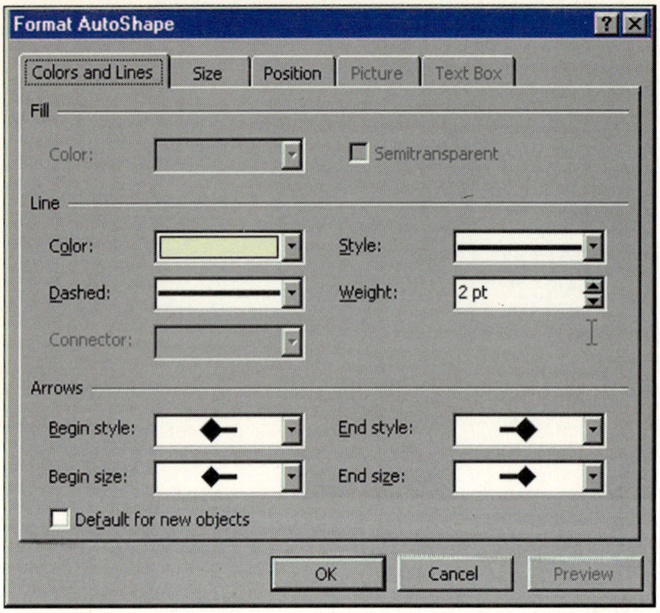

9 Click the star shape you drew earlier to select it and then click the Line Color arrow button.

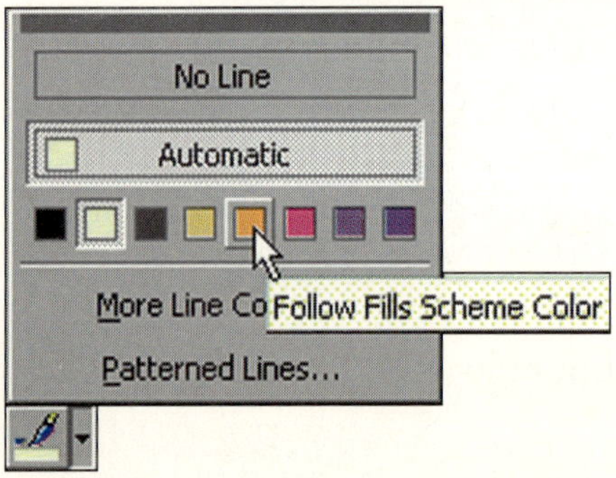

10 Click the Follow Fills Scheme Color box on the Line Color palette. Changing the line color for the star to the same color as the star fill color makes the shape a more cohesive unit by hiding the shape's outline.

11 Click the 3-D button on the Drawing toolbar and select 3-D Style 6.

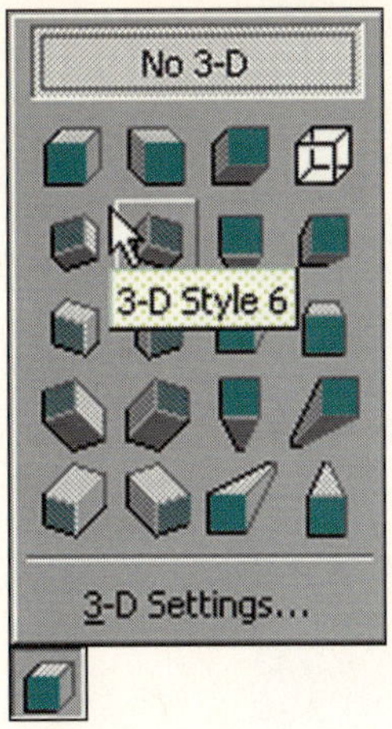

12 Press CTRL+**D** to duplicate the star.

13 Drag the new star slightly up and to the right of the first star.

14 Repeat step 12 two more times and arrange the stars as in:

15 Save the changes to the presentation.

Manipulating Art

Clip art images that you add to slides and drawings that you create freehand often need to be adjusted so that they display appropriately on the slides. Using PowerPoint's special features, you can ***flip*** images to make them face the opposite direction, turn them upside down, ***rotate*** them to create special effects, ***group*** separate objects to make them stick together, and ***ungroup*** grouped objects to change pieces of the objects. You can also rearrange the objects so that different objects appear in front of or behind other objects.

TASK 7: TO MANIPULATE ART OBJECTS:

1 Display Slide 3 in Slide view.

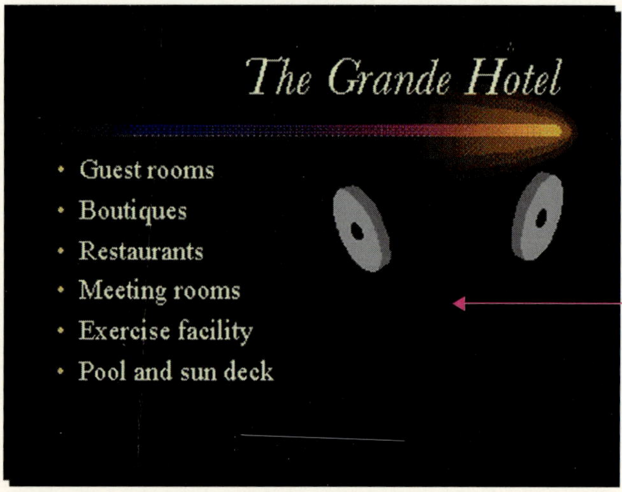

The clip art image you added is lost in the background color

2 Click the clip art image to select it and then click the Draw button on the Drawing toolbar.

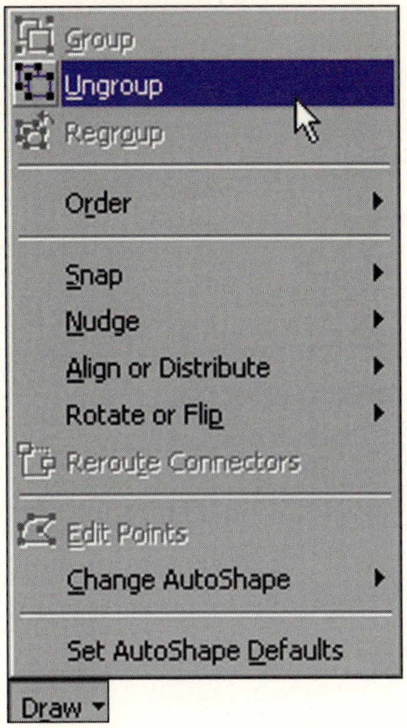

3 Click Ungroup.
A message box tells you that you are about to convert the image to a PowerPoint image. By converting the object, you can edit pieces of the object.

4 Choose Yes to convert the object to a PowerPoint image.

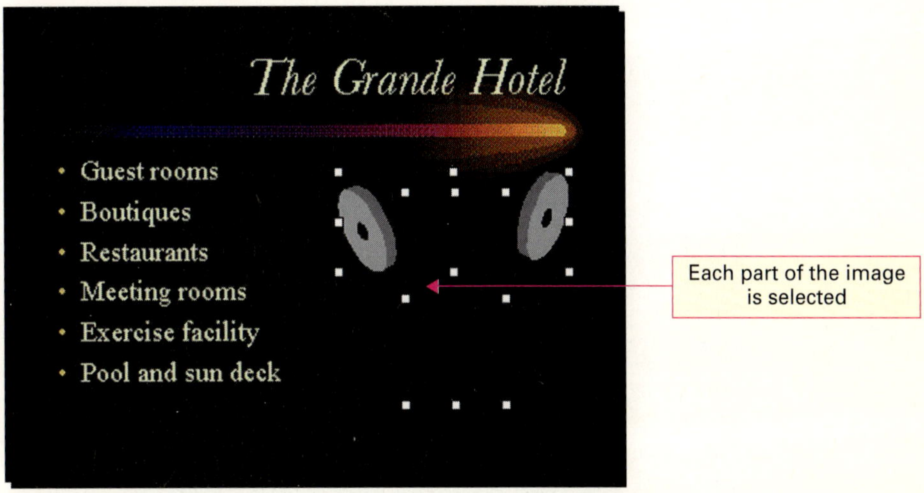

5 Press (SHIFT) and click the barbells to deselect them.
Only the body of the clip art image remains selected.

6 Click the Fill Color button arrow on the Drawing toolbar.

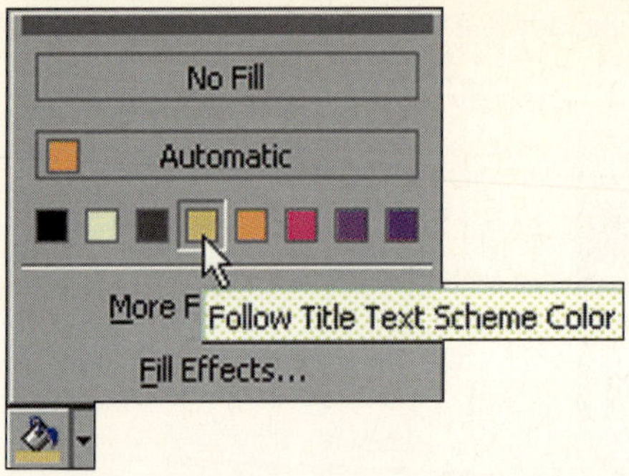

7 Click the Follow Title Text Scheme Color button on the Fill Color palette.

8 Click the barbells and ungroup the object.

Tip If the selected object isn't made up of smaller objects, the Ungroup command on the Draw menu isn't available.

9 Press SHIFT and click each of the gray barbells, leaving only the bar selected.

10 Click the fill color button arrow and click the dark gray color.

11 Click the body of the clip art image and then click the Draw button on the Drawing toolbar and select Rotate or Flip.

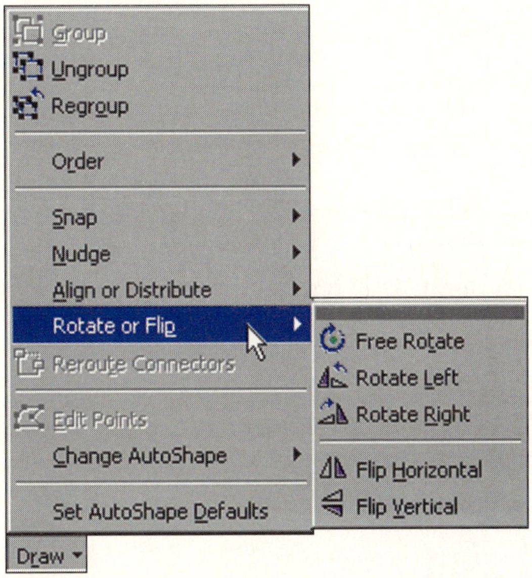

12 Click Flip Horizontal.

13 Position the pointer slightly above and to the left of the leftmost barbell; then click and drag across the clip art image.

A marquee surrounds the pieces of the object

14 Release the mouse button when all pieces of the image are within the marquee.
All pieces of the original clip art image are selected.

15 Click the Draw button on the Drawing toolbar and select Group.
The image is one object again.

16 Display Slide 2, press (SHIFT), and click each of the star shapes.
All four stars are selected.

17 Click the Draw button on the Drawing toolbar and select Align or Distribute.

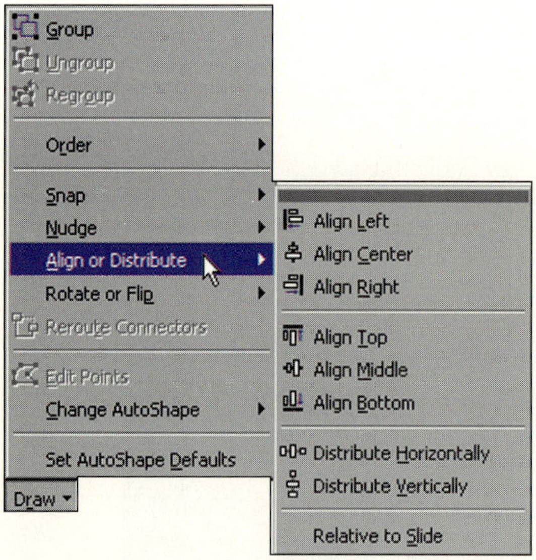

18 Select Align Top.

All stars align with the top point of the star

Tip If you want to position an image behind text on a slide, select the image and choose Draw, Order, and then select the Send to Back option from the cascading menu.

19 Click the Draw button on the Drawing toolbar, select Align or Distribute, and then select Distribute Vertically.
The stars are evenly spaced from each other.

20 Save the changes to the presentation.

The Conclusion

Before closing the presentation *The Willows*, print a copy of the presentation as black-and-white handouts with six framed slides per page. Then, if you've completed your work, close the presentation and exit PowerPoint. If you plan to continue with the Exercises and Assignments, close the presentation and leave PowerPoint running.

Summary and Exercises

Summary

- You can add clip art to any slide in Slide view; AutoLayout formats make accessing the Clip Gallery easy.
- WordArt lets you shape text to fit creatively on your slides. You can apply many of the techniques you use to format slide text to WordArt text.
- PowerPoint's Drawing toolbar provides tools for drawing and formatting shapes and adding special effects.
- Manipulating graphic images includes grouping, ungrouping, flipping, rotating, and aligning.

Key Terms and Operations

Key Terms	Operations
clip art	add, select, move, size, and delete presentation art
flip	create and manipulate WordArt
group	create drawings
rotate	group, ungroup, flip, and rotate art
ungroup	
WordArt	

Study Questions

Multiple Choice

1. PowerPoint comes with a number of images known as
   a. clip art.
   b. pictures.
   c. drawings.
   d. multimedia clips.

2. You can use any of the following techniques to add clip art images to your slide *except*
   a. choose an AutoLayout format that contains a clip art placeholder.
   b. choose File, Import.
   c. click the Insert Clip Art toolbar button.
   d. choose Insert, Picture, Clip Art.

3. To move a clip art image,
   a. delete the existing image, reposition the insertion point, and reinsert the image.
   b. select the image and drag a handle.
   c. select the image, position the pointer on the image away from a handle, and drag the image to a new location.
   d. outline the position you want the image to occupy and then double-click the image to make it move to the new position.

4. When you add clip art images to a document, what toolbar appears?
   a. The Formatting toolbar.

b. The Drawing toolbar.
c. The Insert Clip Art toolbar.
d. The Picture toolbar.

5. To swirl title text on a slide, use PowerPoint's
   a. WordArt feature.
   b. Text Rotate command.
   c. Drawing toolbar.
   d. Clip Gallery.

6. You can edit clip art images to change the color of part of the image by first
   a. redrawing a shape on top of the part you want to change.
   b. ungrouping the image.
   c. changing the size of the image.
   d. editing the image, using Paint.

7. When you want to move two objects together and retain their current position relative to each other,
   a. delete one object, move the other, and then redraw the second object.
   b. ungroup the objects.
   c. group the objects.
   d. relayer the objects.

8. To select multiple drawn objects, WordArt, or clip art images,
   a. simply click each object.
   b. save the slide as a picture and then select the picture object.
   c. position all objects on top of each other and then outline the group of objects.
   d. press Shift and click each object.

9. When you want to draw an object from the center point,
   a. press Ctrl, position the pointer at the object's center point, and draw the shape.
   b. draw the object and then move it so that the center is where you want it.
   c. draw the object and then double-click it.
   d. ungroup all objects on the slide.

10. To size a drawn object, WordArt object, or clip art image,
    a. delete and then redraw the object.
    b. ungroup the object.
    c. select the object and then drag a handle.
    d. select the object, position the pointer in the middle of the object, and drag.

Short Answer

1. What Drawing toolbar button accesses a palette of shapes?
2. How do you copy a drawn object?
3. How do you make a clip art image face the other way?
4. How do you add WordArt to a slide?
5. How do you change the shape of a WordArt object?
6. Name the three basic ways to insert a clip art image.
7. In what shape does the pointer appear when you draw a freehand shape?

8. How does layering affect objects on a slide?
9. How do you change the border color and fill color of a drawn object?
10. What procedure do you use to group objects?

For Discussion

1. What additional formatting techniques can you use to enhance WordArt that are not available for formatting placeholder text?
2. How do the techniques for adding WordArt to slides differ from the techniques used to add text to placeholders?
3. How do you access additional clip art on the Internet?
4. Which of the art features presented in this project do you believe will benefit you the most?

Review Exercises

1. Adding, Moving, and Sizing Clip Art Images

Ruth Lindsey, Manager of The Willows Shops, would like you to add clip art images to slides to enhance the presentation *The Willows Shops*. Suggested graphics are shown in Figure 3.2.

Figure 3.2

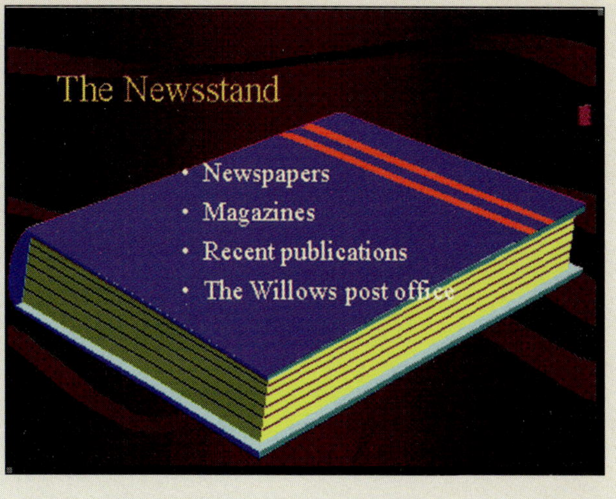

Figure 3.2 *(continued)*

If you do not have the images displayed, insert graphics of your choice or those chosen by your instructor. Use the techniques explored in this project to locate appropriate clip art to add to slides. Follow these instructions to complete the presentation:

1. Launch PowerPoint, if necessary, and open the presentation *The Willows Shops*.
2. Display the presentation in Slide view, display the slides pictured in Figure 3.2, and choose Insert, Picture, Clip Art to locate the image in the Clip Gallery.
3. Position and size the clip art images to appear as shown in Figure 3.2. Rotate and flip items as necessary to create the images displayed in the figure. Ungroup the object on Slide 3 and change the color of the character so it can be seen.
4. Save changes to the presentation and print a copy of the six slides containing clip art.
5. Close the presentation and exit PowerPoint when you've completed your work.

2. Adding WordArt and Drawings to Slides

Ms. Lindsey would also like to change the titles of the three slides pictured in Figure 3.3 from the presentation *The Willows Shops* to WordArt.

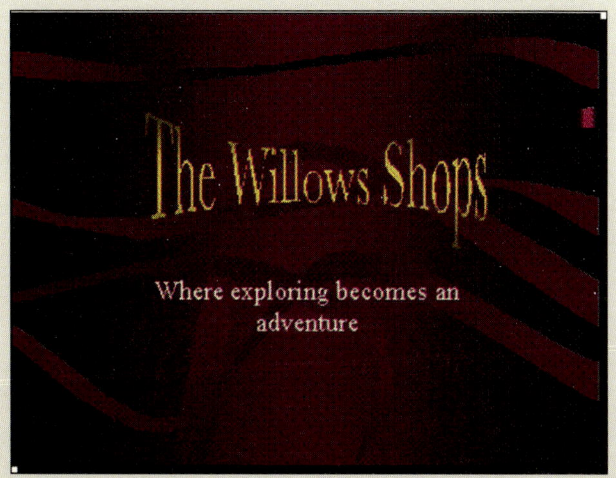

Figure 3.3

Figure 3.3 *(continued)*

Follow these steps to complete the task.

1. Launch PowerPoint, if necessary, and open the presentation *The Willows Shops*.
2. Display Slide 1 in Slide view, delete the title placeholder, add the title text as a WordArt object, and format the WordArt so that it appears as shown in Figure 3.3.
3. Repeat step 2 for Slides 2 and 4.
4. Display Slide 4 and create and format the drawn object shown in Figure 3.3, using a shadowed rectangle and a shaded four-pointed AutoShape star. Edit the colors to show gradient fill effects.
5. Save the changes to the presentation and print copies of the three slides containing WordArt titles as black-and-white handouts with three slides per page.
6. Close the presentation and exit PowerPoint when you've completed your work.

Assignments

1. Adding, Formatting, and Manipulating Clip Art, WordArt, and Drawings

The slides from the *Festivals and Attractions* presentation enhanced with suggested graphics appear in Figure 3.4.

Figure 3.4

Use tools presented in this project to add clip art images, WordArt objects, and drawings to your presentation slides. Edit the clip art images by ungrouping them and changing the colors. Size and position the graphics as shown in Figure 3.4. Save changes to the presentation and print black-and-white handouts with three slides per page. Close the presentation and exit PowerPoint when you've completed your work.

2. Searching the Internet for Pictures to Enhance Presentations

Check with your instructor on how and where to download the Willow graphic. If you have access to the Internet, click the Globe button on the Clip Gallery window to search the Internet Clip Gallery for images you can use in your résumé presentation. Otherwise, search the Clip Art Gallery that is provided in the program.

Add drawings to presentation slides and change the titles of all slides in your presentation to WordArt, formatted to create special effects. Save changes to the presentation and print a copy of your presentation as black-and-white handouts with three slides per page.

Close the presentation and exit PowerPoint when you've completed your work.

4

PROJECT

Viewing and Editing a Presentation

Most of the presentations you create are designed to provide powerful visuals to enhance oral presentations. Slides in a presentation can be formatted and shown on-screen by individuals or projected on an audiovisual screen or flat surface as you present a report to an audience.

Showing your presentations with style has a positive impact on your audience. The PowerPoint slide show feature enables you to show your presentation on a computer screen. Seeing your presentation "live" the first time can be quite satisfying—and exciting. In this project, you learn how to dress up your presentation for on-screen viewing and how to use Slide Sorter view to rearrange slides in the presentation.

Objectives

After completing this project, you will be able to:

- **Present a slide show**
- **Use the slide show shortcut menu**
- **Rearrange slides in a presentation**
- **Add slide transitions**
- **Animate text**
- **Expand slides**
- **Hide slides and display hidden slides**

The Challenge

Francesca Savoy has reviewed the presentation *The Willows* and has approved the design, graphics, and format of slides in the presentation. She now asks that the presentation be tweaked into its final form so that she can present it to the managers at their next meeting.

The Solution

To get the presentation *The Willows* into shape, you need to view the presentation as a slide show and then use Slide Sorter view to make final edits to the presentation. Figure 4.1 shows the final presentation in Slide Sorter view.

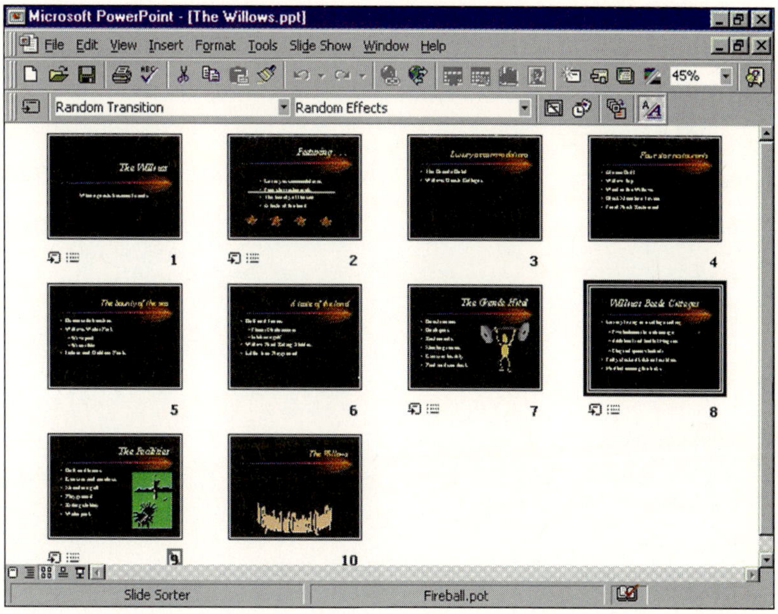

Figure 4.1

The Setup

You're switching to a different view for many of the activities in this section, and you're also going to be using the slide show feature in PowerPoint. As a result, you need to select some different settings to ensure that your screen will match the illustrations shown in this project.

When you switch to Slide Sorter view, make sure that the Standard and Slide Sorter toolbars display. If you don't see them, choose View, Toolbars, and then select them. Close the Common Tasks toolbar if it's open.

You'll also need to work with your presentation window maximized in Slide Sorter view. Click the Maximize button on the presentation window, if necessary. Then set the Zoom control to 66%.

Presenting a Slide Show

Viewing your presentation as a slide show makes it come to life. Slide shows display slides in the presentation window without the PowerPoint toolbars, title bar, and status bar. During a slide show, each slide literally fills the screen and you can focus on slide contents to determine impact. PowerPoint offers a number of ways to launch a slide show:

- Choose View, Slide Show
- Choose Slide Show, View Show
- Click the Slide Show button at the bottom of the presentation window

TASK 1: TO VIEW A PRESENTATION AS A SLIDE SHOW:

1. Open the presentation *The Willows* and display the first slide in Slide view. Slide 1 of the presentation appears as last shown in Project 3.

2. Click the Slide Show button at the bottom of the presentation window.

You can use both the keyboard and mouse to navigate the slides in a presentation during a slide show. Table 4.1 compares the actions for using both techniques. Practice each technique to identify the ones you like best.

Note The slide show starts with the slide displayed in Slide or Notes Pages view or the slide selected in Slide Sorter or Outline view.

2 Click Slide 5 to select it, and then drag it to the left of Slide 4.

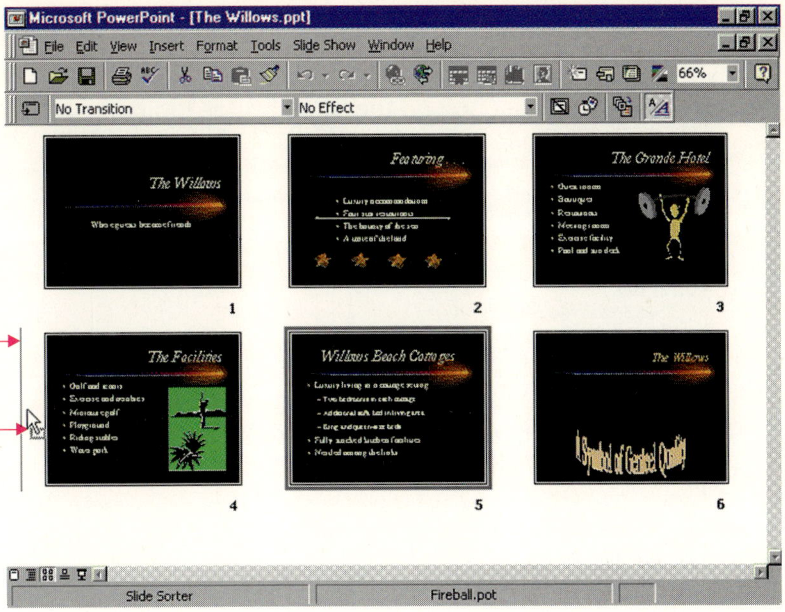

The vertical bar shows the active position for the slide

The mouse pointer changes to a pointer carrying a slide

3 Drop Slide 5 when the vertical bar appears as shown in step 2.

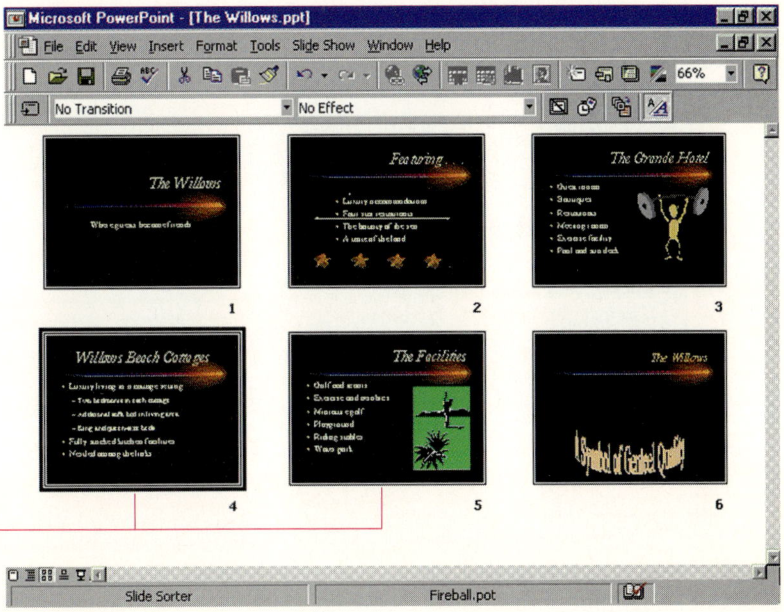

The slide appears in the new order and renumbers automatically

4 Click to save changes to the presentation, and leave it open.

Adding Slide Transitions

Slide ***transitions*** create special effects as your slides go on and off the screen during a slide show. You can use the Slide Sorter toolbar to add transitions to your slides.

TASK 4: TO ADD SLIDE TRANSITIONS:

1 Display the presentation *The Willows* in Slide Sorter view, if necessary.

2 Click Slide 1 to select it and then click the arrow button beside the Slide Transition Effects list box on the Slide Sorter toolbar.

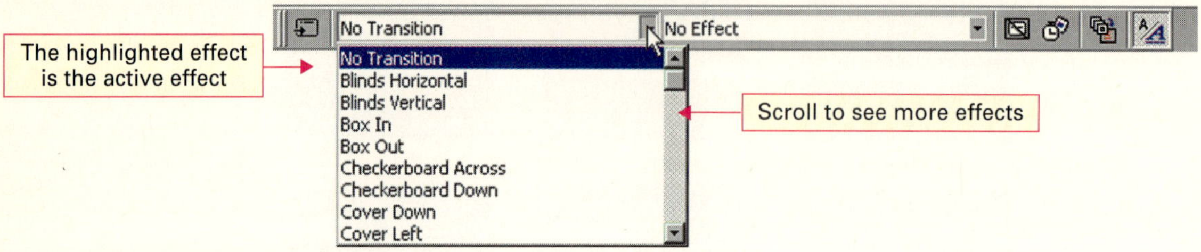

3 Scroll down the effects list, if necessary, click *Dissolve,* and watch Slide 1 closely to view the effect.

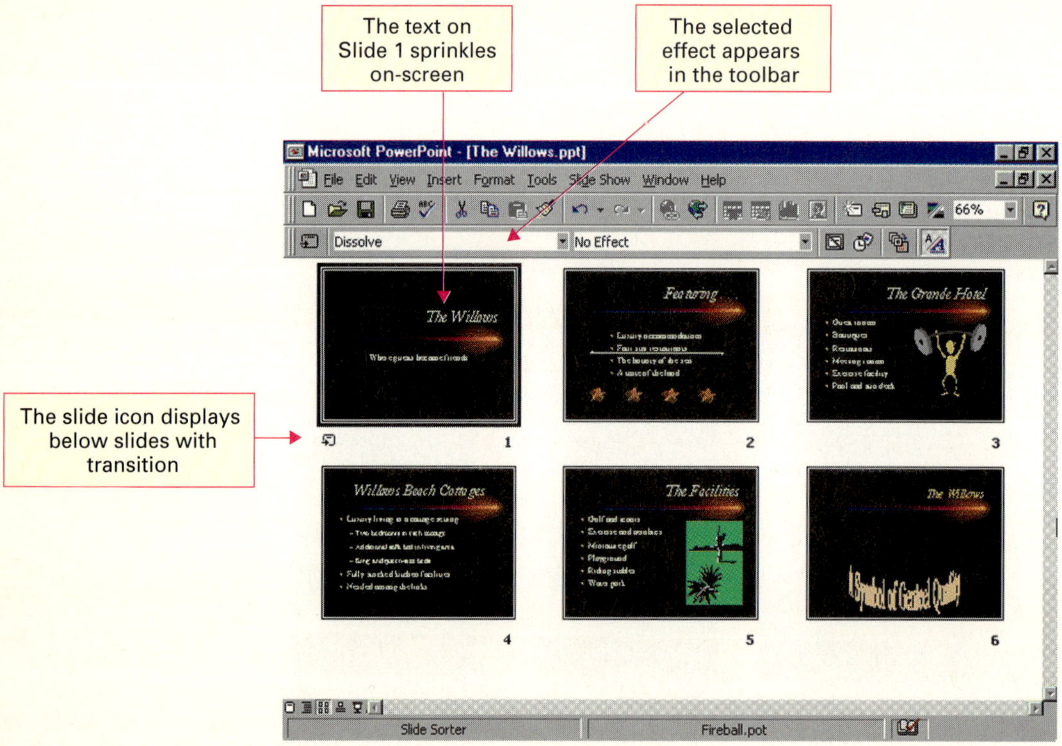

4 Click the slide icon below Slide 1.
The transition effect repeats to show the effect.

5 Click to select Slide 2, and then press (SHIFT) and click Slides 3, 4, and 5.
The four selected slides appear with broad dark borders.

6 Click the Slide Transition Effect arrow button, scroll down the list, and select Random Transition from the bottom of the transition effects list.
An icon appears below each selected slide.

7 Click the transition slide icon below each slide and view the transition effect.
The effect changes each time you click the icon below a slide when you use Random transition.

8 Click .

Animating Text

When you apply ***text preset animations*** (formerly known as *builds*) to slides, each slide title displays on-screen by itself and each bulleted list item is presented separately during a slide show. Text preset animations help focus the attention of your audience on each individual bulleted item as you discuss it and removes the distractions of presenting all bulleted points at once. Text that appears in text placeholders is affected when you apply the text preset animation effects.

TASK 5: TO ANIMATE SLIDE TEXT:

1 Click Slide 1 in Slide Sorter view.
Slide 1 is selected.

2 Click the arrow button for the Text Preset Animation list box in the Slide Sorter toolbar.

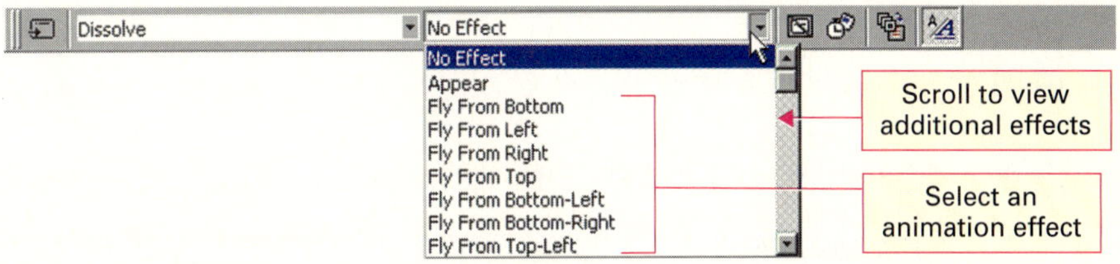

3 Scroll down the list, if necessary, and select Crawl From Right.

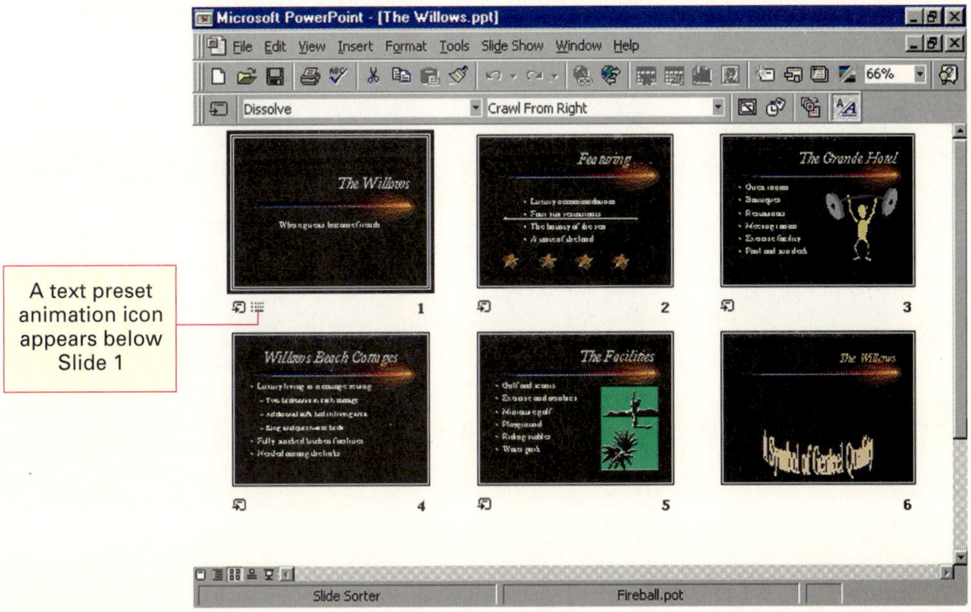

4 Select Slide 2 and select Peek From Left from the Text Preset Animations list.

5 Add text preset animations of your choice to Slides 3, 4, and 5.
Text preset animation icons appear below each slide.

6 Select Slide 1 and then click [Slide Show button] to view the special effects applied to each slide.
Use navigation techniques to review all slides and end the slide show.

7 Click [Close button] when the slide show finishes.

Expanding Slides

When a bulleted list slide contains points that you need to expand (or expound upon), you can use the PowerPoint ***expand*** feature to create new slides. When you expand a slide, each bulleted list item appears as the title of a new slide. Slides you expand are often referred to as ***parent slides*** and new slides created from the parent slide are called ***children***. When you expand a slide, the children appear in bulleted list order immediately following the parent slide.

TASK 6: TO EXPAND BULLETED LISTS:

1 Select Slide 2 in Slide Sorter view.
Slide 2 appears with a broad dark border.

2 Choose Tools, Expand Slide.

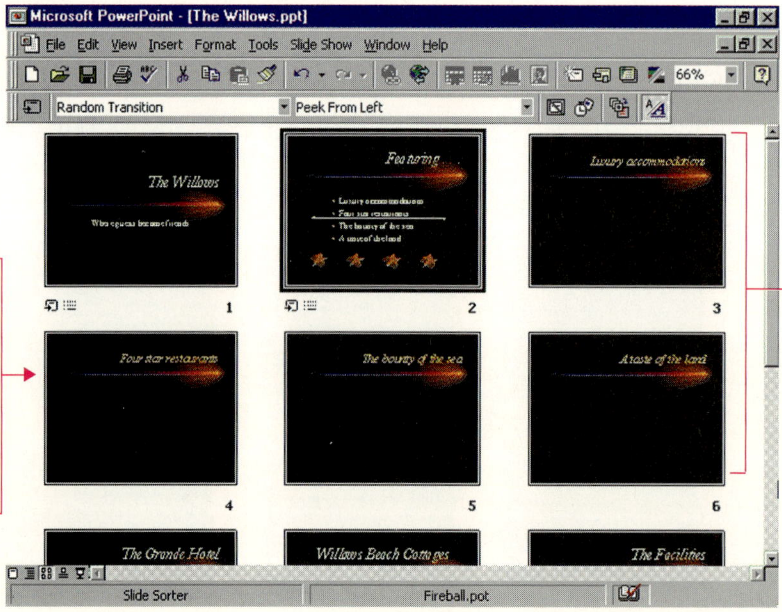

The new slides (children) follow the original (parent). Children slides don't carry the transition effect or the text preset animations of the parent slide.

Four new slides contain titles that parallel Slide 2 bullet points. Titles follow the original template format.

3 Click [Outline View button] to switch to Outline view.

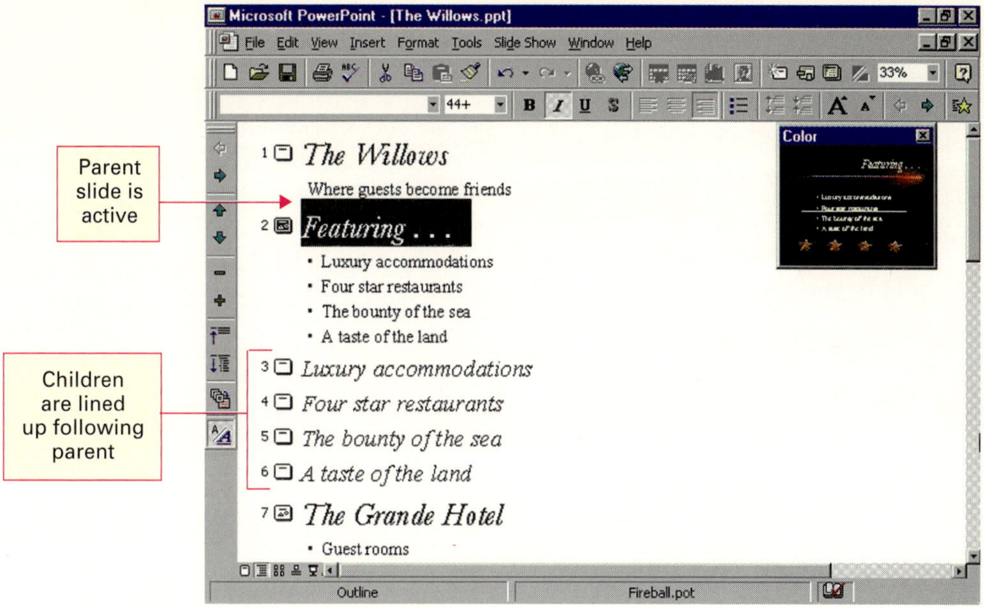

4 Position the I-beam after the word "accommodations" in Slide 3, press (ENTER) and then (TAB), and type additional text, as in:

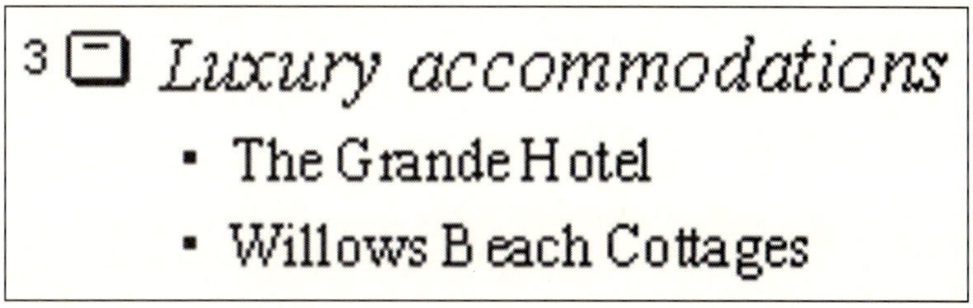

5 Position the I-beam after the last word in the slide titles for Slides 4, 5, and 6, press ENTER, and then press TAB and type the additional text shown here as bulleted lists:

4 *Four-star restaurants*
- Atrium Grill
- Willow Top
- Wind in the Willows
- Black Mountain Tavern
- Front Porch Restaurant

5 *The bounty of the sea*
- Ocean beaches
- Willows Water Park
  - Wave pool
  - Water slide
- Indoor and outdoor pools

6 *A taste of the land*
- Golf and tennis
  - Three 18-hole courses
  - Miniature golf
- Willow Pond Riding Stables
- Little Tree Playground

6 Click to return to Slide Sorter view, click the Zoom box on the Standard toolbar, type **45**, and press ENTER.

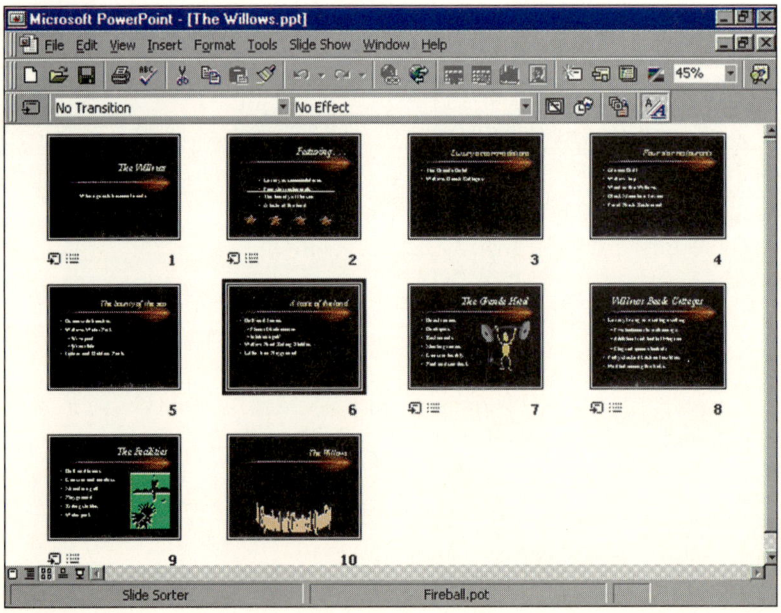

Hiding Slides and Displaying Hidden Slides

Hiding slides enables you to include slides containing detailed information or data in your presentation but display the slides during a slide show only when the audience asks questions or when you need more details about a topic. Hidden slides remain in the background during a slide show and show only when you access them.

TASK 7: TO HIDE SLIDES AND DISPLAY THEM DURING A SLIDE SHOW:

1. Select Slide 9 in Slide Sorter view.
   Slide 9 appears with a broad dark border.
2. Click the Hide Slide button on the Slide Sorter toolbar.

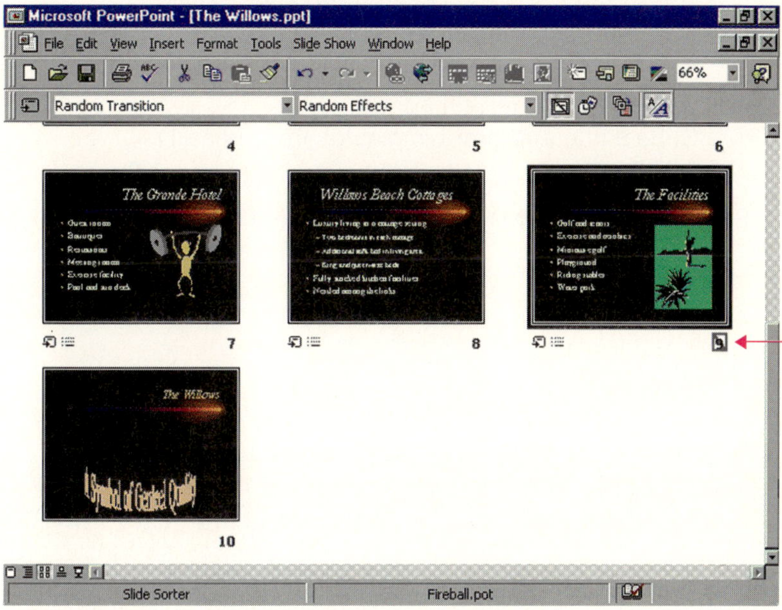

Slide numbers of hidden slides are marked

3. Select Slide 8 and then click .
   Slide 8 displays in the slide show window.
4. Click the left mouse button until the next slide displays.
   Slide 10 now displays after Slide 8 during the slide show unless you call up Slide 9.
5. Press ESC to stop the slide show, select Slide 8, if necessary, and then click to start the show again.
   Slide 8 displays in the slide show window.
6. Press **H** to display the hidden Slide 9.
   Slide 9 title and graphic display immediately.
7. Press ESC to stop the slide show, select Slide 8, if necessary, and then click again.
   Slide 8 displays in the slide show window.
8. Right-click on the screen and choose Go.

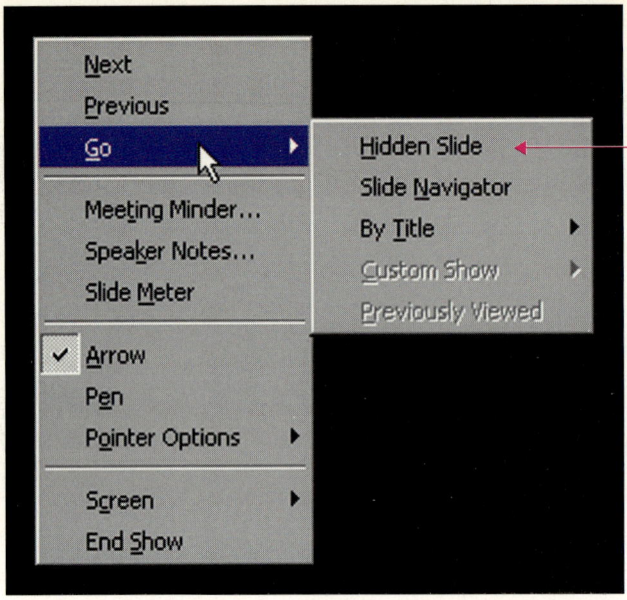

The Hidden Slide option is active only when a hidden slide follows the active slide

9 Choose Hidden Slide.
The Slide 9 title and graphic display immediately.

10 Press ESC to stop the slide show and then click the Save button.
PowerPoint saves changes to the presentation.

The Conclusion

Before closing the presentation *The Willows*, print a copy of the presentation in Outline view. Then, if you've completed your work, close the presentation and exit PowerPoint. If you plan to continue with the Exercises and Assignments, close the presentation and leave PowerPoint running.

Summary and Exercises

Summary

- The PowerPoint slide show feature enables you to show your presentation on-screen.
- Slide shows display slides in the presentation window without the PowerPoint toolbars, title bar, and status bar.
- The easiest way to start a slide show is to click the Slide Show button at the bottom of the presentation window.
- You can use both mouse and keyboard techniques to navigate slides during a slide show.
- You can display the slide show shortcut menu during a slide show by clicking the right mouse button. The slide show shortcut menu displays commands for controlling on-screen features.
- You can also access the slide show shortcut menu by moving the mouse pointer on-screen until a shortcut menu button displays and then clicking the shortcut menu button.
- Slide Sorter view is the most efficient view to use when you need to rearrange slides or apply transitions and special effects.
- Slide transitions affect the way slides move on and off the screen during a slide show.
- Text preset animations present text on slides one bullet point at a time during a slide show. You can also set an animation to dim previously presented bullet points to enable the audience to focus on the point being discussed.
- You can use the expand slide feature to create new slides that use the bulleted list text from a parent slide. Each bulleted list item appears as the title of a new slide.
- Hiding slides enables you to include slides with supplemental information in the presentation and display the slides only when you need them.

Key Terms and Operations

Key Terms

expand
hidden slides
slide show
slide show shortcut menu
Slide Sorter view
text preset animation
transition

Operations

add transitions to slides
animate slide text using text preset animations
display different slides in a presentation
end a slide show
expand and hide slides
rearrange slides in a presentation using Slide Sorter view
start a slide show

Study Questions

Multiple Choice

1. To start a slide show,
   - **a.** click a button on the Standard toolbar.
   - **b.** press Enter after the last slide is completed.
   - **c.** use the slide show shortcut menu.
   - **d.** click the Slide Show button at the bottom of the presentation window.

2. Showing slides as a slide show displays slides
  a. all on-screen together.
  b. in Print Preview mode.
  c. one at a time, using the full screen.
  d. one at a time, as in Slide view.

3. The view that makes it easy to rearrange slides is
  a. Print Preview.
  b. Slide Sorter view.
  c. Outline view.
  d. Slide view.

4. To move a slide in Slide Sorter view,
  a. select the slide and drag it to a new location.
  b. press Delete and then press Insert.
  c. press Ctrl+Insert.
  d. press Ctrl+D.

5. As you move a slide in Slide Sorter view, what identifies the active location of the slide?
  a. The mouse pointer
  b. The slide outline
  c. The ruler scale
  d. A vertical bar

6. To create special effects as slides move onto the screen,
  a. use the slide show shortcut menu.
  b. press the left mouse button.
  c. add a transition.
  d. press Page Down.

7. To advance to the next slide during a slide show, use any of the following techniques *except*
  a. click the left mouse button.
  b. press E.
  c. press Page Down.
  d. press N.

8. To leave a slide in a presentation but display it only when it's needed,
  a. hide the slide.
  b. build the slide text.
  c. skip the slide.
  d. branch out to the slide.

9. One way to move to a specific slide during a slide show is to
  a. press Home and the slide number.
  b. press Ctrl and the slide number.
  c. press Esc.
  d. type the slide number and press Enter.

10. To stop a presentation,
  a. press Enter.
  b. press Ctrl+S.
  c. press Esc.
  d. press Home.

Short Answer

1. Which view enables you to select a transition from a special toolbar?
2. In what shape does the pointer appear when you move a slide in Slide Sorter view?
3. What feature do you apply to slide text so that bullet items appear one at a time?
4. When you drag and drop a slide in Slide Sorter view, how do you know where the slide will appear?
5. On what menu does the Expand Slide feature appear?
6. Name the three basic ways to launch a slide show.
7. To what view in other applications might you compare viewing slides as a slide show?
8. What's the difference between a transition and text preset animation?
9. How do you display the slide show shortcut menu?
10. What view displays the presentation when the show ends?

For Discussion

1. What design concerns should you consider when applying transitions?
2. Why do you add hidden slides to a presentation?
3. What's the advantage of applying text preset animations to slides?
4. How can you control which slide appears first during a slide show?

Review Exercises

1. Rearranging, Hiding, and Expanding Slides and Showing a Presentation

The presentation *The Willows* is almost ready for Ms. Savoy to show to the managers, but it needs a bit more editing. The final presentation outline appears in Figure 4.2.

1 *The Willows*
Where guests become friends

2 *Featuring . . .*
- Luxury accommodations
- Four-star restaurants
- The bounty of the sea
- A taste of the land

3 *Luxury accommodations*
- The Grande Hotel
- Willows Beach Cottages

4 *The Grande Hotel*
- Guest rooms
- Boutiques
- Restaurants
- Meeting rooms
- Exercise facility
- Pool and sun deck

5 *Willows Beach Cottages*
- Luxury living in a cottage setting
  - Two bedrooms in each cottage
  - Additional sofa bed in the living area
  - King and queen size beds
- Fully stocked kitchen facilities
- Nestled among the links

6 *Four-star restaurants*
- Atrium Grill
- Willow Top
- Wind in the Willows
- Black Mountain Tavern
- Front Porch Restaurant

7 *Sandwich Shops*
- Willow Green on the golf course
- The Cola Shop on the Mezzanine
- Grey Fox Deli at The Grande Hotel
- The 18th Hole on the golf course
- Red Rocker at the pool
- The Boardwalk on the beach

8 *The bounty of the sea*
- Ocean beaches
- Willows Water Park
  - Wave pool
  - Water slide
- Indoor and outdoor pools

9 *A taste of the land*
- Golf and tennis
  - Three 18-hole courses
  - Miniature golf
- Willow Pond Riding Stables
- Little Tree Playground

10 *Golf and tennis*
- Three 18-hole courses
- Miniature golf

11 *Willow Pond Riding Stables*
- 15 Gentle rides
- Ponies for the young and young-at-heart
- One-, two-, and three-hour bridle paths
- Bike rentals

12 *Little Tree Playground*
- State-of-the-art equipment
- Sand for a soft landing
- Play counselors on-site from dawn to dusk

13 *The Facilities*
- Golf and tennis
- Exercise and aerobics
- Miniature golf
- Playground
- Riding stables
- Water park

14 *The Willows*

Figure 4.2

Follow these steps to complete the presentation:

1. Launch PowerPoint, if necessary, and open the presentation *The Willows*.
2. Display the presentation in Slide Sorter view and move Slide 7 so that it becomes Slide 4. Then move Slide 8 so that it becomes Slide 5.
3. Select Slide 6; then click the New Slide button on the Standard toolbar and choose the Bulleted List AutoLayout. Double-click the plain new slide to display it in Slide view so that you can add slide text.
4. Type **Sandwich Shops** in the title placeholder and then add the following bulleted list to the bulleted list placeholder:
   - Willow Green on the golf course
   - The Cola Shop on the Mezzanine

- Grey Fox Deli at The Grande Hotel
- The 18th Hole on the golf course
- Red Rocker at the pool
- The Boardwalk on the beach

5. Display Slide Sorter view again, hide Slide 7, and expand Slide 9.
6. Switch to Outline view and add the text for new Slides 11 and 12 as shown in Figure 4.2.
7. View the slide show and then display the presentation in Slide Sorter view to add transitions and text preset animations you find most effective to each slide.
8. Save the changes to the presentation and print a copy of the presentation outline. Demonstrate the slide show for your instructor.

2. Editing, Enhancing, and Viewing a Presentation as a Slide Show

Ms. Lindsey would also like to fine-tune the presentation *The Willows Shops* so that she can include it in her presentation to the managers. Figure 4.3 displays the finished presentation in Slide Sorter view.

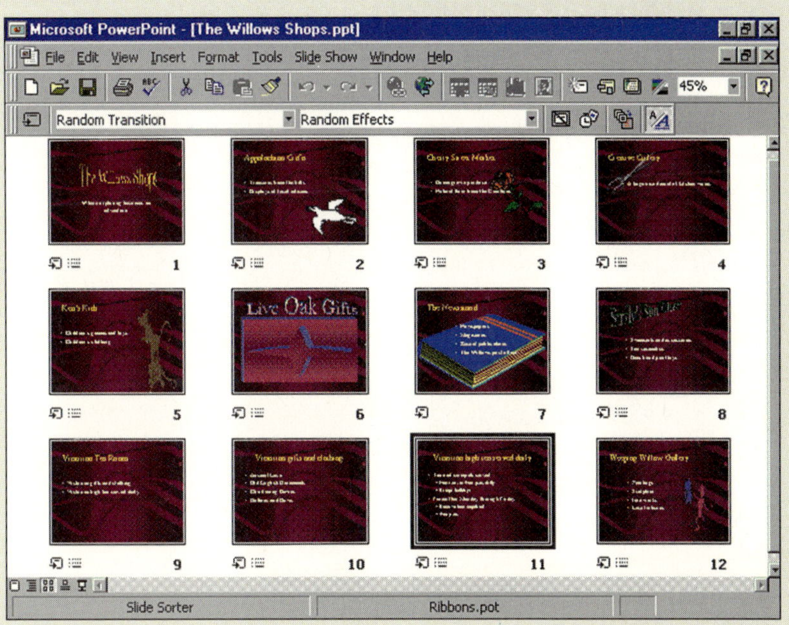

Figure 4.3

Follow these steps to complete the task:

1. Launch PowerPoint, if necessary, and open the presentation *The Willows Shops*.
2. Display Slide Sorter view and rearrange the bulleted list slides into alphabetical order by titles as follows:
    - Slide 9 becomes Slide 2
    - Slide 7 becomes Slide 3
    - Slide 7 (new) becomes Slide 4
    - Slide 9 becomes Slide 5
    - Slide 8 becomes Slide 6
    - Slide 10 becomes Slide 7
    - Slide 10 (new) becomes Slide 9

3. Expand Slide 9. Display the new Slide 10 in Slide view and add the following text to the bulleted list placeholder:
   - Ancient Lace
   - Old English Ornaments
   - Christening Gowns
   - Buttons and Bows
4. Display Slide 11 and add the following bulleted list items:
   - Tea and crumpets
     - 9:00 a.m. to 4:00 p.m. daily
     - Except holidays
   - Formal tea Monday through Friday
     - Reservations required
     - 4:00 p.m.
5. Show the presentation as a slide show and then display Slide Sorter view. Add transitions and text preset animations to the bulleted list slides and show the presentation again.
6. Make any necessary adjustments to the presentation and then save the changes to the presentation.
7. Show the presentation to your instructor and print copies of presentation slides as handouts with six framed pure black-and-white slides per page.
8. Close the presentation and exit PowerPoint when you've completed your work.

Assignments

1. Editing and Enhancing a Presentation and Viewing a Slide Show

The slides from the *Festivals and Attractions* presentation appear in Figure 4.4. Use the tools presented in this project to expand slides, rearrange slides, and add text to slides. Add slide transitions and text preset animations to slides in the presentation. Then view the presentation as a slide show and save changes to the presentation. Present the slide show to your instructor and print pure black-and-white handouts with six framed slides per page. Close the presentation and exit PowerPoint when you've completed your work.

2. Editing and Enhancing a Presentation and Posting It to the WWW (Optional Assignment. Ask your instructor how to proceed.)

Edit and enhance your résumé presentation and then follow one or both of the following options, as directed by your instructor:

- Post the presentation to the Web site identified by your instructor.
- Choose File, Send To, Exchange Folder to file the presentation in Outlook. Select Microsoft Outlook from the Profile Name list and save the presentation in the Journal folder of the Personal Folders drawer or create a new personal folder with your name as the folder name (according to your instructor's directions) and store the presentation in your personal folder. Then launch Outlook, if available, and verify that the presentation name appears on the list of files in the Journal folder or in your personal folder.

Festivals and Attractions
The Willows
North Carolina
Festivals
Stray Fox Arts and Crafts Festival
Grove Park Folk Festival
Willow Park Light Festival
Stray Fox Arts and Crafts Festival
In the Spring when the blush is on the roses
Costumes for an "Old World" fox hunt encouraged
Treasures crafted for those who appreciate "Old World" charm
Antiques and Hunt objects featured
Grove Park Folk Festival
Late Summer on the brink of Fall
Square Dancing all day and into the night
Clogging lessons and fun
Outdoor cooking in the folk tradition
Willow Park Light Festival
See the Hills in their holiday finery
Join the parade of cars as they tour the lighted route
Float the rivers by firelight
Attractions
Sheer Madness Night
Little Pitchers Beach Week
Sheer Madness Night
Visit a world gone mad
Costumes and masks required
Kiss the pumpkin for a special treat
Hang around the eaves with the bats
Little Pitchers Beach Week
Midsummer fun for the young and the young-at-heart
Activities focus on children 12 years old and under
Teen dance Friday night

Figure 4.4

5

PROJECT

Enhancing a Presentation

Okay! You've created a fantastic presentation, edited it, and dressed it up so that you can deliver it with style, and you're ready to take the presentation on the road. A few more features are buried within PowerPoint that will help you set up your presentation to run in different environments. In this project, you learn how to fine-tune your presentations and create materials to use as you show the presentation.

Objectives

After completing this project, you will be able to:

- **Animate slides with sound**
- **Set action buttons**
- **Add slide timings**
- **Set a presentation to run continuously**
- **Create notes pages**
- **Pack a presentation to go**

The Challenge

Francesca Savoy impressed the managers when she made her presentation last week. Now the Board of Directors of The Willows wants the presentation to be set up at strategic locations throughout the resort so that guests and visitors can stop and view it. In addition, the Board has authorized Ms. Savoy, as Marketing Director, to market the resort to large organizations interested in locating resort settings for conventions. She comes to you for help.

The Solution

To get the presentation for The Willows ready for viewing throughout the resort, you need to set the presentation to run automatically. To draw the attention of guests and visitors to the presentation, you need to add some sound to your text animation. Because Ms. Savoy will be traveling with the presentation, you need to package the presentation to take on the road and develop a set of notes pages for her to use as she shows the presentation. A sample notes page appears in Figure 5.1.

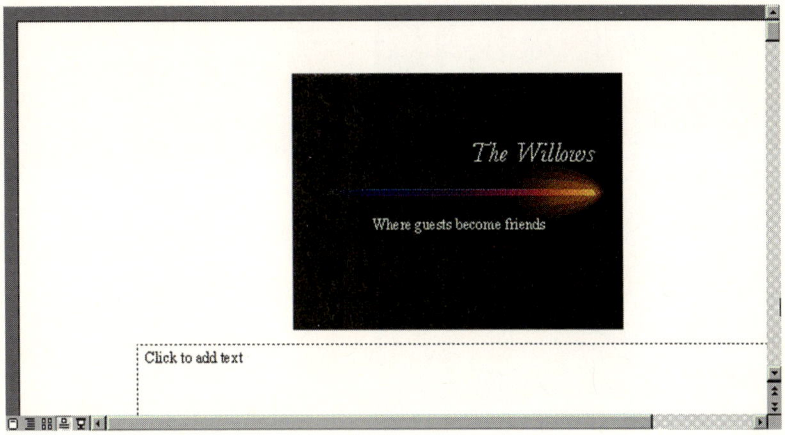

Figure 5.1

The Setup

Most of the default settings you've been using throughout this part of the book should be active as you complete the activities in this project. You'll be using Notes Pages view for part of the project, and the toolbars for Notes Pages view are the same toolbars you see in Slide view. Display the Standard, Formatting, and Drawing toolbars and close the Common Tasks toolbar so that what you see on your computer screen will match the illustrations shown here.

You'll also need to work with your presentation window maximized in Slide and Notes Pages views. Click the Maximize button on the presentation window, if necessary.

Animating Slides with Sound

In Project 4, you animated the slide text using text preset animations. The Animation Effects toolbar contains buttons that you can use to add sound to the animated text automatically or to customize the animation effect and select a sound. When you choose to add ***custom animation,*** you'll use the Custom Animation dialog box. The Custom Animation dialog box displays options that also enable you to dim bullet points for animated text as new bullet points display.

TASK 1: TO ANIMATE SLIDES WITH SOUND:

1. Open the presentation *The Willows* and display Slide 1 in Slide view. Slide 1 displays as last edited.

2. Click the Animation Effects button on the Formatting toolbar.

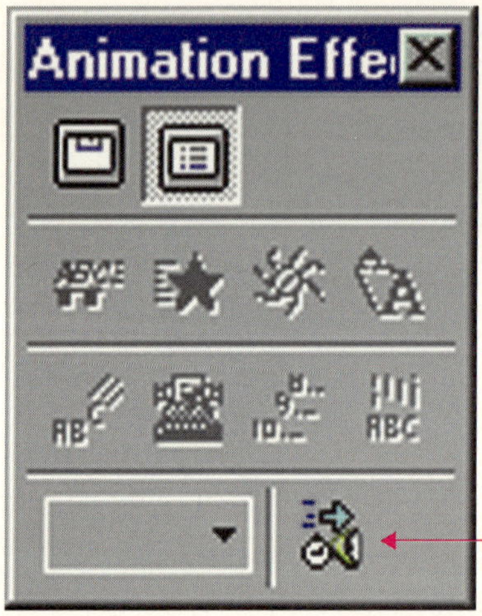

3. Click the Custom Animation button.

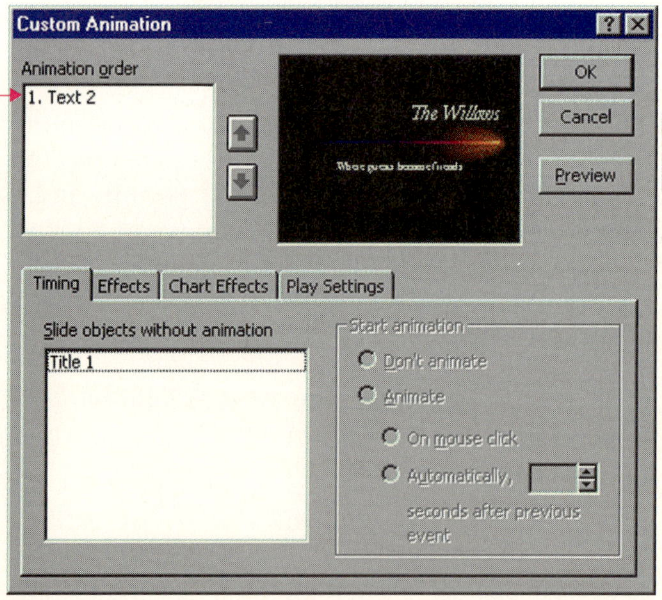

4. Click the Effects tab and then click "1. Text 2" in the Animation order list box.

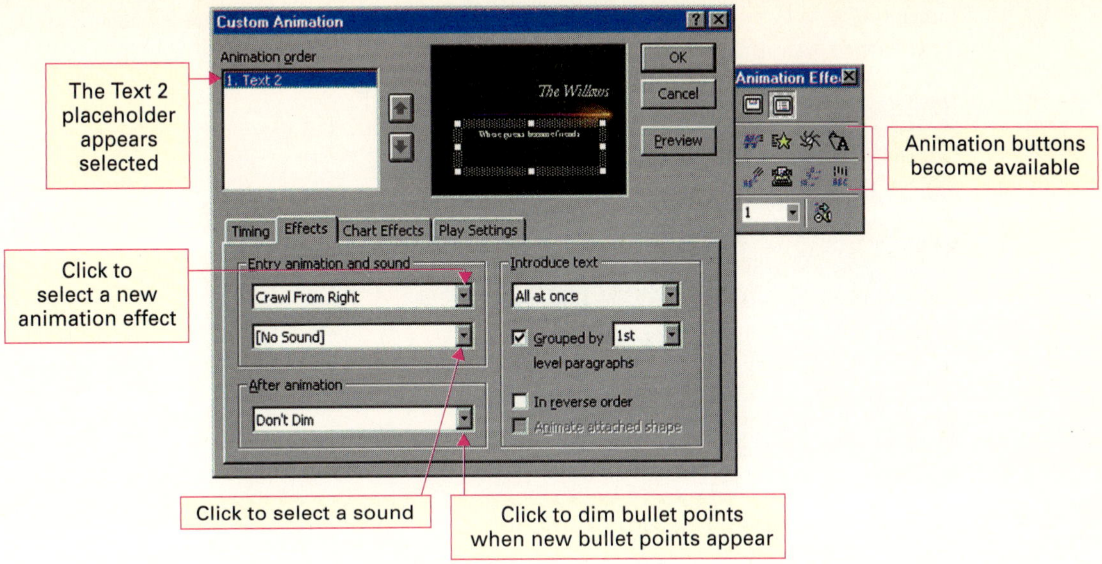

5 Click the arrow button for the sound option and point to Whoosh.

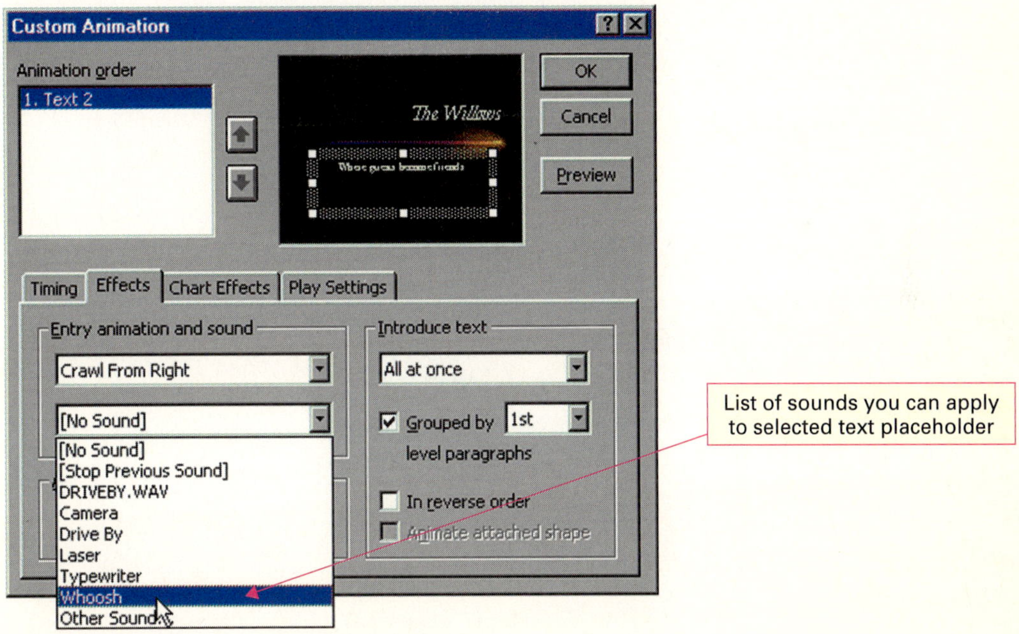

6 Click Whoosh to apply the sound to the animated text.
Whoosh appears in the text box.

7 Click OK to return to Slide 1 and then click the Slide Show View button to show the slide.
Slide 1 displays in full-screen view.

8 Press (ENTER) to display the animated text and hear the sound; then press (ESC) to return to Slide view.
Slide 1 displays in Slide view.

9 Display Slide 2, select the bulleted list placeholder, and click the Typewriter Text Effect button on the Animation Effects toolbar.

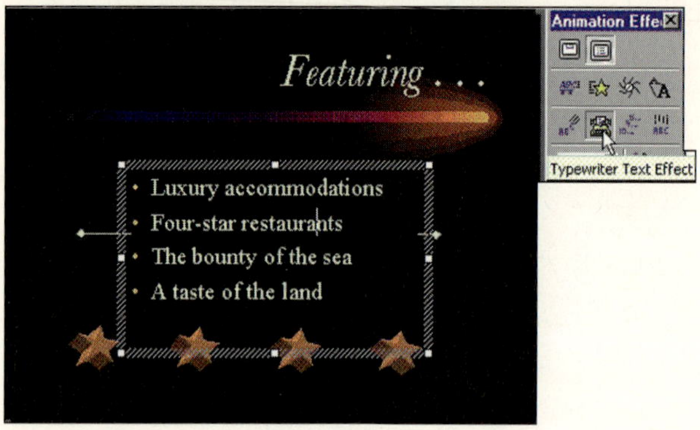

10 Click to open the Custom Animation dialog box.

Text 2 is automatically selected

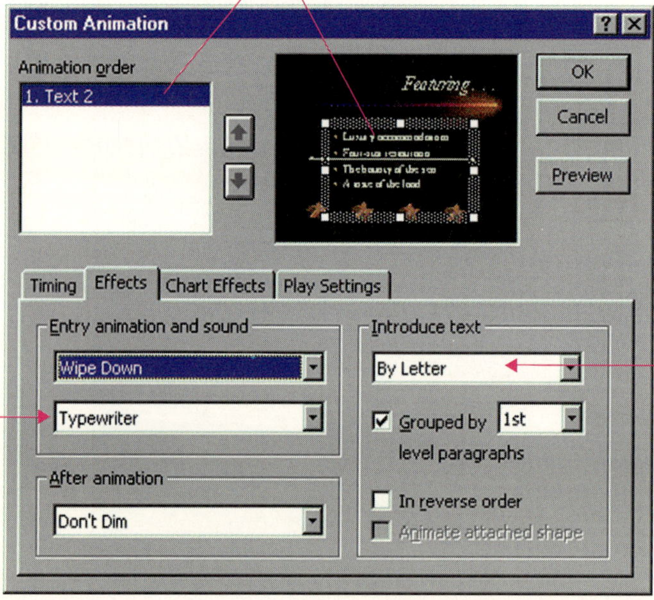

The Typewriter sound is automatically active

The text will display a letter at a time

11 Click the arrow button beside the After animation option.

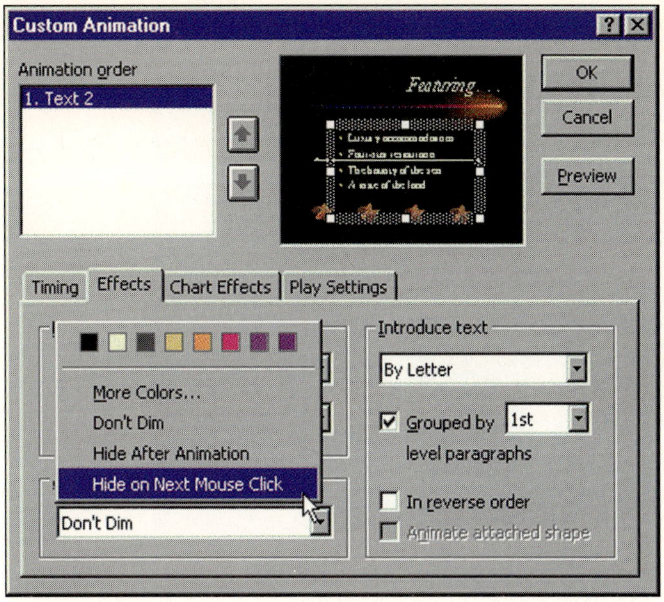

12 Click Hide on Next Mouse Click and then click OK to return to the slide.
Slide 2 appears in Slide view.

13 Show the slide to view the effects, press ESC, and then save the changes to the presentation.
The text displays one character at a time and you can hear the sound of a typewriter as each character appears. Each bullet point disappears when the next bullet point displays.

Setting Action Buttons

Action buttons enable you to control the slide PowerPoint displays when you click the button during a slide show. For the presentation *The Willows,* you can add an action button to display a hidden slide that follows Slide 8. PowerPoint creates a ***hyperlink*** to the slide so that clicking the action button automatically displays the desired slide.

Tip You can also add action buttons to enable users to choose the section of a presentation they want to view or to display documents from other applications. Explore these advanced features as you become more comfortable with PowerPoint.

TASK 2: TO CREATE AND SET AN ACTION BUTTON:

1 Display Slide 6 of the presentation *The Willows* in Slide view.

2 Choose Slide Show, Action Buttons.

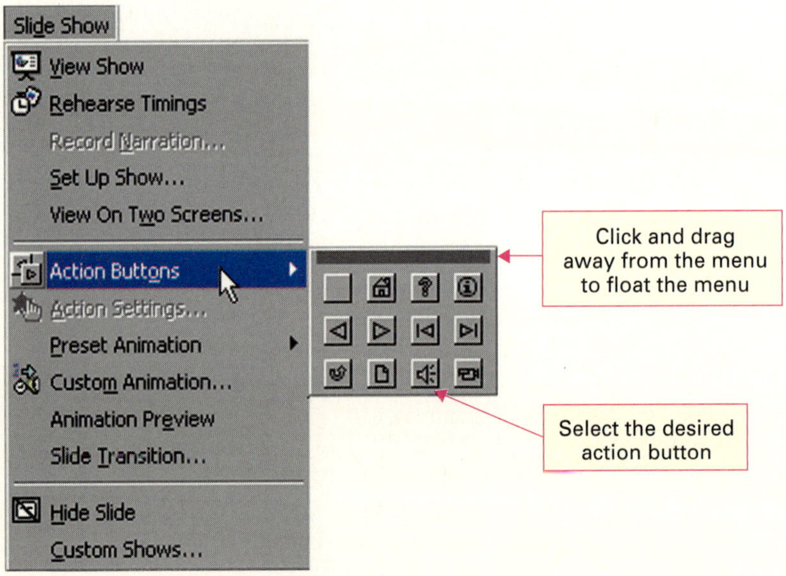

3 Click the Action Button: Forward or Next button. The pointer changes to a plus (+).

4 Position the pointer in the lower-right corner of the slide, click, and draw a small square shape.

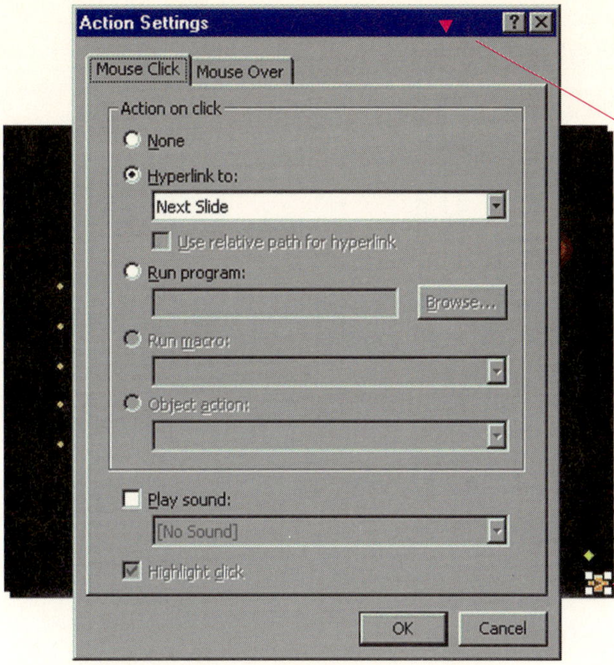

The Action Settings dialog box opens so that you can set the action

The action button displays on-screen

5 Click the arrow button beside the Hyperlink to option and select Slide.

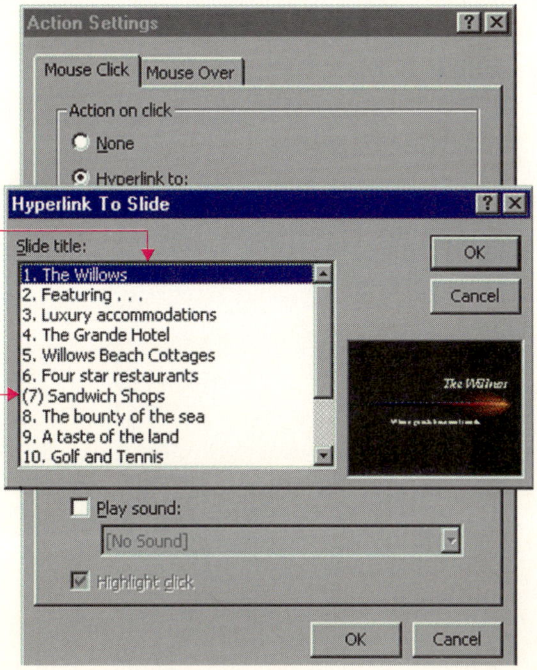

Slide titles display beside slide numbers

Numbers for hidden slides appear in parentheses

6 Select (7) Sandwich Shops and then click OK.
The slide title appears in the Hyperlink to text box.

7 Press (ENTER) to close the Action Settings dialog box and then click the Slide Show button to show the slide.

8 Point to the action button and click to display the hidden slide.
Slide 7 displays immediately.

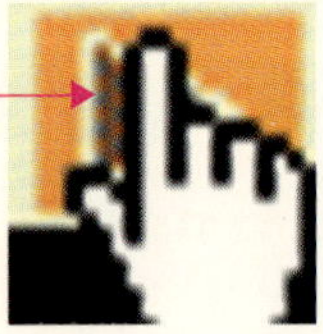

9 Press (ESC) to stop the show, save the changes to the presentation, and close the Animation Effects toolbar.

Adding Slide Timings

Before you set the presentation to run automatically, you need to add slide timings so that each slide displays for a set amount of time before advancing to the next slide. After you add timings, slides move on and off the screen automatically. Of course, viewers can advance slides manually, even when timings are present.

TASK 3: TO ADD SLIDE TIMINGS:

1 Display the presentation *The Willows* in Slide Sorter view.
Thumbnail images appear in Slide Sorter view.

2 Select Slide 1 and then click the Slide Transition button on the Slide Sorter toolbar.

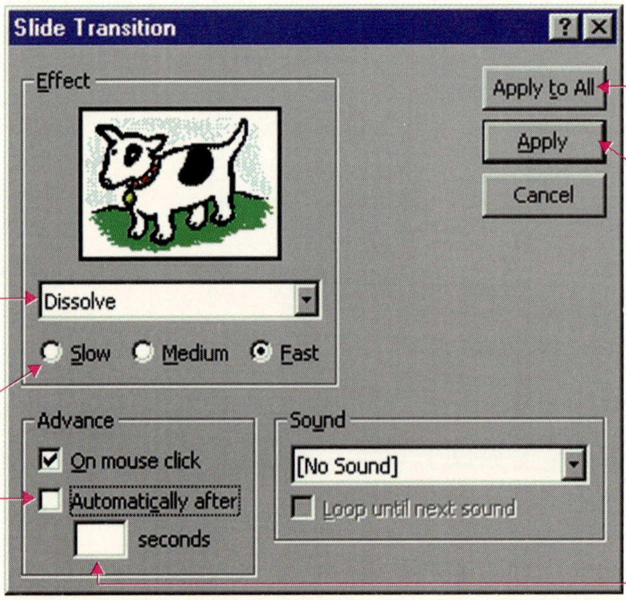

3 Click the check box beside Automatically after, type **25** in the seconds value box, and click Apply.

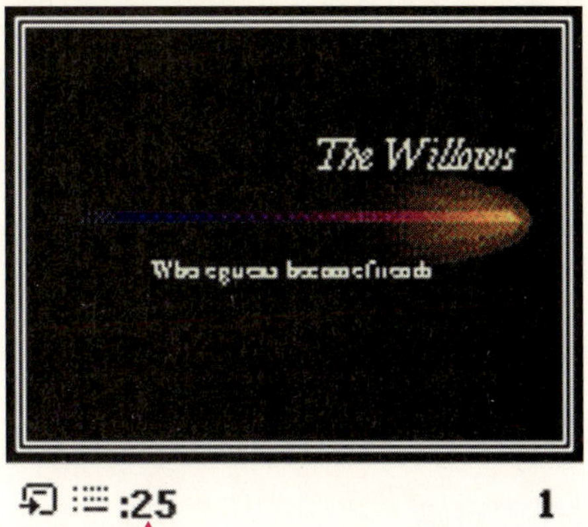

The slide timing appears below the slide

4 Apply the slide timings shown here to all the slides in the presentation.

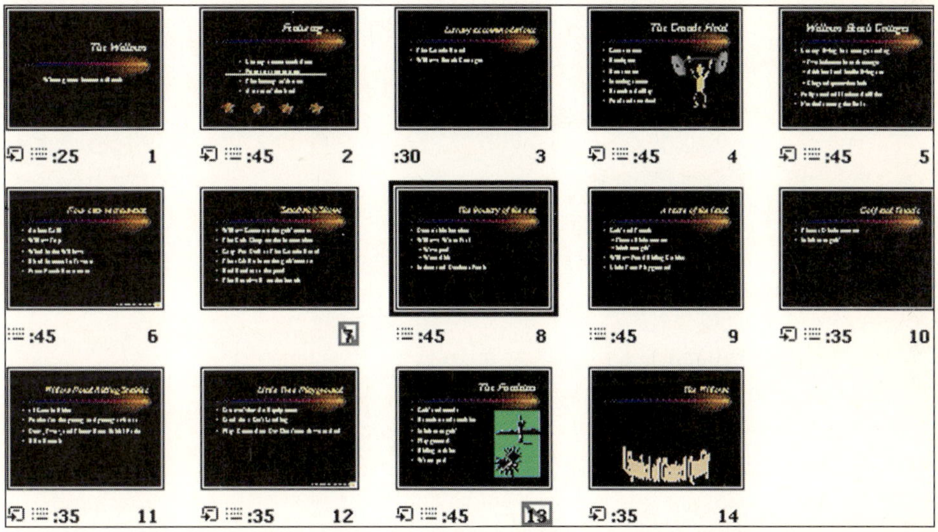

> **Note** If slide text is formatted with a text preset animation, PowerPoint distributes the timing you set among the bulleted list items on the slide. As a result, a four-point bulleted list set to display for 60 seconds would display each bulleted item for 15 seconds before displaying the next bullet point.

5 Save the first few changes to the presentation and then show the presentation, letting the slides advance automatically.

Setting a Presentation to Run Continuously

You may have seen computer monitors set up in stores or at conferences or trade shows that displayed information automatically and gave you an opportunity to review the information. Now that you have the presentation set up to run automatically with timings, you can set it to start over after the last slide displays, so that it runs continuously—or ***loops*** back to the first slide in a never-ending circle.

TASK 4: TO SET UP A PRESENTATION TO RUN CONTINUOUSLY:

1. Choose Slide Show, Set Up Show.

These options control the flow of the show

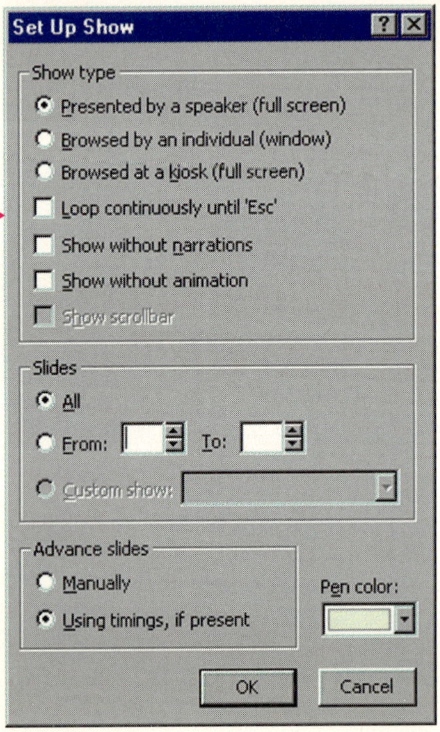

2. Click the Loop continuously until 'Esc' option and click OK.

> **Tip** Selecting the Browsed at a kiosk (full screen) option in the Set Up Show dialog box restricts slide advancement to timings only; manual clicking won't advance slides. Selecting Loop continuously until 'Esc' lets you advance slides manually as well as automatically.

3. Save the changes to the presentation and show the presentation, letting some slides advance automatically and advancing some slides manually.

4. Press ESC to stop the presentation, display Slide 6 in Slide view, and then click the Text Box button on the Drawing toolbar.

The crosshair I-beam lets you add text outside a placeholder

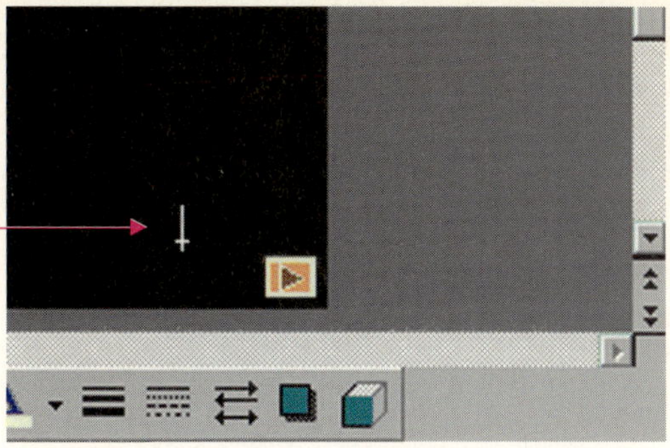

5 Position the I-beam to the left of the action button, click, and type **Click to see facilities summary.**
The text appears shadowed and too large for the slide area.

6 Select the text in the text box, click the Shadow button on the Formatting toolbar to turn off shadowing, and select 14 from the Font Size list box.

7 Click to view the slide and click the action button to display Slide 7.

8 Press ESC to stop the presentation and then save the changes to the presentation.

Creating Notes Pages

Your presentation is ready to be set up at strategic locations throughout the resort and is almost ready to take on the road. All Ms. Savoy needs now is a set of notes to take with her so she doesn't forget important points she wants to make during the presentation. The PowerPoint Notes Pages view enables you to add notes to the bottom of a page that contains an image of the slide at the top.

TASK 5: TO CREATE NOTES PAGES:

1 Display Slide 1 in Slide view and then click the Notes Pages View button at the bottom of the presentation window.
A small image of Slide 1 appears on-screen with a Notes placeholder at the bottom. The zoom percentage makes reading difficult.

2 Change the Zoom control setting to 75%.

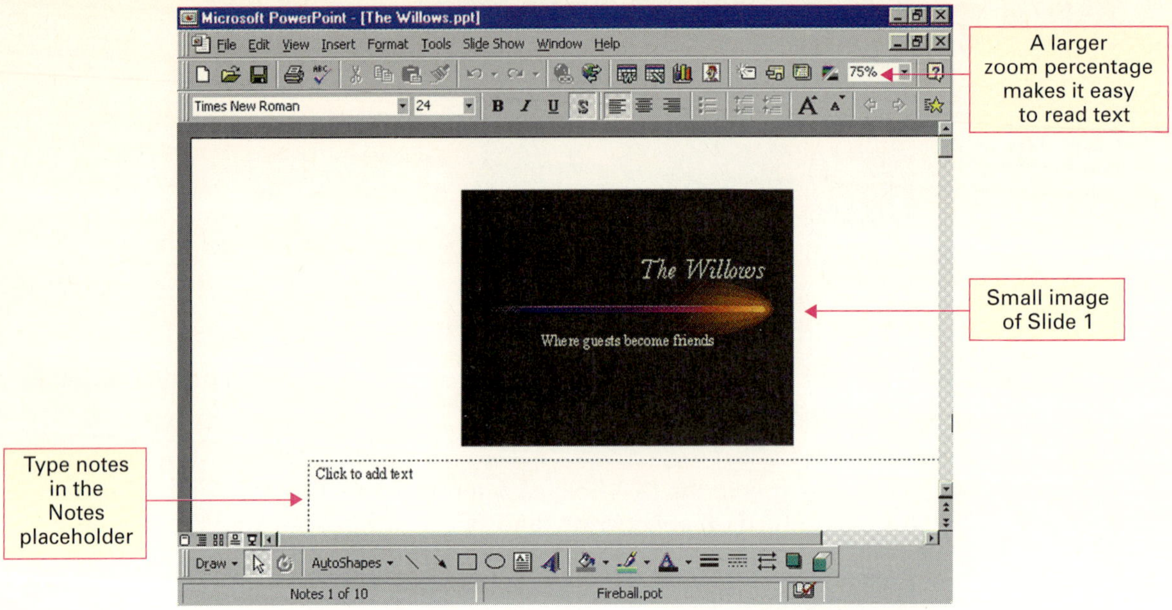

3 Point to the Notes placeholder, click, and type **Introduce myself and explain the purpose of the presentation. Ask audience what facilities they require for their conference.**
The text appears in the notes placeholder below the slide image.

4 Press (PGDN) to display Slide 2, click the Notes placeholder, and type **Review basic features of The Willows.**
The notes appear in the Notes placeholder of Slide 2.

5 Add the following text as notes to the following slides:

Slide 3: **Emphasize that The Grande Hotel has more than 400 rooms to accommodate large gatherings and that the cottages offer more private settings. Review specific features of The Grande Hotel and the cottages as next two slides appear.**

Slide 6: **Cite accolades of recent publications about the quality of our restaurants. Emphasize that there are less formal eateries available as well. Mention catering for special dinners. A hidden slide follows this slide and lists sandwich shops in case someone asks about them.**

Slide 8: **Ask audience what types of activities they like to explore.**

Slide 9: **Compare on-shore activities to the water sports. Stress the "something for everyone" aspect of the resort to show that families will have plenty to do while businesspeople attend meetings.**

Slide 14: **Summarize The Willows features and ask for questions.**

6 Choose File, Print.
The Print dialog box displays.

7 Select Notes Pages from the Print what drop-down list, select the Pure black & white option, click the Slides option, type **1–3,6,8,9,14** in the Slides text box, and press (ENTER).
The notes pages for the selected slides print.

Packing a Presentation to Go

Everything is set—and, as usual, just in the nick of time! Ms. Savoy is about to take off on her first marketing trip and needs the presentation on a disk to take with her. You're in luck—PowerPoint has a Pack and Go Wizard that can have her on the road in just a few minutes with disk in hand. Graphics, templates, and animation effects increase the size of presentations and make them difficult to copy to a disk. When you pack a presentation using the Pack and Go Wizard, however, PowerPoint ***compresses*** the presentation, making it more compact and easier to fit on one disk.

TASK 6: TO PACK A PRESENTATION TO GO:

1 Choose File, Pack and Go.

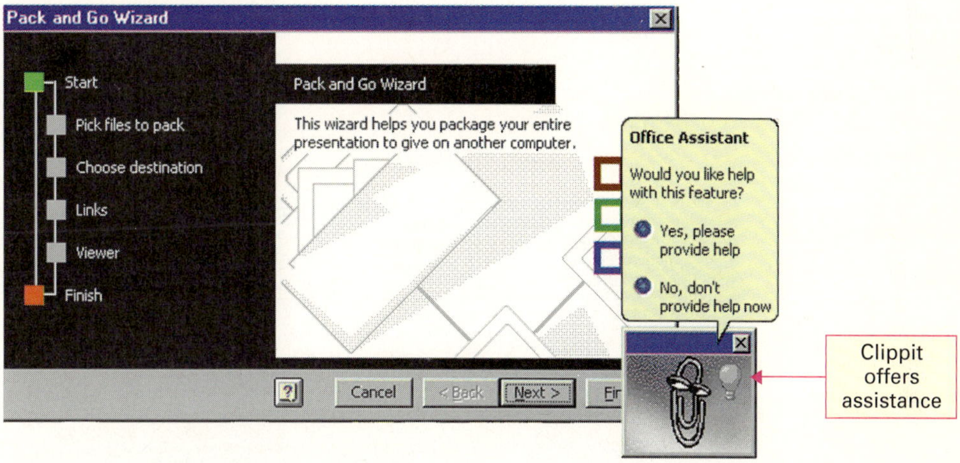

2 Click No, don't provide help now to close the Office Assistant; then click Next.

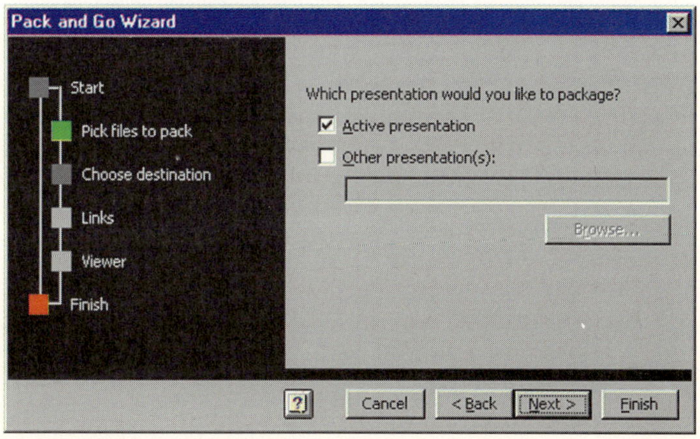

3 Ensure that Active presentation is selected and click Next.

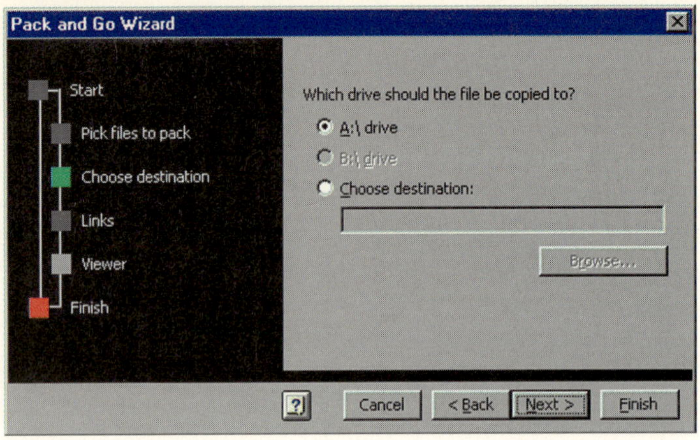

4 Ensure that the floppy drive for your computer is active, place a disk in the floppy drive, and click Next.

> **Note** The disk you use should contain no other files, otherwise your presentation might not fit.

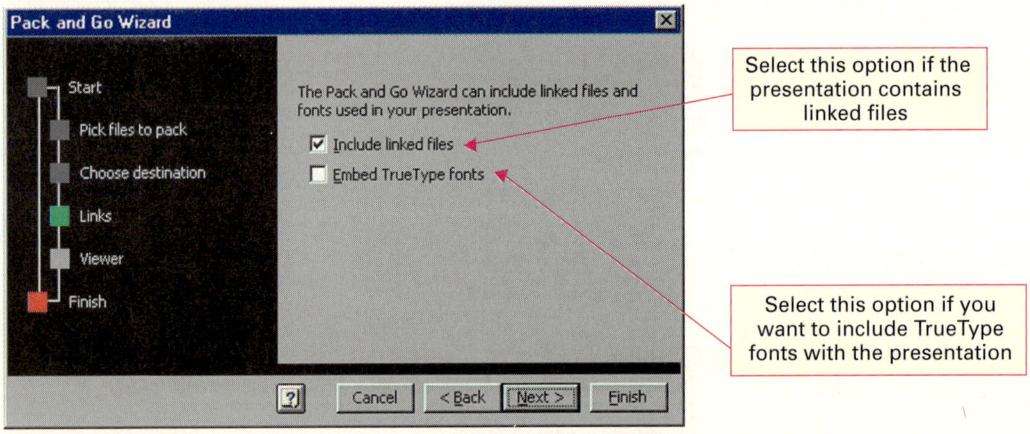

5 For this exercise, deselect the Include linked files option because your presentation doesn't contain links, and select Embed TrueType fonts to ensure that your presentation displays properly; then click Next.

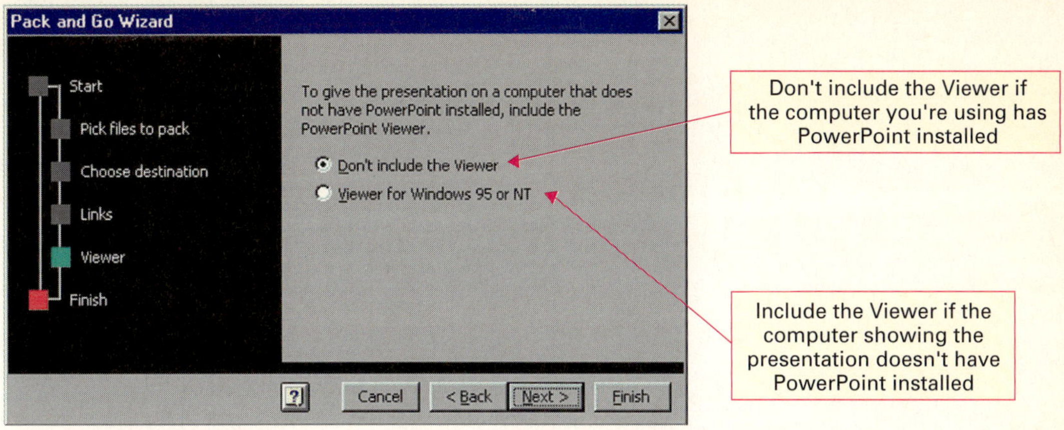

Note If the PowerPoint Viewer isn't installed on your computer, you'll need the original PowerPoint CD to access the Viewer so that the Pack and Go Wizard can find it and pack it with the presentation(s).

6 For this example, click Don't include the Viewer and then click Next.

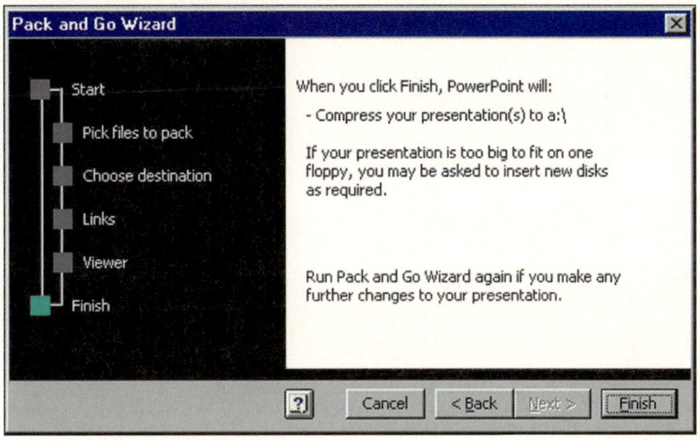

7 Click Finish.
PowerPoint whirs and burps a bit as it packages the presentation on the disk. When the presentation is packaged, a message window tells you that Pack and Go has successfully packed your presentation. If your presentation is too large to fit on one disk, you'll be told when to insert another disk.

8 Click OK to acknowledge the message.
Your presentation is ready to turn in to your instructor.

The Conclusion

Now that you have the presentation on disk, you can show it from any computer that has PowerPoint installed. Simply launch PowerPoint and open the presentation. If you've completed your work, close the presentation for The Willows and exit PowerPoint. If you plan to continue with the Review Exercises and Assignments, close the presentation and leave PowerPoint running.

Summary and Exercises

Summary

- PowerPoint comes equipped with animation effects that can contain sounds. You can apply these effects to slide text by using the Animation Effects toolbar.
- You can use action buttons to control the slides presented and to jump to different parts of a presentation.
- To prepare a presentation to run automatically, add slide timings to each slide to tell PowerPoint how long to leave the slide on the screen. When slide text is animated, each bullet point or animated object gets an equal share of the time allotted to the slide.
- To show a presentation at a trade show or in a location where no one is available to monitor the presentation, you can set the presentation to run continuously until someone stops the show.
- Create notes pages to type reminder notes to use during a show. Notes Pages view presents pages with slide images at the top and a notes placeholder at the bottom of the page for you to use.
- The Pack and Go Wizard prepares presentations for showing at another location. You can include a PowerPoint Viewer with the presentation if necessary.

Key Terms and Operations

Key Terms	**Operations**
action button	add sound to slide text animations
compress	add timings to slides so that they automatically advance
custom animation	create notes pages to accompany a presentation
dim effect	pack up a presentation using the Pack and Go Wizard
hyperlink	set action buttons to control the flow of the presentation
loop	set a presentation to run continuously
Pack and Go Wizard	
timings	
Viewer	

Study Questions

Multiple Choice

1. To jump to a different slide than the one that normally follows the active slide,
   a. create a mini-program that runs the link.
   b. add a text box to a slide.
   c. add a graphic to the slide.
   d. add an action button to the slide.

2. To select a sound for a text preset animation,
   a. record the sound using a microphone.
   b. create an action button.
   c. customize the animation.
   d. add a graphic to the slide.

3. To create a set of notes to use during a slide show, display
   a. Slide Sorter view.
   b. Notes Pages view.
   c. Outline view.
   d. Slide view.

4. You can set up a presentation to advance slides automatically by setting
   a. slide timings.
   b. a hyperlink.
   c. a loop.
   d. an action button.

5. A hyperlink attached to an action button is called
   a. an animation effect.
   b. the slide outline.
   c. slide timings.
   d. a loop.

6. When you want to set up a presentation to run without constant monitoring, set up the presentation
   a. as a slide show.
   b. with timings only.
   c. to run continuously, using a loop.
   d. to advance manually.

7. Notes Pages view displays
   a. a notes placeholder only.
   b. a notes placeholder and a slide image.
   c. a slide image only.
   d. three slides on each page.

8. To prepare a presentation to show on another computer,
   a. use the Pack and Go Wizard.
   b. copy the slide to a disk.
   c. use the Send to command.
   d. branch out to the slide.

9. Slide timings
   a. must all be set exactly the same.
   b. don't work during a regular presentation.
   c. don't let you advance slides manually.
   d. can be different for each slide.

10. When you want to disable the manual advance for a presentation,
   a. simply set slide timings.
   b. set the presentation to loop continuously.
   c. set the presentation to run at a kiosk.
   d. You can't disable the manual advance for a presentation.

Short Answer

1. How can you quickly access the Animation Effects toolbar?
2. How does the slide number for hidden slides appear in a list of slide titles?

3. What page of the Custom Animation dialog box displays sounds and animation effects?
4. What tool do you use to add text to a slide outside a text placeholder?
5. How does the Pack and Go Wizard fit a large presentation onto one floppy disk?
6. To help focus the attention of your audience on the bullet point you're discussing during a slide show, what should you do to other bullet points already presented?
7. What view makes it easy to add slide timings?
8. Where do slide timings appear on-screen?
9. How do you stop a show set to run continuously?
10. What can you change to make the text in Notes Pages view easier to read?

For Discussion

1. What does the dim feature do?
2. What advantage does applying timings to slides in a presentation provide when the time you have for a presentation is limited?
3. Where have you seen presentations set up to run unmonitored?
4. How does attaching an action button help keep track of hidden slides?

Review Exercises

1. Adding Sound Effects to Animated Text, Setting Action Buttons to Display Hidden Slides, Adding Text to a Slide

The presentation *The Willows* includes numerous slides that contain animated text and a hidden slide that you need to format an action button to access. Follow these steps to complete the presentation:

1. Launch PowerPoint, if necessary, open the presentation *The Willows* in Slide view, and display the Animation Effects toolbar.
2. Display Slides 3 through 14 individually and apply an animated sound to the text preset animations already applied to the slides. Select different options to dim bullet points.
3. Display Slide 12 and add an action button to hyperlink to hidden Slide 13.
4. Display Slide 6, press (SHIFT), select the text box next to the action button, and copy the text box to the Windows Clipboard. Then display Slide 12 again and paste the text box onto the slide. Adjust the size and placement of the text box as needed.
5. Show the slide show to view your changes, and make final adjustments to the presentation.
6. Save changes to the presentation and print a copy of Slide 12 in pure black-and-white. Close the presentation.

2. Adding Action Buttons, Animating with Sound, Adding Slide Timings, Setting a Presentation to Run Continuously, Creating Notes Pages

Ms. Lindsey was so impressed with your work on the presentation for The Willows that she would like you to develop the presentation for The Willows Shops using the same techniques, and add a list of notes to notes pages in the presentation. A sample notes page appears in Figure 5.2.

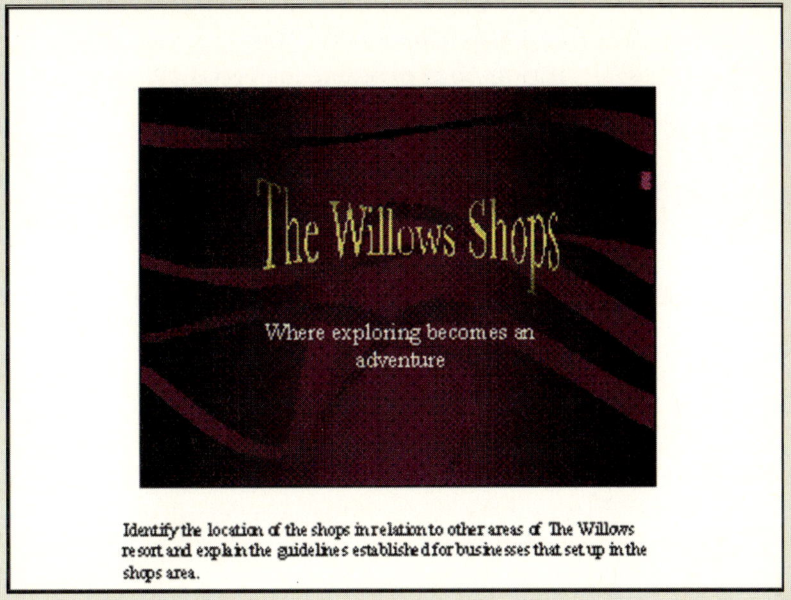

Figure 5.2

Follow these steps to format each slide in the presentation with a sound animation effect, dim bulleted list points, add timings to the all slides in the presentation, and create notes pages for the presentation.

1. Launch PowerPoint, if necessary, and open the presentation *The Willows Shops.*
2. Display Slide Sorter view and review the presentation settings. Then switch to Slide view and display the Animation Effects toolbar.
3. Display each slide in the presentation individually and apply a custom animation effect to the text already formatted with a preset animation. Apply a dim option to bulleted list text.
4. View the slide show and assess the effects. Then return to slide view and make any adjustments to slides in the presentation.
5. Display the presentation in Slide Sorter view and apply slide timings to each slide. Hide Slide 6.
6. Switch back to Slide view and add an action button to Slide 5 to access the hidden slide. Double-click the action button and change the fill and line color to make the action button blend in with the slide background.
7. View the presentation again and make certain that the action button displays the correct slide.

8. Display Notes Pages view and add the following notes to the slides:

Slide 1:	**Identify the location of the shops in relation to other areas of The Willows resort and explain the guidelines established for businesses that set up in the shops area.**
Slide 2:	**A series of slides about different shops starts with this slide and extends through Slide 12.** **Emphasize that the wares displayed in this craft shop are original creations of people living in the Appalachian Mountains.**
Slide 3:	**Stress that produce is brought to market daily.**
Slide 5:	**Mention that sizes for children range from newborn to about age 12.**
Slide 7:	**Mention daily delivery of all major newspapers from across the country, delivered on time, and available for room delivery.**
Slide 11:	**Review operating hours and explain that special arrangements can be made for organizations holding meetings at the resort.**

9. Set the presentation to loop continuously, using the Set Up Show dialog box, and then save changes to the presentation.

10. Print a copy of all notes pages containing notes, close the presentation, and exit PowerPoint when you've completed your work.

Assignments

1. Finalizing a Presentation to Run Continuously

The slides from the *Festivals and Attractions* presentation appear in Slide Sorter view in Figure 5.3.

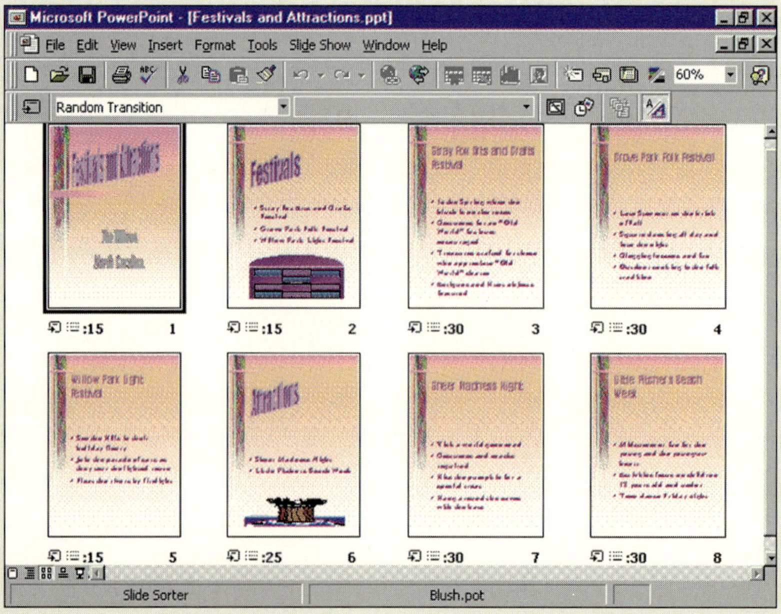

Figure 5.3

Use tools presented in this project to animate slide text with sound, add slide timings, and set the presentation to run continuously. Then view the presentation as a slide show and save changes to the presentation. Use your imagination to develop notes pages for the presentation and print copies of the notes pages that display slides in black-and-white. Set up the presentation on your computer during the next class session so that your instructor can review the special effects you've applied. Close the presentation and exit PowerPoint when you've completed your work.

2. Packing Presentations to Go and Sending Them Via a Mail Message

Package the *Festivals and Attractions* and *The Willows Shops* presentations to go, using the same disk. Exit PowerPoint and launch Outlook or your school mail program.

Create a mail message to your instructor. From the floppy that contains your presentations, attach the *Pngsetup.exe* file to the mail message. Send the message to your instructor.

Notes

Notes

Notes

Glossary

Action button The button that enables you to control the slide PowerPoint displays during a slide show.

AutoContent Wizard A PowerPoint feature that helps you build an outline for specific types of presentations by presenting options for you to choose and enabling you to fill in specific pieces of information about the presentation.

AutoLayout A PowerPoint feature that contains object placeholders.

Clip art A gallery of images supplied by PowerPoint that you can use to enhance your presentation.

Compress To arrange data more tightly so that it will fit on a disk; for example, the Pack and Go Wizard compresses presentations.

Custom animation The special effects you add to animation settings using the Custom Animation dialog box. The Custom Animation dialog box displays options that also enable you to dim bullet points for animated text as new bullet points display.

Dim effect The setting that causes animated text to lighten or dim as new bullet points display.

Expand To create new slides using bullet list text from another slide. When you expand a slide, each bulleted list item appears as the title of a new slide.

Flip To turn images so they face the opposite direction.

Font The type and style of text you use in your PowerPoint presentations.

Group To combine separate graphic or drawn objects into one.

Handles The squares on the corners and sides of selected placeholders and graphic or drawn objects that enable you to size the object.

Handouts Printed versions of your PowerPoint presentation. You can display two, three, or six slides on each printed handout page.

Hidden slides Slides that remain part of a presentation but don't display unless you specifically access them.

Hyperlink The connection that enables you to jump to a desired slide when you click an action button.

Kiosk A booth at a convention or shopping mall where you can set up a presentation to run continuously.

Line spacing The setting that controls the amount of space (such as single, double, and so forth) between lines of text.

Loop To play back continuously, or to go back to the first slide in a never-ending circle.

Master A layout that contains formats for text, bullets, placeholder alignment, headers and footers, and backgrounds.

Menu bar The bar at the top of the window that provides access to commands used to perform tasks. The menu bar changes, depending on the task you're performing.

Notes Pages view The PowerPoint view that displays a small slide image at the top of the page and provides space below the image so that you can type notes about the slide contents.

Office Assistant The new on-the-spot Help feature that pops up frequently to offer help on the task you're performing. Office Assistant enables you to ask questions about the task you want to perform.

Online help The help provided by the software and accessible from the computer.

Orientation The direction of the paper on which you print slides and other materials. Orientation can be Portrait or Landscape.

Outline view The PowerPoint view that displays the title and body text you add to placeholders in a notebook-like format so that you can review the content of the presentation.

Pack and Go Wizard A PowerPoint feature that prepares presentations for showing at another location. The Pack and Go Wizard compresses the presentation, making it easier to fit on one disk.

Page setup The orientation and size of paper used for slides and outlines, handouts, and notes pages. You change these options in the Page Setup dialog box.

Placeholder A predefined area outlined on a slide for placing text, bulleted lists, and objects such as graphs, tables, and charts.

Rotate To turn or spin objects to create special effects.

Slide show The display of slides in the presentation window without the PowerPoint toolbars, title bar, and status bar. During a slide show, each slide fills the screen, and you can focus on slide contents.

Slide show shortcut menu A list that displays commands for accessing navigation features as well as for controlling on-screen features such as the mouse pointer and slide meter. To display the slide show shortcut menu, click the right mouse button during the slide show.

Slide Sorter view The PowerPoint view that displays small images (often called *thumbnail images*) of each slide in the presentation so that you can review the effects of applying a template design to all the slides in the presentation.

Status bar The bar at the bottom of the window that displays information about the program status, instructions for performing selected tasks, active key information, and trouble messages.

Template A professionally developed slide design that you can apply to presentations to give a consistent look to all slides in a presentation.

Text preset animation A slide presentation (formerly known as a *build*) in which each slide title displays on-screen by itself and each bulleted list item is presented separately during a slide show. Text preset animations help focus the attention of your audience on each individual bulleted item as you discuss it and removes the distractions of presenting all bulleted points at once.

Timing The set amount of time a slide appears before automatically advancing to the next slide.

Title bar The bar at the top of the window that identifies the application name and contains the application icon, Maximize or Restore, Minimize, and Close buttons. After you save a presentation, the filename of a maximized presentation appears in the title bar.

Toolbar Bars of buttons that serve as shortcuts for performing common menu commands, displaying special toolbars, or changing screen features.

ToolTips Short explanations that pop up when you point to any toolbar button that identify the task the button performs.

Transitions Special effects that appear as your slides go on and off the screen during a slide show.

Ungroup To separate a grouped object into its individual pieces so that individual pieces of the object can be changed.

View The way in which PowerPoint displays your presentation. Each view is designed to make working with specific features of a presentation easier.

Viewer A software program with which you view slide shows.

WordArt The PowerPoint module you use to change text into words of art. WordArt enables you to curve, skew, or mold the text into a shape that better fits the area of the slide you want it to occupy.

Index

Notes

Notes

Notes

Notes

Notes

Notes

Notes

Notes

Notes

Notes

Notes

Notes